BLACK WOMEN AND THE CRIMINAL JUSTICE SYSTEM

Black Women and the Criminal Justice System
Towards the Decolonisation of Victimisation

BIKO AGOZINO
Liverpool John Moores University

Ashgate

Aldershot • Brookfield USA • Singapore • Sydney

Published by
Ashgate Publishing Ltd
Gower House
Croft Road
Aldershot
Hants GU11 3HR
England

Ashgate Publishing Company
Old Post Road
Brookfield
Vermont 05036
USA

British Library Cataloguing in Publication Data
Agozino, Biko
    Black women and the criminal justice system : towards the
    decolonisation of victimisation
    1. Discrimination in criminal justice administration
    2. Blacks - Legal status, laws, etc. 3. Sex discrimination
    in criminal justice administration
    I. Title
    364'.08996

Library of Congress Catalog Card Number: 97-70346

ISBN 1 85972 643 7

Printed in Great Britain by Biddles Limited,
Guildford and King's Lynn

Table of Contents

List of Figures and Tables

Foreword

Biko Agozino has asked me to write a short foreword to his book and I am happy to do this. I was his supervisor while he was a student in Edinburgh and, therefore, I have been very pleased to see the warm reception that his doctoral dissertation has received. As he records in his preface, his essay, 'The Construction of Criminal Categories', a part of chapter three, won the Mike Brake Prize in Radical Social Policy and Social Work in 1994. I mention this not only because it illustrates the quality of his work but also because it indicates the larger political and moral agenda to which Dr Agozino's research was intended to appeal.

This is an original and provocative work. Its originality lies in its subject matter and its approach. There are very few pieces of research on the position of black women in the criminal justice system and this one ought, therefore, to be seen as a pioneer study which aims as much to pose a new set of questions as to provide definitive answers. This is true also of the methodological approach. Agozino clearly rejects conventional empirical approaches both to collection and presentation of data. The study brings historical and observational analyses together with data derived from official sources and other research reports to provide a broad picture of how black women are processed by the criminal justice system. The book also introduces a series of conceptual distinctions aimed at enhancing knowledge of how punishment and victimisation work. It tries to extend the conceptual vocabulary within which the processes of punishment are conceived.

My view is that this book will generate controversy and debate in all its aspects. I certainly think it will cause criminologists, sociologists and activists to examine the way in which they have thought about this topic. They may well disagree with what it says and how it goes about this, but I am sure they will gain from their encounter with it.

Peter Young, Edinburgh.

Preface and Acknowledgements

This book is guided by the assumption that there is discrimination in the criminal justice system and that any such discrimination is likely to affect poor black women in different ways compared to poor black men and poor white women who are caught up in the system. This is why the book has avoided going through the usual ritual of debating whether there is discrimination or not (and there is a lot of literature on this question from the competing negative or affirmative types of conclusion). The book raises a different type of question on the possible forms that discrimination and disadvantage could take in the criminal justice system of England and Wales with specific reference to black women, black men and white women.

This book is based on a longer piece of work that I completed for the doctorate at the Centre for Criminology and the Social and Philosophical Study of Law at the University of Edinburgh, 1990-1993. I have excluded sections of the thesis that were mainly theoretical and methodological from this book because of the need to make the book more accessible, less volumnous and less expensive. However, the relevant theoretico-methodological issues are reflected in relevant publications that have been cited in the book to be followed up by interested readers.

I, Biko Agozino, hereby declare that this book was composed by myself and that it has not been previously published. An essay of fifteen thousand words with the main title was submitted to the University of Cambridge in partial fulfillment of the requirements for a successful M.Phil in 1990 and a 100,000 words thesis of the same title was awarded the Ph.D. by the University of Edinburgh in 1995. The present book is approximately seventy thousand words long. The first sub-section of chapter three, 'The

Construction of Criminal Categories' was awarded the 'Mike Brake Prize in Radical Social Policy and Social Work 1994'. Thanks to the judges for their useful comments.

Thanks also to my supervisors and examiners for their patience and understanding, to my colleagues for their support, help with proof-reading and constructive criticism, to my family for their sacrifice and encouragement, to the University of Calabar for the Study Fellowship Award, the Cambridge Commonwealth Trust and ODA for the Cambridge/ODA shared Scholarship, to the University of Edinburgh for the Postgraduate Research Studentship, and to the Committee of Vice Chancellors and Principals for the Overseas Research Students Award which helped to finance the study that gave rise to this book. Big thanks to the groups and individuals who provided research information. Although the credits are not mine alone, I am fully responsible for any errors that might be found in this book. Finally, thanks to the editorial team of Ashgate for considerably reducing this burden of errors.

Biko Agozino, Liverpool.

Dedication

To my mother, Inoakamma (or the enemy does not say your praise), who was once charged to court by the colonial authorities in connection with an alleged breach of the peace when she rallied the community with a poetic tonal cry for the arrest of a stranger who was fishing in Omala, our ancestral stream. The fish in Omala symbolised happiness for the villagers because they were never threatened and it was believed that if the fish was killed, the stream would dry up. Proof of this is found down stream towards the distant farms where Omala merged with streams that we could fish in and where the stream dried up during the dry season. Omala was sacred to us as the route through which new born babies return to us from the land of the ancestors. Mothers of new born babies were expected to visit Omala and have their ritual bathe with a troop of children singing a dedication of the new born to Omala. The mother usually returned with water that she would feed to the new born so that s/he would learn the tongue of our ancestors with ease. I once accompanied my mother alone in sorrow when she had a still birth and while watching her bathe with a stream of tears down her face, I pledged silently to live and dry those tears from her face. The man who was caught fishing in the sacred stream was given a good beating by the villagers before the police rescued him. My mother conducted her own successful defence in court and won herself the nick-name, *leyo-maji* or Lawyer-Magistrate (stipendiary as opposed to lay Magistrate), from her fellow peasant women. However, my father allegedly rebuked her for using the 'male' art form of tonal poetry, *iti mpkupko*, to rally the community and so since then, according to her, she lost the talent for this type of performance poetry. Knowledge of this case that happened long before I was born, must have sensitised me to the fact that what is crime and what is justice are not given but are contentious and are contested.

1. Analytical Framework

Introduction

> Brothers and sisters, Hail! Hail! ... As the brothers in the street would say, I man Ire, I man dread, which simply means that whatever pressures may be coming down we are determined to resist. Our will to struggle has not in any way been lessened; on the contrary, today we feel stronger than ever, we feel more confident than ever, not simply in our own ability and capacity, because that would be incorrect. We feel more confident because of the demonstrated ability and capacity of the people as a whole (Rodney, 1981: 5, his last public address exactly one week before he was assassinated on 13 June 1980).

The choice to focus this research primarily on black women is based on the belief that they are marginalised in both society and in criminological research. In education, employment, the professions, commerce, industry, and politics, black women are poorly represented. But in the prisons, their presence is highly disproportionate to their numbers in the wider society.

It was reported by the Home Office that in June 1988,

> About 9.5 per cent of the male prison population and 19 per cent of the females were known to be of West Indian or African origin, compared to 9 per cent and 17.5 per cent respectively in mid 1987 and thus continuing the increases from 8 per cent and 12 per cent respectively, in mid-1985 *(Home Office Statistical Bulletin*, hereafter referred to as *H.O.S.B.* 12/89, 'The prison population in 1988', p. 10).

This is out of line with their proportional distribution of less than three per cent in the total population. It is also out of tune with the relative lack of criminological interest in Black women (Rice, 1990; Agozino, 1995a). Yet some criminologists and administrators interpret these statistics to mean that black people are disproportionately involved in criminality. See Fitzgerald (1993) a Home Office review of the literature on this for The Royal Commission on Criminal Justice. She concluded that it is not possible to tell the level of involvement in criminality by whole groups and categories. She also conceded that it is possible that some of the over-representation of black people in the criminal justice system is as a result of discriminatory treatment at different stages of the criminal justice process. Hudson (1987) is surprised to find similar scepticism among criminal justice officials while it is becoming fashionable for many left-wing and right-wing criminologists. to argue that black people must be more involved in (street) crime simply because black people are relatively poor. It will be argued in this book that this pattern of relative presence (in prisons) and relative absence (in research) is symptomatic of marginalisation which needs to be properly understood in order to be overcome.

Marginalised groups such as the poor, it has been argued, are traditionally the focus of criminological research because of their relative powerlessness and also due to their over-representation in control institutions (Box, 1983). The criminological interest in the poor is justifiable because the majority of those arrested and those held in custody are poor. What is difficult to justify is the assumption of some criminologists that the marginalised poor only constitute problems that could be solved through the discovery of more effective control mechanisms (Wilson and Herrnstein, 1985, for example). This book focuses on the problems that the theory and practice of criminal justice pose for the marginalised.

Another research tendency that has been widely criticised is that of drawing generalisations for all poor people from studies that focus on a specific category of poor men. Women as a category of marginalised people tend to be denied the traditional focus of conventional criminology, perhaps, because most of the researchers are men or because women have not tended to end up in prison as frequently as men. Feminist scholars have convincingly argued that better criminological knowledge could be gained by studying women with equal emphasis and by limiting conclusions to those studied (Smart, 1990). Black women have similarly criticised research in criminology for focusing almost exclusively on white women or on black men while claiming to be writing generally on gender or race relations (Rice, 1990; Chigwada, 1991; Agozino, 1997).

By generalising for black women from studies that do not focus on black women, researchers who exclude black women from their studies give the impression that the problems facing black women are not significantly different from the problems facing those studied. Examples of such studies

2

will soon be discussed under the guiding assumptions of the present research. Whether researchers assume that the problems facing black women are unique or that they are common, there is a need to study such problems compared to the problems of similar categories of people in order to understand them and help to overcome them.

This book assumes that the race and class relations of black women are shared (to a large extent) by black men and that their gender and class relations are shared, to some extent, by white women. This means that race relations reflect and are reflected by class and gender relations and these relations should be analysed together in order to understand fully the problems that face black women (see Daly, 1993; Hall, 1988; hooks, 1984; Agozino, 1991, 1995a-c, 1996a&b, 1997). The nature of the outcome of all three relations for black women can be best understood in this book along with outcomes for categories of people who share these relations to some extent.

There is now a growing literature in criminological research on gender, race, and class but their analyses rarely tend to be brought together and are often treated separately. For example, Hall, et al (1978), *Policing The Crisis*, focused on race and class but made only passing remarks on black women probably because the reaction to the crime of mugging, with which they were concerned, affected black men almost exclusively. Even so. one would like to know how much the policing of mugging affected the women in the lives of the suspects because, as we shall see, there is evidence that the policing of men affects the women in their family or in their lives. Similarly, Naffine (1990) analysed the impacts of gender and class relations on the treatment of people by the criminal justice system but she was silent on race relations even though she writes from a highly racialised society. Australia. Another example is that of the black feminist activist, Ware (1970) who looked at race and gender relations but narrowed it down to quarrels between black men and black women without mentioning the impacts of class relations in this context.

Likewise, although there is a growing literature on black women, most of it relates to their family life or employment opportunities (Gregory, 1987; Crenshaw, 1991; James and Busia, eds. 1993). Those that have direct relevance to criminology tend to be positivistic in the sense of trying to identify what makes black women commit crimes. For example, Carlen (1992), in a review of her earlier work *Women, Crime and Poverty* (1988), indicated that black women were included in her sample but what she wanted to find out from the women was why they broke the law or why they failed to conform to societal norms.

Carlen's approach is inadequate for at least three reasons. Firstly, her questions presupposed that the women had what she called 'criminal careers' or that they were exposed to overcriminalisation or excessive punishment relative to the seriousness of their deviance. The criminal career

3

approach ignored the fact that some of the women were first time offenders who might have normal rather than criminal careers. However, Carlen used the term 'criminal careers' differently compared to longitudinal studies that follow a given age cohort. She seems to have used the term to refer to the occurrence of criminality in the life histories of the women.

Secondly, it is possible that some of the poor and marginalised women that Carlen studied may have been processed through the criminal justice system, not always because their marginalisation forced them into a criminal career as left realists would predict (see Young and Matthews, 1992), but, perhaps, because their marginalisation exposed them to severe surveillance and, possibly, to Victimisation-As-Mere-Punishment (soon to be clarified). If Carlen did not find any such women, it may be because she started with a leading question that is ideologically loaded. Instead of asking them why they broke the law or why they found it difficult to conform, she should have started with an inquiry into the possibility of their innocence. To assume their guilt from court verdicts is to ignore the fact that many convicts go down still protesting their innocence (see Eaton, 1993).

Thirdly, Carlen failed to analyse the impact of race relations on the women she studied. She merely stated in passing that race was an additional factor for the marginalisation of some of the women and presumably, an additional variable for the causation of the criminality of those (black) women. This qualification is inadequate for the first two reasons stated above and also because when Carlen summarised her findings, there was no mention of race at all, implying that the politics of race was irrelevant to how white women were treated in the criminal justice system.

According to Lardner (1987), most criminological writings on black people maintain a 'deviant perspective' because black people lack adequate power to resist the stereotypes and labels applied to them. She argues that future research should abandon the search for 'problems' of (i.e. caused by) the black community and focus on 'the nature of oppression and the mechanism by which institutionalised forms of subjugation are initiated and act to maintain the system intact.' This is the approach that is adopted in this book.

The small amount of literature that exists on the ways black women are treated in the criminal justice system tends to focus on one institution such as the police or the prison (Chigwada, 1991; French, 1981). Some, like Rice (1990), only complain about the relative absence of black women in criminological literature and call for the criminality of black women to be studied alongside the criminality of white women. As we have seen with reference to Carlen (and with reference to the theory and philosophy of the Punishment-Of-Offenders, POO, more on this soon), the prioritisation of the criminality of black women or that of any group of people in the conceptual focus of any research could lead to the concealment or distortion of some of the problems that the criminal justice system poses for some of the people

4

who might be innocent. The contention in this book is that it is necessary to go beyond these approaches by examining the criminal justice system as a whole with a view to understanding the problems different institutions cumulatively pose for black women.

Further, this book contends that it is equally necessary to see the social relations of black women concurrently, as Dill (1987) implies, instead of looking at their race, class, gender, or culture separately as if these do not operate in articulation. In this connection, Dill (1987) and Gilroy (1990) warn that black culture should not be equated with working class culture since black people have variable class relations.

The fact that most earlier studies of race and gender in criminology focus exclusively on black men or on white women implies that the racial experiences of black women could be represented by those of black men and that the gender experiences of black women could be inferred from those of white women (Rice, 1990; Harding, 1987). Some writers have noticed this and called for the study of black women in class relations (Morris, 1987; 1988) but this call tends to be answered in exclusive dualities of race and gender or race and class, rather than in the broad comparative way that has been suggested by Hall (1980, 1988, 1996), hooks (1981, 1984, 1994), Daly (1993), Agozino (1995a-d, 1996a&b, 1997), Crenshaw (1991) and others.

Following Cain's warning against the use of men as false standards in comparing men with women (Cain, 1990), there are no assumptions in this book that black men and white women are standard bearers of social justice against whom black women are to be measured. However, the solution to false standards does not lie in different standards, as Cain seems to suggest, by calling for women to be compared with other women while opposing comparisons of men with women. This book does not see what makes the comparison of black women with black men unacceptable if it is permissible to compare poor women with rich women and black women with white women.

Nevertheless, the warning against false standards - such as regarding female prisons to be holiday camps because they appear to be less over-crowded and better-kept than male ones in what Carlen (1983) called 'female imprisonment (as) female imprisonment denied' - is taken seriously here. There is no assumption that if black women are treated in exactly the same way as black men and as white women, they would have no problem at all or vice versa.

Moreover, differences between black men and black women or between the latter and white women may not be related to gender or racial differences as such. A poor black man may face problems that a rich black woman may escape and a poor black woman may share the problems of a poor white woman. Therefore, there is an attempt here to see what ways class relations articulate with race and gender relations for people with similar and variable class, race or gender relations in the criminal justice

5

system. This means that neither class, nor race, nor gender would be analysed exclusively without indicating how far they are articulated.

Given similar circumstances before the law, this book hopes to demonstrate how the problems faced by black women vary according to their gender, race, class, and the historical point in time when they are confronted by the criminal justice system. The relations of race, class, and gender are analysed in historically specific contexts to make sense of the problems that black women face in the criminal justice system.

This does not mean that these social relations are separate and independent of one another. Rather, the claim in this book is that race, gender and class relations are socially articulated with one another. In other words, the meanings of femininity (for example) vary with race, class, time, and place. Black women are different from white women in many ways but they are similar enough to be classified together as women. A rich black woman may not face significant problems that a poor black woman may share with poor black men and poor white women. This seems to be what Hall (1988) referred to when he said that race, class and gender are socially articulated, disarticulated and rearticulated dialectically. Naffine (1990) has also argued that gender and class, and by extension, race, should be analysed together because their meanings and impacts are compounded. However, this does not mean that they are all identical social relations, it only suggests that although they are different issues, they do not operate separately and so should be analysed jointly.

This book will look at similarities in the class-race-gender (as Daly, 1993, put it) relations of black women, black men and white women in society to see whether or not these can explain similarities and differences in the problems that they face in the criminal justice system. Of course, differences and similarities in problems could be due to factors other than race, gender, or class. They could be due to circumstances surrounding the cases but if different cases tend to raise similar problems or if similar cases raise different problems, they may also have to do with the social relations of the people involved.

Another objective of this book is to examine whether existing theories in criminology adequately account for any evidence of differences in the problems faced, and modes of struggle for survival, by women of different races and classes and those of men and women of one race and class in the criminal justice system. The emphasis is on the tendency to victimise innocent people and in what ways such victimisation follows gender, racial, class, or historical patterns. However, the relative victimisation of offenders through disproportionate criminalisation is also considered.

In line with this objective, three related guiding assumptions that are implicit in existing criminological theories and methods will be examined and debated. These are:

1. Black women do not face unique problems in the criminal justice system compared to white women,

2. Black women do not face different problems in the criminal justice system compared to black men and,

3. Poor black women do not face peculiar problems in the criminal justice system compared to rich black women.

Although very few researchers make explicit claims that all black women, or all black people, or all women, or all poor people face the same problems irrespective of variable race, gender, and class relations, those who do not theorise these internal differences leave the assumption of sameness intact, albeit implicitly, in their generalised conclusions. For example, O'Dyer, Wilson and Carlen (1987: 178) explicitly claimed that 'women in prison suffer all the same deprivation, indignities and degradations as male prisoners. Additionally they suffer other problems that are specific to them as imprisoned women.' The authors could have qualified their claim by adding that black women also suffer additional problems based on race relations.

They did not see the need for such a qualification probably because they were not studying black women as well, otherwise, they would have seen the danger of generalising for all women from the experiences of some. Besides, even if they gave such a qualification, it would prove inadequate for two reasons. First, it still implies that all men face the same problems in prison in spite of different race and class relations. Secondly, such a ritualistic qualification would still beg the question of what the nature of the specific problems facing black women are, demanding that they be directly studied.

Similarly, Hall, et al (1978) and Gilroy (1987a) have made significant contributions towards the understanding of the politics of race in society and in the criminal justice system. However, they based their conclusions almost exclusively on encounters between young black men and the police without showing the unique predicament of black women. The present book is directly aimed at understanding the problems that poor black women share or do not share with poor black men and poor white women in the criminal justice system. The emphasis on poor black women, black men and white women is noteworthy here because a majority of those processed through the criminal justice system are poor. Unless otherwise indicated, wherever these categories of people are mentioned in this book, the reference is to the poor.

This is different from those approaches that represent black women as if they all face the same problems in spite of different class relations. For example, Ruth Hall (1985) talked about 'racist-sexist violence' in the same manner that French (1981) identified a 'double jeopardy' of race and gender as the major problem facing black women. The theme of double jeopardy is reflected in many studies of black women even when a sloganeering call for race, class and gender to be analysed together is made (see Chigwada, 1991). The guiding assumptions of this book, opposite of those stated above, make differences within categories of people problematic without denying that some problems are shared between and within categories.

The above assumptions are closely related because they capture the three major ways in which the relations of race, gender, and class are articulated in the problems facing black women in the criminal justice system. This indicates that an attempt will be made in the pages of this book to understand differences in the problems faced by black men and black women with reference mainly to their gender differences. Differences between the problems facing black women and white women will be partially linked to their racial differences. And we will try to see whether similarities in the problems facing black women, white women and black men in the criminal justice system when offence characteristics and circumstances differ, has any connection with their similar class-race-gender relations.

If the three assumptions enumerated above are upheld by the evidence, then the relative neglect of black women in research could be excused since their experiences could be reduced to those (racial) of black men and to those (gendered) of white women or generalised for all black women irrespective of class relations. Otherwise, ways of reconstructing the relevant theories to avoid this apparent neglect and ways of overcoming the marginalisation of black women in the entire society would be suggested. This is the immediate significance of this book.

The wider significance of this book is as a modest theoretical contribution to the debate over the nature of procedural and substantive equality in the criminal justice system. This significance of the book is related to the theoretical objectives of explaining how race, class, and gender relations are articulated in the problems that face black women in the criminal justice system. The significance is that such an explanation will contribute to the solution of the problems facing black women in the theory and practice of criminal justice.

By focusing on marginalised black women without losing sight of other marginalised categories of people, there is a good chance of understanding the major issues relevant to the problems faced by marginalised black women, black men and white women in the criminal justice system. Irrespective of their differences, it is necessary to understand whether these marginalised categories of people relate to the criminal justice system in similar, though not identical, ways.

Poor white men and poor Asians are excluded from this research for the purpose of narrowing the focus. Moreover, Gilroy (1987a: 39) has argued that racial meanings and identities are not given and constant but are contested, articulated and rearticulated in such a way that 'definitions of black based on the possibility of Afro-Asian unity (has shifted) ... towards more restricted alternative formulations which have confined the concept of blackness to people of African descent.' This view has been supported by Parekh (1987: xii) according to whom, 'The term black is rejected by the bulk of the Asians ....' The extent to which this book has implications beyond the categories of people focused on can only be determined by future research or inferred from previous ones.

The objective of the book, then, is to examine whether the problems that face black women in the criminal justice system are significantly different from those that confront black men, on the one hand, and white women, on the other hand. If so, this book aims at demonstrating how such problems are constituted by the articulation of race, gender and class relations and how these social relations are articulated in the struggles against such problems. There will be no attempt here to hierarchicise these social relations for the purpose of determining respective ranks of significance in specific instances. My focus is on the nature of the problems that confront black women in the criminal justice system rather than on the extent of such problems. However, the nature of the problems that face black women may suggest the seriousness of such problems.

Similarly, attitudes of black women could reflect, to some extent, the problems that black women face and so such attitudes deserve to be studied in their own right. However, the present book is more interested in social structural problems and in problems constituted by institutional practices that may or may not be reflected by the attitudes of individuals. It will be argued here that the problems that face black women can be understood in terms of the structural positions of black women in society, their social relations and the nature of the institutional practices of the criminal justice system. The attitudes of black women will be reflected by the opinions of individuals and groups who provide research information but the author will always try to focus attention on the problems that the women face and not on their attitudes to social institutions.

However, the perception of such problems by groups and individuals is likely to carry the marks of certain attitudes. Nevertheless, it is possible to focus either on the problems perceived or on the attitudes implicit in the perception or on both. This book is analytically focused on the problems and not on the attitudes articulated in their perception although the latter cannot be completely excluded from consideration.

The major significance of this book is that the identification of the problems that black women face could enable activists, scholars, and legal practitioners to be better able to work with black women to overcome such problems and boost the confidence of black women in their power and rights within the criminal justice system in particular and society in general. The extent to which such problems can be shown to be shared by black men and by white women would be the extent to which the implications of the findings could be applied for the purpose of overcoming the problems that

9

face these other categories of people in the criminal justice system and in society.

Discussions were held (by this author) with individual black women in courts and with relevant voluntary organisations such as the 'Africa Prisoners' Scheme', 'Black Female Prisoners' Scheme', NACRO's 'Women Prisoners Resource Centre', 'Women In Prison', 'Akina Mama wa Africa', 'Society of Black Lawyers', 'Society of Black Probation Officers', and 'Hackney Community Defence Association' to understand the problems that face black women, white women, and black men in the criminal justice system.

Description of Outline

This book is structured into six chapters. The first chapter is a summary of the theoretico-methodological objectives and gives an indication of the significance of the book. This chapter also contains a brief review of existing literature to see what leads they can offer towards the formulation of questions on race, gender, and class relations in the criminal justice system. Moreover, this chapter considers the alternative background models or frameworks for the book. The major models of social relations in the judicial process are reviewed here to see to what extent they are applicable to problems of race, class, and gender relations in the criminal justice system.

Chapter two is historical in the sense that it attempts to show what links there are between the problems that face black women in London and the slavery, colonial and neo-colonial techniques of control which created problems for black women in Africa and America. This chapter also considers the historical experiences of black women in British society. The aim of this chapter is not to prove the universality of the victimisation of black women in the criminal justice system, but to see what can be learnt from the specific form(s) of victimisation in the different epochs and thereby arrive at a better understanding of recent instances. Similarities in the experiences of black women in the different epochs would not be simplistically seen as evidence of gradual evolution of victimisation practices from the past to the present. Any similarities among specific instances of victimisation would be seen as being suggestive of similar social relations and similar material conditions of repression and resistance which form part of the historical consciousness of most black people in particular and the oppressed poor in general, corresponding to the historical lessons learnt by agents of the criminal justice system.

Chapter three considers how the construction of black people as a crime-prone category of people could lead to the victimisation of innocent black women. The chapter also points out that the problem of victimisation in terms of policing is not merely that of the attitudes of individual police officers but also an institutionalised process of power relations. The chapter also analyses the ways that the black community and black women organise autonomously or in alliance with others to resist perceived injustice.

Chapter four analyses the court-room observations of this writer against the background information from relevant publications, voluntary organisations and affected individuals. The observations on disparity and discrimination, support and isolation, the hierarchy of discreditability and observations on procedure go to suggest the forms that discrimination could take in the courts. It is true that observations about the relative isolation of the female defendant in court and those about a possible hierarchy of discreditability do not directly reflect discrimination. However, they serve to point out how the problems that face black women in courts reflect or affect problems that are faced by black women and people like them in society.

Chapter five concludes the presentation of evidence for the forms of victimisation and discrimination which face black women in the criminal justice system. This is done by looking at the race and gender composition of prison populations in England and Wales. An analysis of the ways that relations in prisons are racialised and gendered is presented with relevant evidence from the US and Britain. The special plights of foreign black women in prisons are also highlighted to emphasise the assumption of this writer that impoverishment and imperialist power relations are important elements in the analysis of the ways that discrimination and victimisation affect black women in the criminal justice system.

Chapter six focuses mainly on the theoretical and practical implications of the methodology and the framework in view of the findings. This involves a general discussion of issues raised and the conclusions they point to. This includes a review of the theoretical assumptions that guided the book and a re-assessment of the methodological approach. This is followed by a general discussion on the agenda for future research and by a general bibliography. Full references for information from newspapers or bulletins are given in the body of the text.

Clarification of Concepts

To end this general introduction, there is a need to clarify further the key concepts introduced in this book. Victimisation-As-Mere-Punishment (VAMP) is used here to refer to what is sometimes referred to in jurisprudence (see Lacey, 1988) as the Punishment-Of-The-Innocent (POTI). Victimisation-As-Mere-Punishment differs from Punishment-Of-The-Innocent in three important ways.

Firstly, they differ in terms of theory because punishment is rightly conceptualised but not always practised as the Punishment-Of-Offenders (POO). This suggests that to term what is done to the innocent as a form of punishment would be a misconception. Secondly, from a conceptual point of view, punishment is the operative word in Punishment-Of-The-Innocent

11

whereas victimisation is the operative word in Victimisation-As-Mere-Punishment. This suggests that Punishment-Of-The-Innocent still colonises victimisation within the empire of punishment. Thirdly, from a practical perspective, Punishment-Of-The-Innocent would be willing to forgive what is done to the innocent as an error whereas Victimisation-As-Mere-Punishment would like to see the offenders punished in the interest of those who were victimised.

Victimisation-As-Mere-Punishment recognises that some people who are 'punished' are not offenders and so such people can be said to have been victimised. The central point of Victimisation-As-Mere-Punishment is not the simple one that the criminal justice system makes mistakes but the critical one that the system also institutionally violates the rights of some people because of the ways that power relations are structured within the system (see McConville, Sanders and Leng, 1993).

Victimisation-As-Mere-Punishment is, therefore, not my invention. It is adopted from popular consciousness of the reality of victimisation whereas the philosophical concept of Punishment-Of-The-Innocent still talks about victimisation as if it is a form of punishment. Moreover, victimology does not include Victimisation-As-Mere-Punishment in its discourse while the philosophy, theory and practice of Punishment-Of-Offenders simply colonise it and present it as part of their territory by denying its autonomous existence. Notable exceptions are sections 2.8 and 2.9 of the Race Relations Act 1976 that recognise the existence of victimisation but define it restrictively in civil rather than criminal terms as the subsequent unfavourable treatment of a person as a result of proceedings brought, evidence given, or allegations made by such a person under the Act.

Examples of Victimisation-As-Mere-Punishment in this book include the imprisonment without trial of wives of army officers whose husbands were suspected of planning or attempting a coup, mothers or sisters of suspected robbers or terrorists or supporters of suspects and convicts who are themselves imprisoned, harassed, killed, maimed, put under surveillance or have their freedom of movement restricted sometimes because they are mistakenly regarded as conspirators or accomplices and sometimes because their victimisation is calculated to affect the elusive or unapologetic suspects who are socially proximate to the victimised. In England and Wales, an extreme case of Victimisation-As-Mere-Punishment resulting in the conviction of a whole family was that of the Maguire Seven, the surviving six of whom were subsequently cleared of the terrorism charges (see Hillyard, 1993, for a detailed analysis of this and similar Irish cases of what he called a 'suspect community'). This book will show that such assumptions of guilt by association affect black families also not only in terms of harassment and brutality by the police but also in the form of false accusations and malicious prosecutions of black people who happen to be close to suspected black communities.

12

When the innocence of the victimised is not in doubt, such as in the case of the married sisters whose millionaire brother is suspected of funding a coup, Victimisation-As-Mere-Punishment can be said to be direct or deliberate. In the former case, when the significant others are also (rightly or wrongly) suspected, arrested or convicted and later found to have been wrongly so treated, as in most cases of the miscarriage of justice, Victimisation-As-Mere-Punishment can be said to be institutional rather than direct or deliberate. See Agozino (1996a) for the institutionalised ways that collective responsibility is assumed in sports law and in the criminal justice system.

Sports are not the only areas of life where team ethics are operative. Families, groups, nations, etc. can be and have been seen as sharing a common goal and deserving shared sanctions. In England and Wales, for example, the 1991 Criminal Justice Act gave magistrates and judges the power to directly fine the parents of juveniles between the ages of 16 and 18 for offences that such young people committed. The same act also empowered the courts to bind parents over to make sure that their children do not re-offend. The significance of these provisions for black women is that many of them are single parents on low incomes and that young black people are even more over-represented in the criminal justice system than adult blacks. This suggests that poor black women face serious risks under the clause of parental responsibility for the alleged conduct of children.

The London-based Institute of Race Relations has documented cases of Policing Against Black People (re-published in 1987). The most striking fact in the document is that the black women who were affected by repressive policing were mostly affected, not because they were suspects themselves, but because they were mothers, sisters or wives of suspected black men. One of the women was shot and paralysed when the police came looking for a son who no longer lived with her, at her house in London. Another one collapsed and died of a heart attack during a police raid that was connected with her son.

There is no need to overstretch the analogies in order to illustrate the point that the knowledge of guilt is not necessary for the unleashing of the control mechanisms that are often popularised as 'the Punishment-Of-Offenders' (POO). Some people who are 'punished' are known to be innocent and some people who are known to be guilty are not punished at all. Many officials of the criminal justice system would accept the second part of the preceding sentence and apply it exclusively to those poor (or even rich black men like O.J. Simpson) defendants and suspects who manage to win their acquittal or secure their escape even while the officials believe that they are guilty without satisfactory evidence to prove it.

However, such people are not always assumed to be guilty until proved innocent; they could also be given Victimisation-As-Mere-Punishment through repressive actions that are taken, supposedly or initially only against suspected individuals who are close to them even when they themselves are known to be innocent. This is the ancient plough of the criminal justice process: collective responsibility and guilt by association that the football analogy tried to illustrate (Agozino, 1996a).

The Punishment-Of-Offenders discourse is relatively silent on Victimisation-As-Mere-Punishment and even on Punishment-Of-The-Innocent also because it is supposed to be a barbaric practice that is no longer present in the industrial societies of today (see Cohen, 1993 for a powerful explanation of this 'culture of denial'). However, even when the pre-industrial past is the subject-matter of theorising and research, the subject remains offenders (see Durkheim, 1973; Garland, 1990). When the existence of guilt by association is acknowledged, it is applied restrictively to the past as if it is completely absent in modern society (Kennedy, 1976) contrary to the incontrovertible documentation by the Institute of Race Relation in Britain (IRR, 1987).

Coming from an African culture where the concept of human beings as victims is non-existent, this writer wishes to emphasise that Victimisation-As-Mere-Punishment does not suggest that the victimised are victims. Rather, the victimised are seen in this book as survivors who fight militantly against victimisation. As Cornel West (1993) put it, the acknowledgement of victimisation does not mean an acceptance of the status of a passive victimhood.

VIP or Victimisation-In-Punishment is what is usually called 'over-criminalisation' or excessive punishment relative to the nature of the offence. Instances of Victimisation-In-Punishment would be the imprisonment of some convicts for offences that other defendants with similar or even worse previous records could get non-custodial sentences or shorter prison terms, the disproportionate provision of services and discrimination within the prison, and the militarised policing of certain categories of suspects when other categories engaged in similar activities could be more civilly policed.

This book recognises that Victimisation-As-Mere-Punishment is more likely to occur at the level of policing and the investigation of allegations (because of high degrees of discretion given to rank and file officers by the Police and Criminal Evidence Act) but such occurrences could be reinforced institutionally, rather than deliberately if such Victimisation-As-Mere-Punishment is not recognised for what it is at subsequent stages of the criminal justice process. Consequently, Victimisation-In-Punishment is more likely to be the form that victimisation would take in the courts and prisons even though Victimisation-As-Mere-Punishment cannot be said to be absent in these institutions as well.

Central to this book is the theory of articulation. This theory was introduced to this writer by Stuart Hall in London during the fieldwork. Although this writer was familiar with the theory of the articulation of

14

modes of production before this meeting, credit goes to Hall for pointing out its potential for the analysis of social relations. This writer met him along a busy London road and was pleased to get an appointment to visit his house and talk about the research that led to . After a brief summary of the research, Professor Hall immediately identified articulation as the key theoretical concept. He lent his copy of Hall (1980a) and this writer went away with a feeling of 'eureka!'

It is sufficient to say here that this writer uses articulation to indicate that race-class-gender relations are joined together and that they give expression to one another in the experiences of real people and so their analyses should be concurrent and made to reflect their interconnectedness. This approach differs from unifocal perspectives that single out race, class or gender and analyse it by denying or belittling the importance of other relations. I extend this perspective to social policy impacts by looking for ways that penal policies articulate with victimisation and with welfare to give rise to Victimisation-As-Mere-Punishment, Victimisation-In-Punishment and even VAW - Victimisation-As-Welfare.

The concept of Victimisation-As-Mere-Punishment is not the same as what Pitch (1995) described as the sociological movement 'from oppression to victimisation' and 'from victimisation to autonomy'. The first movement refers to what she saw as the movement away from critical criminological focus on the victimisation of criminals by sociologically deterministic criminogenic conditions and their subsequent victimisation by the criminal justice system itself. VAMP differs from both these two instances because it is focused on the innocent and not the 'victim' as such (whereas Pitch talks about 'innocent victims' only in relation to victims of individual crimes and in connection with a 'collective responsibility' by the whole society to care for the needy in a welfare state) and also because VAMP is not an aetiological concept about what causes crime. However, the second idea that the criminal justice system is capable of victimising even the criminal is close to what is called in this book, Victimisation-In-Punishment. The second sociological movement identified by Pitch is that of the empowerment of the victimised to the extent that they organise collectively to protest, lobby or pressurise for policy reforms as working class, civil rights and feminist groups have demonstrated. This second movement will be visible in the autonomous organisations that support mainly black women in the criminal justice system through whom much of the evidence for this book was received.

I suggest that Victimisation-As-Mere-Punishment can be explained by the articulation of unequal race, class and gender relations because the people who are relatively marginalised on the bases of these social relations appear to be the ones most vulnerable to Victimisation-As-Mere-Punishment. This explanation is persuasive because the power and material resources available through these social relations could make certain

15

individuals relatively immune to Victimisation-As-Mere-Punishment because they could more successfully defend themselves against Victimisation-As-Mere-Punishment or even participate in its perpetration through the manipulation of available resources. Articulation is important here because none of these social relations could be isolated to offer a satisfactory explanation for Victimisation-As-Mere-Punishment.

For example, a poor black woman would be more vulnerable to Victimisation-As-Mere-Punishment because subordinate race relations make her more suspect than a poor white woman, subordinate gender relations make her to be more readily seen to be dependent and therefore more likely to be targeted as an accomplice (of suspected black men) than a poor black man (when a black woman is a suspect), and subordinate class relations locate her more closely in the internal colonies that are more militarily policed while also denying her the necessary resources for more effective legal defence than a rich black woman.

It follows that the class of a rich black woman would relatively disarticulate her subordinate gender and race relations and thereby give her a degree of protection, the gender of poor black men could disarticulate their race and class and even make some collaborators in victimisation, while the race of a poor white woman could relatively disarticulate her gender and class by offering her relative protection. However, the class of the rich black women who become targets when their husbands, brothers or fathers become suspects of subversive activities could be said to be disarticulated by their gender just as the race of the white women who are victimised due to their proximity to poor black men could be said to have been disarticulated by their gender relations.

This is not a privileging of class over race and gender relations. It is a recognition of the specificity of the criminal justice system as a terrain where most defendants are poor irrespective of race and gender differences. However, the anti-hierarchicisation perspective of articulation demands that the importance of class relations in the criminal justice system cannot be understood unless they are viewed as class-race-gender relations.

The concept of articulation is being used in this book in the sense that Stuart Hall employed it as a way of avoiding the usual critique that historical materialist analyses tend to be economically deterministic. The concept of articulation allows us to take other forms of social relations seriously without abandoning class relations as many of the critics of historical materialism tend to do. According to Hall (1980a: 325) articulation results in 'a structure in which things are related, as much as through their differences as through their similarities'.

This suggests that I will be interested in differences as well as similarities between black women, black men and white women in the criminal justice system. This is important because the complexity of articulated structures means that such structures do not correspond to any one component but reflect and are reflected by the articulated relations. Hall (1980a) has shown how widely the concept of articulation has been used with reference to relations between different modes of production (Wolpe, 1972; Marx, 1981). I follow Hall by abstracting this theory from modes of production analysis and applying it to social relations and social policies.

Race-Class-Gender Articulation in Criminal Justice

There are four possible models of social relations in the judicial process - the zero, unitary, binary, and articulated models. This book is based on the model of articulation which emphasises that although race, class and gender relations are different, they are not separable in theory or in practice (Hall, 1996, 1988, 1980; Daly, 1993; Crenshaw, 1991; hooks, 1993; Agozino, 1991, 1995a-c, 1996a&b, 1997).

Zero models claim that the administration of justice is not influenced by social relations but is based on rationality, equality before the law, and the treating of like cases alike. The ideal zero model of the impacts of social relations on the administration of justice could be said to be the Weberian rational-bureaucratic model. As Weber (1954) stated in 1914, no existing system of justice approximates the ideal bureaucracy. However, Weber took the technical superiority of the ideal bureaucracy for granted as a measure of its superiority to all other models of administration which Weber dismissed as irrational. In this sense, Weber was arguing along the lines of the classical moral philosophers like Beccaria and Bentham who called for the application of rationality as an alternative to the arbitrary administration of justice in pre-enlightenment times. At one level, it appears that the rational model is a prescription rather than a description but in either form, it has been rightly criticised for assuming that what is rational-bureaucratic (like the Nazi holocaust) would necessarily be just or good. As Bauman (1989) pointed out, Weber has no prescription for the intended or unintended consequences of the bureaucratisation of genocide. Yet the Weberian model is still the dominant self-image of the relationships between juridification and social relations (Relationships? What relationships? Asks the zero model of Michael Howard as he proposed to reduce Bill Clinton's baseball rule of 'three strikes' to two strikes and you're out; you, of course, never them).

Unitary models focus on one social relation and ignore others. Conventional criminological models are almost always unitary - they focus on either race or class almost exclusively. Some critics suggest that even feminist models have extended the focus to gender but very many feminist researchers remain unitary by focusing on one gender (Agozino, 1995a). Some economistic Marxist models have also been very unitary until recently by trying to explain race and gender in terms of class alone.

The chivalry thesis (Pollak, 1950) is unitary because it holds that women receive favourable considerations from officials who treat men more harshly. Official sentencing statistics tend to support this thesis because many more men are sentenced to imprisonment. Empirical research has shown, however, that the less severe sentences given to women reflect the less serious offences that they are charged with and their fewer previous records rather than being evidence of favouritism (Farrington and Morris, 1983). Like cases tend to be treated alike and all women are not treated alike. However, it has been pointed out (Allen, 1987) that when offence seriousness is similar, courts tend to see violent women as victims of nature or emotions, to treat them as non-responsible infants and to neutralise their guilt more readily than men similarly charged. This is paternalism, not favouritism. In other words, if the courts treat women as they are treated at home, it is more likely to be unfavourable to the women given that patriarchy is oppressive to women contrary to the assumption of the chivalry hypothesis (Agozino, 1997).

Furthermore, it has been argued that different socialisation patterns make girls more ready to apologise and be cautioned while boys are more ready to bluff and thus be charged (Gelsthorpe, 1986). Discriminatory stereotyping produces subtle sexism which reinforces the inequalities between men and women in society.

Unitary class models (such as the under-class thesis of Charles Murray and some left-wing variants) would point out that male and female defendants are similar in class and so class is determinant. Unitary race models, as in Hood (1992), try to 'isolate specific race effects' while supporting the chivalry hypothesis but the politics of race is never experienced in isolation from those of class and gender.

Heidensohn (1986) offers a dichotomy or binary model of Portia or Persophone which correspond to male and female law. This still retained a feature of the unitary model by focusing only on gender while appearing to be binary. Race and class are ignored in the critique of the chivalry thesis except in a few cases where it is recognised that poor men are equally disadvantaged and poor black women more so.

Race-and-class models as in *Policing the Crisis* (Hall et al, 1978) almost ignore black women and focus on poor black men. Gilroy (1987a) offers a similar model because black men are more often targeted in the policing of 'the myth of black criminality' but even men are also gendered in ways that race-and-class articulation fails to address.

Research that is focused on black women more easily offers a better articulated model because it is more difficult to ignore the intersections of race-class-gender when looking at black women. Carlen (1988, 1992) attempted this but left race unanalysed probably because her concern was mainly for the white women. She researched the relationships between gender, poverty and criminality and she included some black women in her

18

sample. However, her conclusion was that racism was probably an additional cause of criminality among some (black women). She did not analyse how racism could result in the criminalisation or victimisation of poor black women in the criminal justice system, nor did she attempt such an analysis for poor women and the poor in general.

This author, following Angela Davis, bell hooks, Kimberley Crenshaw, Patricia Hill Collins, Ruth Chigwada, Marcia Rice and others, has attempted to balance the account by focusing on black women. However, some of those who focus on black women (e.g. Rice, 1990) tend to simply bemoan the absence of black women in feminist criminological theory without offering any alternative theoretical accounts. Chigwada's work tends to be empirical but descriptive and largely untheorised. The works of Davis and hooks are more theoretical but much less criminological. Hudson and Cook (1993) regret not having any black writer to contribute to their volume but that was not a good excuse for not having a chapter that focuses on black women. However, Hudson (1987) has analysed the 'non-legal factors in sentencing'. By identifying race, class and gender as factors, her analysis tends to present them as though they are separate social relations rather than simply different but strongly articulated ones. See also Daly (1993) in *Social Justice* for an advocacy of race-class-gender analyses - a call that is frequently taken up nowadays like a mantra but which is rarely applied in many analyses.

The theory of articulation is being developed by Stuart Hall (1980, 1988) as a way of avoiding the limitations of the zero, unitary, and binary models. The articulation model assumes that people do not experience the politics of race separately or practise it in isolation from the politics of gender and the politics of class. It is therefore very important to tell us whether the subjects of a theoretical account are poor-black-women or rich-white-men and vice versa.

The major criticism against the articulation model is that it is capable of being reduced to a muddle to the extent that everything could be assumed to be everything else and nothing is itself anymore. If we must only talk in triplets, does it mean that all three relations are equally important to all persons at all times? The articulation model emphasises that the differences among these social relations must be recognised but that their lack of separation must not be forgotten. This view is clearer in the Marxist political economy of capitalist underdevelopment according to which a dominant mode of production could co-exist with a subordinate mode of production without assuming that the two modes operate independently of each other (Marx, 1981; Wolpe, 1972).

Stuart Hall abstracted this theory of articulation from political economy and applied it to the analyses of social relations of race-and-class (Hall, 1980) and race-class-gender (Hall, 1988). In other words, it is not only modes of production that are joined and that give expression to each other (or, simply, are articulated). Social relations are also articulated in societies structured in dominance, according to Hall. This emphasis on dominance suggests that specific social relations would have unequal impacts on certain people under specific conditions but Hall argues against a hierarchicisation of these social relations. Such a hierarchicisation is found in claims that one type of oppression is worse than another.

2. Black Women and Justice in History

Introduction

This chapter will try to compare the treatment of black women with those of black men and white women to find out if black women were faced with similar or significantly different problems in the criminal justice system under different historically specific ideological formations. The historical materialist theory of articulation demands that the starting point for analysis should be the historically specific material basis of the cultural forms of interest. This chapter will attempt to demonstrate that the political economies of plantation slavery, colonialism, neo-colonialism, and 'internal colonialism' manifested in their specific legal systems, the punishment, care, victimisation and repression of black women in particular and poor black people in general.

Black Women and Slavery

'Much of the rhetoric of the "New World Order" promulgated by the American government since the end of the Cold War', writes Edward Said, cannot fail to remind us of the odour of the bloodshed that greeted the other New World 'discovered' by Cristobal Colon five hundred years ago 'with its redolent self-congratulation, its unconcealed triumphalism, its grave proclamations of responsibility ...' (Said, 1993: xiv). There is no need to rehash the well-documented history of the violence of the slave economy that built the old New World. The aim here is to reinterpret that history with emphasis on the struggles of black women against its manifestations and how black women were victimised in the name of punishment.

At the 1996 meeting of the American Society of Criminology when this author (Agozino, 1996c) presented parts of this chapter to a very appreciative audience, the presentation started unorthodoxly by asking them to close their eyes and imagine that they were any criminological theorist of their liking before looking at a 1792 London cartoon, 'The Abolition of Slave Trade' (see Midgley, 1992 for a reproduction). Only two members of the audience saw the cartoon as depicting human rights abuses against Africans instead of seeing it simply as an instance of the Punishment-Of-Offenders. The interesting thing is that none of the members of the audience could interpret that cartoon in a classicist or positivistic criminological way. This was probably because criminology deals with crime and punishment whereas the African woman who was hoisted on one leg and flogged to death by one Captain Kimbler had not committed any offence. Some of the onlooking white male crew members were credited with comments like; 'By G-d that's too bad. If he had taken her to bed, to him it should be well enough, split me (sic). I'm almost sick of this Black Business'; 'My eyes lack (sic) our girls back at Wapping are never flogged for their modesty'; and from the crew member holding the rope that hoisted the woman, 'Dam me if I like it. I have a good mind to let go.' Midgley reports that the woman was murdered so brutally simply because she refused to dance naked for the pleasure of the captain. The pleasure of the captain at torturing her to death was intended by the cartoonist to contrast with the moral reservations of the crew. It seemed that the captain killed this woman because he was an evil, sick or mad man. Yet the captain presented the torture as punishment and we will search in vain from Durkheim to Foucault for a concept that will accurately describe this victimisation instead of regarding it as a form of punishment, albeit depraved. However, historians, especially those of African descent, have come closest to recognising that the executed woman was not being punished, that she was only being victimised in the name of punishment and that her victimisation was not the isolated act of a crazy pirate but part of a systematic genocide inherent to the Trans Atlantic Slave Trade at the height of the Enlightenment (Gilroy, 1993).

A classic example of such a reinterpretation could be found in The Black Jacobins (James, 1980: 6-26) which shows how severe the victimisation of enslaved black women was in San Domingo, now Haiti. James chronicled the scourge of the slavers who organised expeditions by arming rival societies with gin and gunpowder, exacerbating their struggles for domination. The propagandists of slavery claimed that the enslaved Africans were happier than their ancestors but James debunked this by showing that Africa was relatively peaceful before the commencement of the slave raids. One of the consequences of the unnecessary wars in which Africans were forced 'to supply slaves or be sold as slaves themselves' was that 'the captive women became concubines and degraded the status of the wife' (James 1980: 7).

The fact that they became concubines and not slaves disproves the propaganda or mistaken view that slavery was indigenous to Africa and that the slavers were only following a tradition which also allowed them to bring Christianity to the heathen. Mack (1992) wrote as if slavery - especially the enslavement of women who served as concubines and as domestic or agricultural workers for affluent families - was traditional to Hausaland in West Africa. Rodney (1972: 46) countered such arguments with the observation that, unlike the Europe theorised by Marx, 'in Africa after the communal stage there was no epoch of slavery arising out of internal evolution, nor was there a mode of production which was the replica of European feudalism.' The point being made by Rodney can be illustrated with the fact that enslaved people in parts of Africa could rise to become great kings like Askia Mohammed and King Ja Ja. However, Rodney was opposed to using a few kings to illustrate the history of Africa. He would have preferred to use the example of the tradition of allowing enslaved people to marry their enslavers' sons or daughters as enough indication that the content and the context of enslavement wherever that existed in Africa were not identical to what is known in the West as chattel slavery. Rodney (1972, 1970) showed the class character of the Africans who collaborated with the slavers. According to Rodney (1970) this was the role of the chiefs and feudal lords who had much to gain from the slave trade.

James (1980) provided a graphic account of the incessant revolts against the slave trade that were widespread in the interior and which continued at the port of embarkment and on board the ships in spite of the practice by which the enslaved were chained 'right hand to right leg, left hand to left leg, and attached in rows to long iron bars' (James, 1980: 8). Without going into the details of the inhumanity of the Middle Passage or how the enslaved Africans were worked like farm animals on the plantations, it is sufficient for our purpose to see the forms of victimisation which James called the 'harshest punishment' but which the slavers called the 'torture' that the enslaved received for the 'least fault' (James, 1980: 12).

The 1685 Negro Code authorised whipping, though later, attempts were made to limit the permissible number of lashes beyond which the slavers should hand over the matter to the authorities of the plantocracy. In 1702 the maximum number of strokes any individual was free to inflict was 100. This was reduced to 39 and later increased to 50 (two less than Rodney King received from the hands of the Los Angeles Police Department in 1992 plus two stun gun shots, all seen by an all-white jury as representing reasonable force, an indication that reasonableness is racialised, gendered and class-specific). However, the colonists never bothered to count the strokes and the enslaved were frequently beaten to death. Apart from whipping or in addition to that, the enslaved were also chained to blocks of wood to prevent escape, they were forced to wear tin-plate masks to prevent them from eating

23

the sugar cane that they produced, hot wood was applied to the lacerations on the buttocks in the midst of whipping (James, 1980: 12-13).

All these may seem to have no relevance whatsoever to the problems that face black women in the criminal justice system today. The relevance is that many of these practices were what could be called the miscarriages of justice today because the Negro Code only authorised a certain number of strokes of the lash. Nevertheless, just as the so-called miscarriages of justice today cannot be understood as external intrusions into the criminal justice system, the victimisation of the enslaved could only be understood as part of the criminal justice system of the colonists.

As Sellin (1976) argued, the distinction between domestic justice for slaves and the official criminal justice system is misleading because many of the penal measures applied in the official criminal justice system emerged originally as punishments reserved for the enslaved in ancient Europe. According to him, such 'slave justice' was gradually extended to the wider population due, perhaps, to the end of slavery in medieval Europe. Similarly, those harsh penal measures were again applied to enslaved Africans in the New World at a time that they were disappearing from the penal codes of Europe. This appears to be a confirmation of the 'truism' by Rusche and Kirchheimer (1968) 'that specific forms of punishment correspond to a given stage of economic development.'

However, the correspondence theory of the relation between economic stages and penal forms is inadequate for understanding the complex nature of legislation. In the case of enslavement in the Ante-bellum South, economic determinism of punishment ignores the non economic ideologies of racism that also inform legal formation, as Bell (1973) demonstrates. Sellin talked about the enslaved as a class separate from the 'master class' of slavers and this is very true. However, the class formation of slavery is not all that there is to it. The race and gender formation of enslavement are equally important for understanding the nature of criminal justice. Sellin may have overlooked this because he was trying to generalise from ancient Europe to modern times without making allowance for the relative racial homogeneity of both the enslaved and the slavers in the earlier period. Again, Sellin ignored the warning of Rusche and Kirchheimer that punishment does not correspond exactly with crime and so he missed the point that it was not all the enslaved who were 'punished' that committed any offence.

In this connection, Tombs (1982: 5-7) argues that 'the ethic of individual responsibility for conduct (is a) "legal fiction" which makes it possible for the slave status to be simultaneously recognised and denied by a legal system which regarded human beings as property and also as responsible agents'. By characterising individual responsibility as a fiction comparable to the fiction of equality before the law, Tombs suggests that the chattel status of the enslaved, their lack of property and deprivation of liberty reflect the conditions of 'the propertyless members of the nation states emerging in the sixteenth century who, in turn, came to be regarded as the "dangerous" classes, and from whose ranks the bulk of the "convicts" were, and continue to be, drawn.' Again, by putting 'dangerous' and 'convicts' in inverted commas, Tombs appears more sceptical than Sellin who saw what was being done to the enslaved under the law simply in terms of punishment similar to the Punishment-Of-Offenders, past and present.

Moreover, Sellin presented the enslaved as being incapable of fighting back even through or because, according to him, the laws were created to keep them down. Just as people struggle in various ways against every manifestation of Victimisation-As-Mere-Punishment today, the enslaved engaged in similar struggles for liberation. The most relevant aspect of the evidence presented by James is the methodological question whether it is permissible to make a general claim on the basis of particular evidence. We will come to this question again later in this book but let us see how James posed and pondered the question:

> Were these tortures, so well authenticated, habitual or were they merely isolated incidents, the extravagances of a few half-crazed colonists? Impossible as it is to substantiate hundreds of cases, yet all the evidence shows that these bestial practices were normal features of slave life. The torture of the whip, for instance, had 'a thousand refinements', but there were regular varieties that had special names, so common were they. When the hands and legs were tied to four posts on the ground, the slave was said to undergo 'the four post'. If the slave was tied to a ladder it was 'the torture of the ladder'; if he was suspended by four limbs it was 'the hammock' etc. The pregnant woman was not spared her 'four-posts'. A hole was dug in the earth to accommodate the unborn child. The torture of the collar was specially reserved for women who were suspected of abortion, and the collar never left their necks until they had produced a child. The blowing up of a slave had its own name - 'to burn a little gunpowder in the arse of a nigger.' Obviously this was no freak but a recognised practice (James, 1980: 13).

The normality of the torture and victimisation of the enslaved was illustrated by James with the Le Jeune case that came up in 1788, more than 100 years after the Negro Code of 1685 attempted to standardise torture. Le Jeune was a coffee planter who suspected that the high mortality among those he enslaved was not due to their under-nourishment by him but due to poisoning - a method of resistance widely used by the enslaved to sabotage the plantation economy. As 'punishment' Le Jeune killed four enslaved persons and tried to extort confessions from two women by roasting their feet, legs and elbows while also gagging them to stifle their cries. Contrary to the contention of Sellin (1976: 136) that the enslaved 'would find it difficult to defend themselves against accusations brought by whites and impossible to appear as witnesses against whites charged with crime', fourteen of the people whom Le Jeune enslaved went to court and denounced him even though he had warned them not to do so.

The judges appointed a commission that investigated Le Jeune's plantation and confirmed that the allegation was true. The two women were found to be still barred and chained, to be still alive though their elbows and legs were decomposing, and to have made no confession of any conspiracy to poison. The neck of one of them was so lacerated by an iron collar that she could not swallow. Le Jeune said that they were guilty of poisoning and produced as an exhibit a box that he said contained poison but which was shown to contain only tobacco and rat dung. While the court indulged in unnecessary delays, the women died in torture and Le Jeune escaped to avoid arrest. Finally, at the trial, the fourteen witnesses repeated their allegation but seven white witnesses testified in favour of Le Jeune and two of his stewards absolved him of any guilt. Other planters demanded that the fourteen prosecution witnesses should be given fifty lashes each for denouncing Le Jeune. Finally, the governor of San Domingo wrote, 'To put it shortly, it seems that the safety of the colony depends on the acquittal of Le Jeune.' He was eventually acquitted both at the primary trial and on appeal (James, 1980: 22-24).

This seems to support the claim by James that such forms of victimisation were widespread and not as isolated as they seem. Similarly, the practice of victimising innocent black women who are close to suspected black men today cannot be said to be a freak occurrence. It is impossible to say how widespread this practice is today: it is not possible to discern patterns or degrees from particular incidents. Nevertheless, the incidents we will examine later suggest the tendency or the form of Victimisation-As-Mere-Punishment as it affects black women.

Having briefly outlined the nature of the victimisation of enslaved black women as presented by James, it is important to note that rape was also used as a form of victimisation to which black women were particularly vulnerable and resistance against which exposed them to different methods of torture (Davis, 1981). Just as black women were said to have lost more to colonialism (Mba, 1982), it is argued that the oppression and exploitation of black women as slaves were qualitatively different from those of black men. This is because the former worked equally hard in the fields, were brutalised for little mistakes like the burning of the breakfast if they worked at home, were tormented by having to watch their babies being tortured, were sexually exploited and forced to breed people to be enslaved or breast-feed orphans over whom they had no claim or control, and were forced to endure the sexism of black men besides the jealousy and hatred of white women (hooks, 1981: 15-49).

Many of the women accepted their fate without question but most of them resented their dehumanisation and practically interpreted their oppression as a 'crime'. The three commonest ways in which enslaved black women resisted sexual exploitation were the risking of torture for abstaining from sex with the master, his sons, or enslaved black men; the practice of abortion to sabotage the forced reproduction of slave labour; and the smothering of infants to save them from the agony of slavery (Hine and Wittenstein, 1981).

However, some of the black women saw the need to fight alongside black men for the forceful termination of slavery. Such was the case of the legendary Nanny who led a military attack against the plantation farmers in Jamaica in the 1730s, that of Harriet Tubman who conceptualised and led, in South Carolina, a guerrilla action that started on 2 June 1863 and resulted in the liberation of hundreds of enslaved people, and that of the women among the maroons led by Toussaint L'Ouverture in the Haitian revolution that defeated three imperialist armies and hastened the abolition of slavery (Bilby and Steady, 1981; James, 1980; Davis, 1981).

The rebelliousness of the black slave woman earned her the label of a 'bad' woman or that of a sexual object for white men, an image that continued to be applied to black women explicitly or implicitly to excuse their victimisation with rape even after the formal end of slavery in the United States (Davis, 1981). Davis argued that it was possible for enslaved black women to participate equally with enslaved black men in the struggle against slavery because of the relative equality and similarity between their conditions. She also pointed out how the suffragette movement developed from lessons that women learnt through their participation in the struggle against slavery. Yet the early women's movement in America exhibited racism against the emancipated former slaves when they insisted that black men should not get the vote before white women and tried to prevent black women from participating in the suffragette club movement as equals. This was what prompted Sojourner Truth to make her legendary speech deconstructing hegemonic femininity, 'ain't I a Woman?' (hooks, 1981).

Black Women and Colonial Law

Slavery was horrendous. It was abolished in most countries a long time ago. We have turned to the history of slavery to see what lessons there are for understanding the present problems facing black women in the criminal justice system. The major lesson learnt is that the victimised black women in slavery were not passive 'victims' but activists against victimisation. The history of the victimisation of black women in slavery has also contributed to our aim to move towards the decolonisation of victimisation from the colony

27

of punishment. The realm of penalty remains inadequate as a concept for understanding the articulation of policies and social relations in the criminal justice system. Punishment tends to colonise some forms of victimisation and reconstruct them in analysis and policy as part of what is unproblematically known as the penal realm. The history of the Victimisation-As-Mere-Punishment suffered by the enslaved contributes towards the decolonisation of victimisation.

A similar historical look at the colonial situation of black women in Africa would yield similar lessons for our purpose. The torture of the whip was the most common form of 'punishment' under slavery. In the colonial situation, whipping was also used to victimise Africans. This can be illustrated with the painting, Colonie Belge 1885-1959 by Tshibumba Kanda-Matulu. What is offered here is only one possible interpretation of this historical painting.

See paintings of 'Colonie Belge' or Belgian Colony by Zairean painters the most prominent of whom was Tshibumba Kanda-Matulu, in Young and Turner, (1985:4, black and white) and Jewsiewicki (1991, colour). Kanda-Matulu was the popular painter-historian from Lumumbashi who mysteriously 'vanished' in the early 1980s. The comments here will be based on the black and white copy that was the form in which this writer first saw the painting. A woman had used it in a seminar to illustrate her claim that the 'the punishment of the whip' was not applied to women in the Belgian colony, though this writer offered a completely different interpretation. However it is important to mention a few differences between that version and the version that was exhibited in the Tate Gallery in Liverpool (first colour event). Notice that the colour version might also be an original account of a similar occurrence as the event in the black and white copy. The women do not have the parcels at their feet in the colour picture, one of them was almost framed out of the picture in colour and she was wearing a different dress. This suggestion that the two pictures might be episodes in a similar story rather than copies of each other is supported by the second colour photocopy that shows the same theme treated by different artists who claim to be reporting acts of repression from different parts of the Belgian Colony. Of course this might also be a case of a popular piece of work inspiring imitations in a competitive market for scarce income from artistic work. However, according to Jewsiewicki (1991), 'The work is guided by the desire to establish painted history in the realities directly known to the public.' The work should be seen as a metaphor for the neo-colonial state in Zaire that is presided over by Mobutu Sese Seko who assassinated the Pan-Africanist hero, Patrice Lumumba, with the help of the imperialists (Rodney, 1972) and enriched himself beyond the dreams of the kleptocrat, King Leopold II, who started the Congo Free State as a fraudulent private business concern. This suggests that the white man in the painting might be an image of Mobutu who makes a fetish of the national flag.

If this picture was shown to Durkheim (1982) he would probably argue tautologicaly that punishment is punishment is punishment is punishment by assuming that what makes an act penal is not its content but the definition of such an act, by the collective conscience of society, as penal sanction. If 'Belgian Colony' was to be shown to Durkheim, he would say that the person being victimised in the picture is being punished for a conduct that the colonial society regarded as a crime. This exposes the weakness of the Durkheimian approach which emphasises value consensus and ignores the fact that the colonial conscience (for instance) is more conflictual and contentious than collective.

If the same picture were to be shown to Magrite who painted a pipe and titled it, 'This is not a pipe', he would have exclaimed, 'This is not punishment' (see Greeley, 1992). However, the two statements have completely different meanings. The former refers to the difference between an object and its representation while the latter refers to the nature of the object and not its representation. To say that this is not punishment is to say that what is represented in the painting is not punishment but victimisation. This is not simply because the painter understood the work in these terms; it would be presumptuous to assume that the author understands the text best. The point being made here is that the painting belongs to social realism rather than to the dream world of surrealism.

It is easy to dismiss this picture as irrelevant to the understanding of the problems that face black women especially because the only women in the picture seem to be dressed up like dolls and pedestal-placed, they are the only ones sitting down in the picture. They are not the ones lying prostate and receiving the whipping on bleeding buttocks and so it could be said that the whip was reserved for men in the Belgian Colony (although this is contradicted by one of the episodes in the second set of colour paintings where a woman was kneeling down while being whipped on her palm). However, the women do not seem to be in the picture as Foucault's public who were supposedly summoned to be entertained and controlled through the spectacle of the punishment and discipline of offending bodies. The parcels at the feet of the women suggest that they went to the prison of their own accord to take food to their loved ones. Furthermore, unlike Foucault's public who occasionally rebelled against a particular sentence or a particular judge, Colonie Belge is an indictment on the bulk of Belgian colonial policies in the Congo from 1885-1959 and not merely a protest statement against prison conditions, against the torture of the whip, or against a particular colonial official.

Foucault could see the pipe-smoking colonial officer as the pan-optic representative of the power of the colonial state, conducting surveillance on everyone at once and on no one in particular. However, Foucault (1977) would not say this because, although he identified wide-ranging surveillance as one of the key features of disciplinary and penal institutions and although he analysed the growth of what he called the carceral society, he emphasised that surveillance is carried out institutionally and mechanically rather than through individual officers. Furthermore, Foucault believed that surveillance, like other control mechanisms, was becoming increasingly individualised contrary to the suggestions of Cohen (1985) and Mathiesen (1983) that it is going to be increasingly generalised. The contention in this book is that it has always been generalised. Foucault recognised the phenomenon of 'the generalisation of punishment' but he analysed this with specific reference to 'the offender'. Finally, Foucault focused on the 'micro-physics of power' or on what is done to the individual but was curiously silent on imperialist power relations.

The expression on the face of the officer wielding the whip appears even more sorrowful than that of the person with the lacerated buttocks. It could be the case that the colonial Sergeant is forced to strike harder and harder or he himself would be struck to teach him the proper way to handle the whip. Commenting on the complexity of this sort of victimisation, Lumumba (1962: 80-83) details that, 'The majority of Europeans in the Congo are not in favour of the abolition of flogging' because, according to them, 'If flogging is abolished that will be the end of discipline among the natives, they will no longer stand in awe of the Europeans and the representatives of authority, there will be disorder, etc'.

Lumumba dismissed such argument as invalid because, 'You do not win the confidence, respect or obedience of a subject people by wickedness, cruelty or harshness, but by good administration, respect for the rights of citizens, and just and humane treatment.' He went further to discuss the class character of whipping by noting that a circular dated 31 August 1947 exempted the colonial elite from being flogged but, according to Lumumba, 'this prohibition is a dead letter' since some African members of the exempt categories get flogged if only to coerce them into repressing their own people even more brutally.

Lumumba shows the class-gender-race character of such victimisation when he talked about the rising problem of prostitution and the exemptions of chiefs, mixed race people and educated Africans from the punishment of the whip that guaranteed its efficiency and thereby suggested that Colonie Belge is not a work of fiction as such but a historical documentation. Note that Lumumba never described what was going on as the Punishment-Of-Offenders but correctly identified the people affected as 'victims' of wickedness. He also suggested that the viciousness of the Non Commissioned Officers could be explained by the fact that they were trained as part of an army of occupation who were themselves vulnerable to victimisation unless they distinguished themselves as victimisers of their own people.

The number on the chest of the bare-footed, dark-uniformed African officer who is administering the whip adds to this impression that there were thousands more watching the colonised. Note that there are six officials of colonial law in the picture, neatly matching the number of the colonised African men in the picture. The fact that the women were not matched by officials in the picture suggests that the women were marginal to the drama unfolding or that they were marginalised as low security risk.

It seems that the suit-wearing Belgian official ordered the whipping of the prisoner in the presence of his loved ones. This might be because the man on the ground seems to be in meditation rather than in pain. The presence of his loved ones may have been ordered to make him show that he feels the pain, perhaps, by weakening his resistance through the outpouring of emotions by his loved ones. Since the women are the ones who seem emotionally disturbed by the whipping, it cannot be argued that they are unaffected by the 'punishment'. From this point of view, these women are being victimised. The woman on the left might not have started weeping probably because the man who is just pulling down his pants as if he is next in the line of those to be whipped, could be the one more closely related to her. Alternatively, maybe she is closely related to the man on the ground but chose to deny the colonial officials the pleasure of seeing her cry. Perhaps she is determined to take in the beating with dry eyes like the man on the ground. This reading is supported by Jewsiewicki (1991) who states that, 'In the Belgian-colony subject, ... women usually express the sufferings of victims of violence. Thus a major trait of Zairean social structure appears in these paintings: the ideological and normative domination of women by the patriarchy.'

Furthermore, the women are not the only ones being victimised here. The man being whipped is also being victimised. Whipping as a form of torture is bad enough but whipping in the presence of loved ones seems to be calculated to emasculate the man on the ground. The prisoner seems to be a victim rather than an offender not simply because most of Belgian colonial policies were criminal in themselves but because his uniform was the same as that of those who are doing public works in the picture. The two men near LA POLICE building carry a bucket labelled T.P.M. which stands for the Public Works Department. The only indication of the type of public work contained in that bucket is the baton-wielding official who appears to be literally holding his nose against the stench of the bucket latrine that Fela Anikolapo-Kuti analysed as a symptom of imperialist crimes in his classic criminological song, 'ITT: International Thief Thief'. However, the nose-holding gesture could also be interpreted as a move to blow the whistle against a possible escapee, though the calm of the other officers suggests otherwise. This suggests that the people being victimised may not even be prisoners, they may have been mere suspects being detained by the police for alleged offences and being tortured to extract confessions necessary for convictions before they are sent to Le Prison.

However, it could be that La Police also served as Le Prison under the colonial situation, just as some prisoners are detained or held in police cells today due to overcrowding in prison institutions. If the victimised were actually prisoners, it means that the colonial administration relied on prison labour for menial jobs which Africans saw as befitting of slaves. In the specific instance of Belgian Congo, forced labour was the basis of the plantation economy. Those who resisted this form of slavery ended up in jail to be tortured, killed, or forced to do the work that the threat of imprisonment for tax default alone could not get them to perform for the colonial authorities (Rodney, 1972).

The situation in the Congo is not representative of all colonial experiences. The British and the French did not rely on forced labour as much as the Portuguese and the Belgians did. The British and the French did not use whipping as a major form of penal policy probably because they preferred the more intimidating gun-boat diplomacy of massacres that all colonial states practised (Cashmore and McLaughlin, 1991). What Tshibumba's painting is pointing to is the nature of Victimisation-As-Mere-Punishment which affected black men and black women. The picture also carries the theme of resistance to victimisation especially in one of the second set of colour paintings where a prisoner is striking down an official in an apparent escape attempt.

The colonial system introduced new forms of legality to selectively and partially strengthen or replace existing ones. Black men and women responded by selectively compromising with, accepting or resisting the colonial institutions and practices that they found oppressive. As Fanon argued, 'The violence which has ruled over the ordering of the colonial world, which has ceaselessly drummed the rhythm for the destruction of native social forms ..., that same violence will be claimed and taken over by the native' during the anti-colonial struggle (1963: 31), just as they did against slavery.

The rest of this subsection describes manifestations of the resistance organised by black people as a whole, and by black women in particular, for the purpose of countering colonial domination and challenging its imposed hierarchy of credibility. The analysis shows that the militancy of black women is not evidence of the docility of black men as some people assume (see Isikalu, 1988; Ndem, 1988), but a pointer to the fact that women, like men, were affected adversely by colonial law and order and that they fought along with men to overcome this form of oppression. The question is whether or not black women were victimised differently compared to black men in similar circumstances under colonial law?

The impact of colonial laws and courts on black women is seen by black women and their allies to have been more adverse than their impact on black men (Mba, 1982). Some accounts of the impact of colonialism conclude that black women were pulled down from positions of relative equality with men, in traditional African society, to positions of relative powerlessness (see Steady, 1981). This is opposed to the official view that colonialism had a civilising and liberating impact on black women. A former colonial administrator, Adebayo (1985: 108), for example, in his suggestively titled *White Man in Black Skin*, contended that 'the quality which most impressed the local communities was the sense of integrity, justice and fair play transparently demonstrated by British administrators.'

The basic error in the above two views of the position of women in pre-colonial Africa is that they try to explain the dynamics of a socio-economic formation with the aid of its ideological manifestation alone. The romanticists are right in asserting that Africa had queens and female warriors and that Africa has the highest incidence of kinship systems based on matrilineal descent. However, queens were mere figure heads and were succeeded by kings in patriarchal African societies and it is a 'matrilineal puzzle' that it was the mother's brother who controlled children and property in matrilineal societies (Richards, 1950).

On the other hand, the official view that African women were wallowing in repugnant traditions and powerlessness until colonialism liberated them begs the question, why did African women militantly resist colonial rule? It is most probable that African women had a tradition of resistance to domination. Sudarkasa contends that in many parts of Africa, the 'domestic sphere' of influence and the 'public sphere' of power 'considerably overlap' to the extent that, though subordinate, African women exercised a substantial degree of power, authority and influence by reason of their domestic power (Sudarkasa, 1981: 52). The imposition of an alien hierarchy upon the existing one further intensified their resentment and resistance. The way the protests of black women were repressed can be compared with the way black men were suppressed.

The religious, political, economic, and ideological domination imposed by colonial capitalism meant that most African women 'experienced a substantial loss in their economic and political status' (Ibid). This does not mean that African women did not benefit from colonial law in any way. The outlawing of child sacrifice in those parts of Africa where it obtained and the limited promotion of literacy and modern health technology were of benefit to men and women, but such benefits could still have been introduced without exploiting and repressing African women in the way that colonialism did. Moreover, Rodney (1972) has persuasively argued that such 'benefits' were largely the unintended consequences of colonialism - a system that was based on exploitation and repression. They were not intended as welfare policies in aid of the colonised but as strategic measures for the maximisation of the goal of exploitation. They were therefore limited by their ability to disempower rather than liberate the colonised.

The most crucial reason why the colonial administration was set up was to ensure a conducive atmosphere for the expropriation of African natural resources to Europe. This was done through the exploitation of the surplus values of African labour. This is what the 'maintenance of law and order' practically meant - 'the maintenance of conditions most favourable to the expansion of capitalism and the plunder of Africa' (Rodney, 1972: 179).

In pursuance of this grand design, colonial taxation was imposed to finance the repressive apparatuses of imperialism and, more importantly, to coerce the indigenous labour force into wage slavery. Although women were not directly taxed or forced into wage labour, the imposition of 'hut' taxes made women very vulnerable since most African polygamous husbands housed their wives in different huts. To make this burden light, African men with many wives built larger huts and housed all their wives in one hut, at the risk of increasing tension among the competing co-wives. The colonial authorities reacted by taxing every man for every wife in a system of poll tax that Shivji (1982: 43) called 'wife tax'.

The fact that women were not directly taxed in Tanzania could mean that they were policed and victimised in different ways compared with black men since the former would not be arrested for tax evasion. However, since they must have contributed to their husbands' or adult sons' payments of the poll tax without being recognised as tax-payers, they can be said to have faced double exploitation in this respect. First, they would be inconvenienced by being housed together in one hut or by the arrest of their male supporters and secondly, they were exploited through indirect taxation without being given due recognition.

The aim of such taxation was to extract surplus labour from the men who must leave the farms to their overworked wives to go and earn their taxes in the plantations, the mines or the domestic establishments of colonialism. If there were no women left to work the farms, few of the men could have afforded to migrate seasonally or permanently. Furthermore, those who were convicted of tax-evasion were victimised with forced labour on colonial plantations or on the construction of roads for the evacuation of surpluses (Shivji, 1982: 46). There is some record that black women were victimised in this particular way.

Wipper (1989) documents how African women spontaneously took over the leadership of a mass demonstration organised by the East African Association under the leadership of Harry Thuku. The Association and its leadership were almost exclusively male but one of the issues that it fought to abolish was the system of conscripting young girls and beautiful women to work without pay in the plantations of the settlers or on the new roads being constructed for the evacuation of cash crops. Harry Thuku alleged that some of the colonial chiefs used this as an opportunity to seduce the beautiful wives and daughters of peasants and some of the young girls returned to the village with unwanted pregnancies.

The campaigns of Mr Thuku, 'Chief of Women', landed him in detention without trial and EAA called a general strike and a mass demonstration to set him free. The colonial authorities tried to negotiate with three of the men leading the demonstration and they returned to persuade the people to disperse. Some of the men actually started dispersing but one of the women, Mary Muthoni Nyanjiru, confronted the men by lifting up her dress and challenging them to exchange it for their trousers if they were cowards. This traditional form of insult associated with the female genitals was said to have incensed the men so much that they joined the women who were already marching towards the prison with bayonets pressing against their throats. It was then that the Askaris were given the order to shoot and many women and men were massacred (Wipper, 1989). This was the high price that was paid to end the use of women for forced labour in Kenya. However, forced labour remained for the women in the sense that they were traditionally repressed through forced marriages that were supported by colonial authority (Mbilinyi, 1988).

Women resented the intensification of the exploitation of their labour when most of the peasant farms were left for them to work alone. Many of them were victimised for the 'offence' of running away from home. Single women were denied access to land and this meant that married ones could only flee from one marriage to another, resulting in violent confrontations between spouses and between husbands and the men to whom their wives fled (Mbilinyi, 1982: 7-8).

However, it appears that the running away of wives was a practice that antedated colonialism since the local people had a way of settling the matter by restitution. It may have been escalated by the crisis of colonial exploitation because the treatment of marital instability as an offence which women alone could commit was a severe victimisation of women who could be fatally beaten by husbands, though some of them fought back and killed their husbands in the process (Ibid).

Since the fines imposed on runaway wives, with the approval of the colonial administration, were paid by the men to whom they fled, it can be said that men were also severely victimised. The privileged treatment of men is evident, however, in the fact that there were no cases of runaway husbands being tried even though some men must have abandoned their wives and children. Moreover, women who had no men to flee to would either continue suffering in silence or go into prostitution to face more insulting kinds of victimisation.

To this process of disempowerment, African women, just like their male counterparts, responded with widespread militancy that shook the colonial edifice. This can be illustrated (mainly, but not exclusively) with the case of the 'Women's War' against colonialism in Nigeria because it is one of the best documented independent struggles against colonial authority by black women. Some historians and colonial anthropologists wrongly labelled it

'Aba Women's Riots'. On the contrary, the uprising spread far beyond Aba and was called 'Women's War', Ogu Umunwanyi or Ekong Iban by the Igbo and the Ibibio activists respectively (Afigbo, 1972).

The depression that hit Europe after the first imperialist world war meant intensified exploitation of the colonies. Writing about the 'double squeeze' of African peasants by multinational trading companies which control prices of both cash crops and manufactured goods, Rodney (1972: 172-173) reported that:

> Prices of palm products were severely reduced by the UAC and other trading companies in Nigeria in 1929, while the cost of living was rising due to increased charges for imported goods. In 1924 the price for palm oil had been 14/' per gallon. This fell to 7/' in 1928 and to 1/',2d in the following year (of the 'women's war' and this continued after the second imperialist world war when) .... a yard of khaki which was 3/' in pre-war days went up to 16/'; a bundle of iron sheets formerly costing 30/' went up to 100/' etc.

At the same time, heavier taxation was being imposed on the people whose resources were being depleted. Women played a significant role in the resistance against taxation in particular, and against colonialism in general especially because the processing and marketing of palm oil was almost exclusively a source of income for women. Men usually escaped into the bush on sighting tax-collectors or the colonial police. In Biaseland of Nigeria, members of the women's secret society, Egip, usually confronted the invaders by parading nude in front of them and thereby embarrassing them into withdrawal (Attoe, 1988).

Why were such women not arrested? It is likely that if men had adopted a similar mode of struggle, they could have been arrested in spite of their nakedness. It can only be assumed that the women were spared because they were not the target suspects and there was no law against nakedness as such. The withdrawal of the colonial police when confronted by naked women suggests that the femininity of black women was a symbol of abuse since the 'sexist expectations of chastity and racist assumptions of sexual promiscuity combined to create a distinct set of issues confronting black women' in a world ruled by white men (Crenshaw, 1991: 69). It seems that those women used their sexuality to abuse or attack the colonial authorities in a way that black men could not. They adopted a morally insulting mode of struggle rather than a militarily challenging one probably because they faced qualitatively different problems.

Since the poll tax was imposed on men in Nigeria after a census of adult men, the attempt by the unpopular Warrant Chiefs to conduct a census of women and their personal possessions in Nigeria was seen by the women as an exercise in tax assessment. Women rose up against the Warrant Chiefs and the corrupt 'Native Courts' where they presided. Women in Aba took the lead by marching to the house of Warrant Chief Okugo and following an assault on one of their members by the chief, the women destroyed his house. They also burnt down the Native Courts and attacked branches of the United African Company and other trading companies in the area (Afigbo, 1972). Their actions show that their 'war' which is deliberately trivialised as a tax riot was a far-sighted (or at least, a deep-rooted) uprising.

Through the long-distance trading networks of the women, the news of their militancy spread quickly to the surrounding areas. Characteristically, the colonial administration refused to negotiate directly with the women. Rather, the oppressors tried to use the new elite of men they had created to discourage the women in other areas from joining the uprising. The fact that the colonial administration never attempted to negotiate the grievances of men through women in Africa illustrates the qualitative difference in the domination of black women by the two hierarchies of domination. However, it was only a minority of men who were co-opted by the colonial administration. Most men whose subordinate masculinities were repressed supported the women and the demands of the women covered the interests of men regarding taxation and village-headship.

The collaborators of colonialism appeared to have succeeded in restraining the women of Utu Etim Ekpo village. However, as soon as their 'fire brigade' reached the next village, they heard that the women of Utu Etim Ekpo, nevertheless, burnt down the Native Authority and Native Court buildings in the village. As a result, the Divisional Officer ordered his men to open fire and twenty-one women were killed while nineteen others were wounded (Isikalu, 1988: 59).

This must have taught the colonial officers that the women were acting independently of the men and that they deserved to be listened to in their own right. Thus Mr A. R. Whitman, the Divisional Officer for Opobo, summoned all the women in the area to a meeting for the purpose of discussing their grievances. The women demanded the following:

1. Government must not tax women.
2. Personal property such as boxes are not to be counted.
3. Any woman who practises prostitution should be arrested.
4. Women should not be charged rents for the use of common market stalls.
5. Licences should not be paid for the holding of plays.
6. Women do not want Chief McPepple to be head of Opobo town.
7. Women do not want any man to pay tax.
8. Women are speaking for Opobo, Bonny, Ogoni, and Andoni women. (Isikalu, 1988: 60).

It should be noted how the women democratically stated that they were representing themselves even when their demands covered the interests of men and those of other parts of the country. It was as a result of the misunderstanding of the principles of village democracy that Lord Lugard (1965) generalised the 'expedient' administrative hybrid, which he was forced to extend from the highly feudal Northern Nigeria, to the whole country. However, the Southerners, and especially the Easterners, were more used to village democracy in which everyone was given audience. Thus, they rejected the system of 'dual mandate' or indirect rule as a system of double exploitation and domination.

Note also the concern of the women about the commercialisation of sex that may have threatened their power and prestige. They stated their willingness to support the colonial administration in its control, perhaps, to show that the colonial law and order were busy repressing protests that the women considered legitimate while doing nothing at all to check what the women considered dangerous enough to attract penalty.

Naanen (1991) has linked this unprecedented concern about prostitution to the dynamics of the colonial administration that disempowered traditional institutions of social control or abolished them completely. He argued that although the people of the Cross River Basin were sexually permissive before the advent of colonialism, the commercialisation of sex on a large scale was virtually unknown in the region. However, when the colonial regime widened the territory available for men and women to explore with relative ease and safety, colonial cities soon swarmed with disproportionate numbers of unaccompanied men who were engaged in wage labour. These opened up a lucrative alternative to many women who escaped from the domination of authoritarian patriarchs.

The hostility of respectable black women towards black prostitutes strengthens the argument of this book in the sense that neither Victimisation-As-Mere-Punishment nor Victimisation-In-Punishment assumes that black women are diametrically opposed to the politics of law and order. What these concepts suggest is that the priorities and practices of the politics of law and order do not always reflect the interests of the marginalised. The women appeared to support some legislation while opposing other measures or calling for new ones.

The women, meanwhile, asked Mr Whitman to sign their demands as an agreement but he merely promised to inform the government about them. The women insisted and he became annoyed. At that moment, more women arrived by boat from the surrounding river areas. As they alighted with war cries and ran to join their comrades, Lt. J. N. Hill shot their leader, Madam Mary Adiaha Edem, and ordered his troops to shoot the rest. Twenty-nine women were killed and thirty-one others were wounded. The Legislative Council in Lagos regretted the killings but rejected a motion to prosecute the murderers by thirty-five to two votes (Isikalu, 1988).

The three African Chiefs appointed to the Council predictably voted with their colonial masters and only the elected members for Lagos and Calabar voted for a trial. The three Nigerians who voted with the colonial government did not do so simply because they were men, as Isikalu (1988: 62) alleged. They voted in accordance with their class interest as chiefs who were dependent on the colonial authorities for patronage. Even if they had voted otherwise, the motion would still have been lost by a scandalous margin.

This massacre illustrates the point made by Boerhinger (1977: 60) that 'under colonialism, there are changes in both the legal system and methods of ideological domination.' This refers to the inconsistency between the principle of individual responsibility professed by the imposed legal system and the practice of collective repression for the purpose of political and economic domination. What this account illustrates is that when black women militantly opposed colonial law and order, they were confronted with similar problems compared to men who did so.

It could be said that women reacted collectively and militantly against colonialism because they were used to mass movements of their own and also because men were reacting in much the same way. Perhaps, the reaction of women was more spectacular because, according to Mrs Ransome-Kuti, women lost more economic and political power to colonialism than men (Mba, 1982). The major grievance of the Abeokuta Women's Union (AWU) was that they provided half of district revenues without having any say about expenditure due to the fact that they were not represented in the system of indirect rule. Taxes were introduced in the region in 1918 and since then, women were forced to pay from the age of fifteen whereas men did not pay until the age of seventeen. This was probably because young girls started trading very early in life by acting as hawkers for their parents or for older traders. The women were particularly provoked because tax collectors insulted them, chased them around, and were fond of stripping young women under the guise of assessing their age (Johnson, 1982).

After a series of petitions failed to elicit any positive response from the colonial authorities, AWU mobilised tens of thousands of women to refuse to pay any more taxes and to picket courts during the trial of their comrades. They organised an overnight sit-in at the palace of Alake, the so-called traditional ruler of Abeokuta who acted as the chief tax-collector for the colonial administration. As the women kept vigil, they sang abusive songs against Ademola, the Alake, and against the white men he represented. Two of the songs went like this:

Even if it is only one penny
If it is only a penny Ademola,
We are not paying tax in Egbaland
If even it is one penny

Ademola Ojibosho!
Big man with a big ulcer!
Your behaviour is deplorable.
Alake is a thief.
Council members thieves.
Anyone who does not know Kuti will get into trouble
White man you will not get to your country safely
You and Alake will not die an honorable death (Johnson, 1982).

The response of the colonial administration was typical. The women were told off for insulting the Alake and their leaders were tried for tax evasion. Kuti was fined in court and she tactically chose to pay the fine rather than accept one month in prison because she was the only woman on the delegation to the Nigerian constitutional conference that was leaving the next week. In London for the 1947 conference, Mrs Kuti gave an interview to the Daily Worker - organ of the British Communist Party - in which she criticised the poverty, exploitation, repression, and oppression that faced Nigerian women under colonialism. At home, the conservative Nigerian Women's Party that aimed at acquiring British citizenship for Nigerian women, among other things, condemned Kuti for giving the interview but the radical Lagos Market Women's Association expressed their solidarity with Kuti and passed a vote of confidence in her.

The Alake and the colonial administration tried to intimidate the women but that failed. They promised to reform the tax but the women wanted it abolished. The Alake went on leave to let things quieten down but the women insisted on his abdication. Eventually, the Abeokuta Women's Union forced the Alake to abdicate from the throne in 1949; female taxation was abolished and four women, including Kuti, were appointed to the interim council that replaced the discredited Sole Native Administration system of dual mandate (Mba, 1982: 136-64).

This is consistent with the recognised power of women to intervene collectively in some parts of Africa to discipline members of their family or to ritually cleanse the community (Meek, 1955). Nigerian men overwhelmingly supported this autonomous struggle of the Abeokuta Women's Union which soon expanded to become the Nigerian Women's Union with branches all over the country (Johnson, 1982). This supports the claim made by different scholars that although black women were oppressed and exploited under traditional African societies, they were not completely submissive to the dominant men. The type of radicalism exhibited by those women under colonial domination is likely to have borrowed from traditional strategies of organisation and militancy by African women in traditional societies.

There is unfortunately little evidence for the comparison of the problems that faced black women and white women in the colonial criminal justice system. This is because of the obvious reason that there were few 'Victorian' ladies in the colonies and the few present were paternalistically protected. However, even if there had been many white women in the colonial societies, there is no reason to believe that they would have faced exactly the same problems compared to black women and no reason to expect that they would have organised in similar ways around similar issues. The only comparable situation was in South Africa where the mining corporations turned a blind eye to prostitution - so long as it involved only black women. The moment white prostitutes appeared, the authorities responded by repressing brothel-keepers and arresting women for soliciting or for living on immoral earnings (Van Onselen, 1982). It would be absurd to say that white women were controlled in the same ways that black women were victimised because it seems that the control of the former was protective rather than repressive as was the case with black women.

This section has tried to demonstrate that black women were victimised in different and similar ways compared with the victimisation of black men. Moreover, they were subjected to the authority and influence of black men in addition to those of the colonial administration. This seems to support the feminist theory of the state (Mackinnon, 1989) regarding the systematic repression and control of femininity. It also shows that men who were equally repressed may have participated in the intensification of the repression of femininity. However, it goes beyond a feminist theory of the state by indicating that men and women who were marginalised struggled together and independently in similar and variable ways to overcome their marginalisation, to empower themselves, and contribute to a better future free from racism, sexism, and class exploitation instead of blandly calling for gender separatism as many western feminists do.

This means that the forcing of the colonial police to withdraw, the refusal to be forced into submission by black male collaborators of colonialism, the attack on the structures of colonial power - including their offensive against colonial chiefs - were expressions of power by the organised sections of black women against the colonial state that was based on racism, sexism, and class exploitation.

Such militancy by African women reached its highest stage in the Algerian revolution with the result that the colonial administration defined its political doctrine as follows: 'If we want to destroy the structure of Algerian society, its capacity for resistance, we must first of all conquer the women .... Let's win over the women and the rest will follow' (Fanon, 1965: 15-16). This corresponded to a stage in the struggle when Algerian women carried bombs, grenades, and machine guns concealed under their veils and when they were 'arrested, tortured, raped, and shot down', according to Fanon. Algerian women were not so militant because Algerian men were docile. Rather, 'this was the period during which men, women, children, the whole Algerian people, experienced at one and the same time their national vocation and the recasting of the new Algerian society' (Fanon, 1965: 40).

Black Women and Neo-colonial Law

Fanon did not live to witness how neo-colonialism effectively blocked the aspirations that anti-colonial struggles inspired. Benalligue (1983), Urdang (1983), and Jacobs (1983) have highlighted how little women had gained from political independence in Algeria, Mozambique, and Zimbabwe, respectively, in spite of their immense contributions to the liberation struggles and in spite of the professed socialist orientations of those governments. Benalligue suggests that part of the reason for the continued exploitation of Algerian women compared to the men is that the contributions of the women to the liberation movement were reluctantly accepted by men who still harboured patriarchal ideas. Urdang argues that Mozambique under Samora Machel recognised the unique plight of women and tried to address these seriously. Furthermore, Jacobs identified the process of land redistribution in Zimbabwe which favoured family holdings under the control of men as the main reason why women still laboured without recognition.

These accounts are typical of studies of the conditions of women in neo-colonial Africa. They rightly focus on the economic problems that face women. The few that venture into law restrict themselves to family law 'because it was identified by women throughout the region as one of their greatest concerns, and in many cases a major legal problem' (Letuka et al, 1991: 9-10). The limitation of such exclusive focus on the economic conditions of women and on family law is that statistics easily show that men were better off on the whole while concealing the fact that most men suffer severely under neo-colonialism. To compare men and women on the basis of gender without also considering the articulation of gender with class usually results in the conception of the emancipation of women 'as mechanical equality between men and women' against which Samora Machel warned (quoted in Urdang, 1983: 20).

Another limitation in the exclusive focus on family law is that the extent to which the familial ideology is reinforced by the criminal law is largely neglected. The few that focus on criminal law simply assume from statistics the fact that African women share the global 'mystery' of women being less involved in criminality than men (Clifford, 1970: 40) or concentrate on why the criminality of women is fast increasing (Oloruntimehin, 1981). I am not concerned with rates of criminality but with the specific problems that men and women face in the criminal justice system whether or not they have committed any crime. There is hardly any comprehensive account of the victimisation of African women in the name of criminal punishment.

However, something can be fleshed out from incidents and studies that slightly touch on this theme while focusing on other concerns.

The colonial instances of ideological repression of women by vested political and economic interests became more important under neo-colonialism. This is because the state acquired relative legitimacy with the acquisition of political independence and 'crime' now replaced 'race' as the major category of repressed phenomena except in Mauritania where Arabs still enslaved black Africans and in South Africa where racialism was still a major issue.

The methods and types of victimisation characteristic of the colonial state were partially and selectively carried over by the neo-colonial state in order to uphold and consolidate the inherited political and economic hegemonic ideology of capitalist underdevelopment (Nkrumah, 1968). This was the point echoed by Fabian and Fabian in their androcentric analysis of the painting by Tshibumba:

> Colonial experience, although chronologically a thing of the past, remains an active element of present consciousness. Paintings of Colonie Belge express the omnipresence of powerful, organised, and bureaucratic oppression of the little man as he feels it now, in a system whose decolonization remains imperfect and which constantly uses the former oppressor as a negative counter-image (in Young and Turner, 1985: 6).

Race was directly repressed under colonialism and yet it is a largely unacknowledged basis of colonial rule. Racial rule was implicit in the assumption of the racial superiority of the colonisers (Fyfe, 1992). This rule and hegemony of 'white power' have continued to be the case in the multi-racial African and Caribbean countries even where the leading politicians have become black men (Rodney, 1969). The colonial politics of racialism has been partially replaced with that of ethnicity and nationality in most African countries. However, the focus of neo-colonial law is not the preservation of the moral superiority of one ethnic group or another except in the caste system of Burundi and Rwanda, but the repression of the activities of the subordinate men and women whose liberation was considered dangerous to the neo-colonial state and whose continued subordination was necessary for the maximisation of neo-colonial exploitation.

However, the conflicts in Rwanda and Burundi are not simply along ethnic or caste lines given that the predominantly Hutu army of Rwanda was suspected of shooting down the plane that was returning from peace talks in Tanzania with the Hutu presidents of Burundi and Rwanda just as the 7th Pan African Congress was ending in Uganda, April 1994. Moreover, the Hutu prime minister of Rwanda was also alleged to have been killed by Hutu soldiers probably because the army saw the government as making too many concessions to the mainly Tutsi Rwanda Patriotic Front whose president happens to be a Hutu as well. To understand the conflict adequately, it is necessary to look at the ways that ethnicity/caste articulate, disarticulate and rearticulate with gender and class to ensure that, even while the conflict was being reported as Hutus against Tutsis, peasants of both castes intermarried and fled together as refugees while the French who trained and armed the government troops (Hutu dominated) that were implicated in the genocide moved in quickly to secure a portion of the country for the defeated oppressive army (see Abdulai, ed., 1994).

The specificity of the victimisation of black women is evident in the strict regulation of women in neo-colonial Africa. As Mamdani (1983: 54) describes in the extreme case of Idi Amin's Uganda, 'Amin banned mini-skirts, "hot pants", "maxi-skirts with a V-shaped split in front", long trousers, "tights and such like dresses", abortion, "beautifying and skin-toning creams and lotion which change the natural beauty of women and make them look as half-castes" and so on.

This shows that the excuse of preserving African customs and traditions has been added to the familiar one of maintaining law and order to justify the repression of women. This is likely to affect poor women more because they are more exposed to the 'hooligans' who police cultural purity. It was not directed against men though poor men could suffer materially and emotionally when their wives or daughters were victimised. Again, such decrees were not expected to affect white women who have no need for 'skin-toning creams' and who could sun-bathe in hot pants and swimming dresses without Amin's hooligans lifting a finger. However, this was an extreme case of the victimisation of black women in the criminal justice system and it was not formalised into law anywhere else in Africa except in Malawi under 'life-president' Kamuzu Banda where it was a crime for women to wear trousers.

The hypocritical campaigners for cultural independence in the face of political and economic domination pretend to be ignorant of the fact that the material and ideological bases for traditional culture have been completely disarticulated by imperialism. This disarticulation reduced the ability of men to contribute their quota to the upkeep of their families and at the same time denied women equal opportunities to participate in the imposed capitalist economy.

Alice Lenshina was a Zambian woman who was recognised by a white missionary for her spiritual gifts. However, when the white missionary went on leave, his African assistants felt threatened by Lenshina and excommunicated the prophetess. She was forced to found her own church in 1955 and she borrowed ideals from traditional beliefs about morality and village communalism, while repudiating the authority of the village chiefs and condemning the worship of only male ancestors (van Binsbergen, 1979).

Her vision of the new society - headed by herself, collectivised and autonomous from the criminal justice system - was such a threat to the ideology of the hegemonic order that the colonial police burnt down her model 'Sioni Village'. Her followers moved into villages that belonged predominantly to her Lumpa sect. They bypassed the corrupt criminal courts and took cases to their trusted prophetess for arbitration and she collected exploitative tributes in cash and labour to expand the property of her church and grow food to feed her touring choir.

The local chiefs ganged up against her and the rivalry between her Lumpa sect and the nationalist party, United National Independence Party (UNIP), led Kenneth Kaunda to decide, three months before independence, to unleash military might on the Lumpas even though (or because) they were his former allies, his elder brother was a leading member of the sect, and he (Kenneth) and Alice had gone to the same school and come from the same area (van Binsbergen, 1979: 379). Kaunda used the same colonial excuse that Lenshina's followers were living in an 'unauthorised' village to order them to quit. In July 1964, when the ultimatum expired, two policemen on patrol in the village were thought to have come to effect the eviction and were killed. Kaunda retaliated by unleashing the army on them and 1500 villagers, mostly women, were killed, the sect was banned, Lenshina was detained until 1975, and thousands of her followers went into exile in Zaire.

Kaunda justified the massacre on the ground that Lumpa adherents were criminally attacking and killing people who did not share their faith. However, official figures show that before the two police officers were killed, UNIP attacks on Lumpa left 14 dead while Lumpa killed only seven UNIP members; UNIP burnt 121 houses compared to Lumpa's two; UNIP destroyed 28 churches and 28 grain bins while Lumpa destroyed only two grain bins; UNIP committed 66 assaults to Lumpa's 10; UNIP committed 22 acts of intimidation, destroyed one cattle kraal and 18 goats by arson while Lumpa did none of these (van Binsbergen, 1979: 414). The brutal response of the state can be explained by the fact that:

> Lumpa had ... struggled to regain local rural control and to create new relations of production (like tribute labour) not dominated by the rural community's wider incorporation in capitalism and the state. Once Lumpa had taken this road, the (secular) state, and nationalism ... were out of the question (van Binsbergen, 1979: 415).

This shows that any challenge to conventional morality was repressed by the neo-colonial state in the same way the colonial state did. It can be argued that the murder of the policemen provoked Kaunda into bombarding the villages, but the murder could not have been committed by all the villagers and their collective repression was like the 'gun-boat diplomacy' of colonial administrators - implying guilt by association and causing Victimisation-As-Mere-Punishment.

It is not likely that a man could found a church and organise it against the ruling patriarchal interests the way that Lenshina did. However, it is likely that if such a church encouraged the subversion of the criminal justice system to the extent of inciting the murder of policemen, the reprisal could be as severe. The Watchtower and Kibangu sects were also banned by Mr Kaunda for being in opposition to a neo-colonial state desperately in need of legitimation. Probably because these other sects did not attempt to develop a mode of production that was disarticulated from the hegemonic one and because they did not resist militantly, their suppression was not as bloody (van Binsbergen, 1979: 378). Lenshina became hostile to conventional morality and the state mainly after the missionary churches tried to repress her spirituality, the chiefs and patriarchs refused to sell land to her so that she could establish a settlement for her followers and after the ruling UNIP started intimidating her followers with violence.

Many black women were forced or chose to go into prostitution which attracts harassment from state officials but which was usually not punished as crime (Clifford, 1974: 131). There is no evidence of the harassment of male prostitutes in neo-colonial societies except in the case of the 'beach bummers' or 'toy boys' who earn a living off middle aged European women who visit the Gambia as tourists (*The Sunday Times*, 28 August 1994). The young men had their hair forcibly shaven by the soldiers who recently seized power in that country. The young lieutenant who led the military government was reported as protesting that 'our people are not sex machines.' He suggested that the hair of the bummers was shaved to make them less attractive to women.

Although men and women are equally prosecuted for keeping brothels and women are specially prosecuted for soliciting, there is no record of the prosecution of men for buying sex in neo-colonial societies. Poor black women are therefore differently repressed in the sex industries of neo-colonial societies compared with black men or 'respectable' white women engaged in prostitution who operate from five-star hotels.

Analysing the popular protests by men and women in the Caribbean, Mahabir (1985: 1) writes that 'when ... majorities aggressively challenged the rule of law, resorting to acts of violence in many instances in order to secure their freedom ... they did not consider themselves criminals.' To consider such militants to be criminals would amount to taking the terms of abuse applied by the state as a given.

The perspective of articulation that is adopted here recognises the legitimacy of the resistance organised by the people against the oppressive state. The perspective of articulation is theoretically clearer than the law and order approach because many people who are 'punished' as criminals turn out to be 'victims' of criminalisation. This does not mean that African women did not accept many of the colonial and neo-colonial laws dealing with personal safety and the safeguard of property. Thus, it is not everybody who breaks the law that can be seen as consciously fighting for freedom.

In different African countries, women are detained without trial for being the wives, sisters, or even the girlfriends of men who are suspected of treasonable felonies. There is no reason why such women are victimised except that they are assumed guilty by association. Moreover, it is not the case that they are being held in order to compel the suspected men to give themselves up, a popular police tactic for dealing with lesser offences. In the case of the widow of Gen. Mohamed Oufkhir who was detained with her children for 18 years in Morocco, her husband was known to have committed suicide to avoid capture (Amnesty International, 1992).

When Mrs Dora Mukoro, the wife of an army officer wanted in connection with an abortive coup, escaped with her maid and five children aged 1, 6, 8, 10 and 11, from detention in Nigeria and fled into exile, The Directorate of Military Intelligence questioned the Human Rights lawyers who had filed suits for their immediate release from detention. Some people started talking about how lax the national security was when the real issue was that, according to Article 7, Section 2 of the African Charter on Human and People's Rights, (OAU, 1981), 'Punishment is personal and can be imposed only on the offender.' Otherwise, the 'punishment' should be seen for what it is, victimisation of the innocent, and it should be internationally justiciable and punishable. See Agozino (1996/97) for a detailed critical analysis of the African Charter from the perspective of articulation.

It could be argued that the women who have suffered victimisation in the bizarre ways documented above were not exactly poor and so they must have been victimised on the basis of their gender rather than their class or race. Wives of army officers, preachers and their children are among the most privileged in Africa. However, we must not ignore the class character of their victimisation because class relations are not completely determined by class positions - that is why it is possible for middle class people to be involved in working class politics.

It is interesting that these women and children were victimised specifically because of the subversive nature of the felonies that the men who were close to them were alleged to have committed. It is true that any such felonies were not by or for poor people, but being associated with them must have excluded some of the relatively privileged from special immunity and exposed them to practices that are the daily experience of thousands of the poor.

According to the Committee for the Defence of Human Rights, other detainees who were related to men suspected of taking part in the planning or execution of the 22 April 1991 coup in Nigeria were quickly moved from the detention camps of the Directorate of Military Intelligence to Kirikiri Maximum Security Prison following the escape of Mrs Mukoro. These other detainees were Mrs P.T. Obahor and Mrs C.O. Ozeigbe whose criminality constituted entirely of being married to fleeing army officers wanted in connection with the coup. Others were Mrs Gloria Anwuri and Mrs Rhoda Heman-Ackah who had the misfortune of being sisters of Chief Great Ogboru who was suspected of having financed the coup. Also affected was Miss Gloria Mowarin, the pregnant lover of Mr Felix Aigbe - a business-man also wanted in connection with the coup.

However, it was not only women who were detained oppressively in this manner. The men also detained without being accused or charged were Mr Ufuoma Onakpaya who transgressed gender boundaries by taking care of the children of Mrs Heman Ackah since her arrest and Mr Sarro Akpeneyi, a former Public Relations Officer of a company owned by the wanted business man, Ogboru. Also moved to the Maximum Security Prison was the 14 years old son of Mr Felix Aigbe, the other business-man also wanted (African Concord. 16 September 1991).

The fates of these women, men and children illustrate the fact that Victimisation-As-Mere-Punishment (VAMP) affects men and women. However. the women were affected in gender-specific ways that differed from those of the men even though Mr Onakpaya could be said to have been repressed for crossing the gender boundary into child-care. It is true that no man was detained because his wife was suspected of having anything to do with the coup since no woman was suspected in that manner. However, women are often suspected of other serious crimes like drugs trafficking, and there is no record to show that their lovers, husbands, brothers or children are arrested as part of the punishment for the crimes allegedly committed by women.

Toni Morrison addressed this issue in her enchanting novel *Jazz*. She asked, 'Did police put their fists in women's faces so the husband's spirits would break along with the women's jaws?' (Morrison, 1992: 78). The question should be whether the police do so and not whether they did so at some isolated time in the past. Isabella Allende (1991) answered Morrison's question affirmatively in her story, 'The Judge's Wife', in which the judge caged the mother of a wanted criminal and tortured her in order to dare her son to surrender or attempt to rescue her and be damned.

These creative accounts prove nothing in fact but only serve as illustrations of a more general point. What is important for our immediate purpose is that Mrs Dora Mukoro escaped into exile. This is what many women in similar circumstances would do but, unfortunately, foreign countries would not recognise all of them as refugees and most of them cannot afford the money to finance the trip. It is true that Mrs Mukoro was a political refugee because of the political nature of her persecution. However, many women, men and children face no less serious oppressive economic conditions from which they would be glad to escape at the least opportunity. This brings us to the constant efforts by many poor women, men and children to escape to Europe or America in search of economic and political safety. Unfortunately, the conditions they flee from at home are not completely absent in the safe havens they seek abroad.

Ama Ata Aidoo (1992: 28) addressed the issue of political exile in her poem, 'Speaking of Hurricanes', dedicated to Micere Mugo and all other African exiles:

But speaking of very recent events, my sister,
have you met any of
the 'post-colonial' African political refugees
shuffling on the streets of
London
Paris
Washington
Stockholm and
The Hague?

Minds - and bodies - discarded
because they tried
to put themselves to good use?

Please,
don't tell me how lucky they are.

They know. We know.
They are the few who got away

Mrs Dora Mukoro was one of the lucky few who got away. The fates of those who were not so lucky remain shrouded in the secrecy that surrounds government, law, force, death and disappearances. It is an open secret that those who remain behind dream of escape too. But why the emphasis on European and American cities when most African exiles and refugees are still found in Africa? The emphasis is on European and American cities because they are more attractive to political refugees of various shapes and shades. They are more attractive, not just because of their relative affluence but mainly because of their relative security against trans-continental hit squads. Those who remain behind in Africa do so out of the belief that they could help change things by being closer to home or because they are too poor to afford the cost of escape. Most of the poor ones are those whom the immigration officials detain on arrival and deport at the slightest opportunity. At the same time, rich and powerful political refugees are routinely protected and encouraged to invest what they looted from their own people in foreign-owned industries. What is even more disturbing,

49

according to Aidoo (1992: 45), is that there is a flood of criminals from Europe to Africa:

> who remarked, somewhat wryly,
> that the trouble with neo-colonialism is that
> we have to cope with the same crimes, but
> there are no colonial sergeants to drill
> their own criminals and ours?!
> He must have referred to
> the current human flood from
> European Houses of Correction to our homes.

It is not fair to talk about the flood of criminals from Europe to Africa because a lot of Europeans in Africa are genuinely interested in helping to find a solution to the crises in Africa. Perhaps it is an overstatement to talk about a flood of human beings comparable to the transportation of convicts to Australia and Canada. Besides, Rudè (1978) has convincingly argued that, far from being all criminals, many of the transportees, especially Irish women, were merely political activists whose crimes, mainly arson, could be better understood as acts of political protest often committed out of a desire to join loved ones who had earlier been transported to relatively better prospects.

Nevertheless, just as Hannibal the Cannibal escaped to a hot tropical climate in the 'Silence of the Lambs', it is easy to imagine Europeans being deferred to in Africa even though some of them may be considered undesirable elements in Europe. However, Aidoo is right because some criminal activities involving fraud, for instance, might be sources of wealth and prestige for Africans and Europeans in Africa or in Europe. Yet no African country has any policy of excluding Europeans or of restricting the access of their crime films and television to Africa. On the contrary, the presence of Europeans is actively canvassed with blanket no-visa status for them. In contrast, many Africans need visas to enter some African countries and poor Africans are being deported en-masse from neighbouring African countries.

Rich and powerful Africans also find it relatively easy to secure sanctuary in Africa compared to the impoverished 'victims' of authoritarian regimes. For example, Nigeria's Ibrahim Babangida eagerly granted political asylum to Siad Barre, who presided over the devastation of Somalia. Civil Rights campaigners in Nigeria say that Siad Barre was a suspected criminal in Somalia and so it was unconstitutional to offer him political asylum in Nigeria. What is more, the campaigners point out that it is unjust to offer protection to a dictator like Barre while at the same time deporting innocent Chadian refugees who stood chances of being executed for opposing arbitrary rule in their own country (*The Campaigner*, Vol. 1, No. 3).

These are part of the reasons why many Africans are pushed towards seeking refuge in the domestic colonies of Europe. Furthermore, the then Home Secretary, Kenneth Clarke, was pushing for tough European Community policies to 'force refugees to seek protection in their own countries' (*The Observer*, Sunday, 29 November 1992).

Black Women and Internal Colonialism

The theory of internal colonialism was popularised by Hecter (1975) but Williams (1983) recognised that Lenin used the term much earlier to describe the development of capitalism in Russia. Hecter adopted this concept and applied it to the 'Celtic fringe in British national development'. Hecter argued that the areas within, but peripheral to, the metropole of imperial powers were exposed to forms of exploitation comparable to the 'colonial situation'. According to him, this is because there are two unequal and objectively distinct cultural groups within the nation, created by the historical accident of the uneven spread of industrialisation. As he put it, 'the existence of a culture of low prestige within a peripheral region is justification enough for the establishment of an internal colony category: without it, there can be no cultural division of labour' (Hecter, 1975: 349).

This formulation has been severely criticised for not being structuralist enough even while claiming to be a structuralist analysis. The major weakness of studies based on the Hecterian model is that they failed to account for internal colonialism in terms of imperialism (Williams, 1983: 12). This weakness is noticeable in the fact that the original formulation by Hecter talked about a 'British national development' as if there is anything like a British nation. If Hecter had recognised that the Irish, the Scottish, the Welsh and the English are different nationalities that are culturally distinct, he would have seen the need to go beyond his narrow intra-national focus. In this light, the Irish sociologist, Liam O'Dowd (1990) argues that 'Northern Ireland is not only a domestic Irish, British or British Isles problem but, in many senses, part of the wider story of global colonialism.' Hecter (1983) hoped that, by extending the theory of internal colonialism to Eastern Europe, some of the criticisms of the theory would be overcome. However, that is not necessarily so, especially if Yugoslavia, for instance, is analysed as a nation instead of as a multinational state and if such an analysis fails to take into account the role of global imperialism. The intra-national focus therefore remains the limiting feature of Hecter's theory.

'Internal colonialism' is used in this book to refer to three different but closely linked processes. First, internal colonialism is used to refer to institutional colonialism whereby one institution colonises another. This is the sense in which Habermas (1987) talks about internal colonialism as representing the reification of the judiciary by monetary power and vice versa. In this sense, this book regards the institution of punishment to be imperialist because it tends to colonise other institutions and processes like welfare and victimisation.

Secondly, internal colonialism will be used in the Hecterian sense to describe conditions in industrialised countries where black people form a sizeable proportion of the citizenry but live mainly in poor locations that are the targets of special policing. The term is applied correctly here because the alienating conditions of such 'ghetto colonies' (Hall, et al 1978) and the special police tactics aimed at their residents are reminiscent of (though not identical with) what was experienced by the colonised people in Africa, Asia, Latin America and the Caribbean.

Thirdly, internal colonialism is used here to refer to the process of imperialist domination that links black people abroad with those at home through policies like immigration controls and the war on drugs that are funded by the imperial powers and waged by the nominally independent neo-colonial states. Accordingly, this book will touch upon the need for decolonisation in the institutional, intranational and global senses of the term. Institutionally, decolonisation of victimisation would aim at recognising the relative autonomy of victimisation from punishment and welfare. Intranationally, decolonisation would address the marginalisation of the relatively powerless in the internal colonies and neocolonies of today. Globally, decolonisation will be used to emphasise the incompleteness of earlier decolonisation processes and the growth of what Said (1993) described as the recolonisation of the world by imperial powers.

The victimisation of black women in apartheid South Africa is illustrative of the continuity of colonial relationships in its classical, neo-colonial and internal colonial forms. No example illustrates the resistance against victimisation under colonialism, neo-colonialism and internal colonialism by black women better than the example of their struggles against apartheid. The most dramatic of these was the Cato Mano beer hall protests and the anti-pass demonstrations of 1959.

The government had outlawed the sale and consumption of liquor in places other than halls controlled by the white mercantilist class (Kuper, 1965). Illicit beer brewing was the mainstay of the income of black women who were denied equal opportunities to earn wages at the mines and were victimised for exploiting their own sexuality (Van Onselen, 1982). They rose up to wage their own version of the 'women's war'. With characteristic colonial arrogance, the apartheid regime refused to negotiate with the women and asked them to tell their grievances to their husbands who would report them to the chiefs for onward transmission to the government. After a series of street battles during which women marched chanting 'Wathint' abafazi, wathint' imbokotho' - you have struck the women, you have struck the rock (CIIR, 1988), 624 Africans, mainly women, were sentenced to a total of 168 years and/or fines totalling 7,130 pounds (Kuper, 1965: 16-18). The militancy of South African women continued the focus of the Women's War in Nigeria by demanding that men too should not carry passes and by using the exposure of their buttocks as a serious form of abuse. This militant contribution to liberation was recognised by the ANC-led government in 1994 when the constitution clearly stated the objective of building a non-racist, non-sexist, non-exploitative democracy in South Africa, very much in line with the theory of articulation on which this book is based.

Most of the examples of the struggles engaged in by black women against imperialism given so far in this book concern manifestly political struggles. This is deliberately so because I am trying to avoid the emphasis placed on street criminality by many writers of the right and the left when discussing the politics of race in the criminal justice system. With the manifestly political protests of black women as a background, it is now easier to see that discussions of 'black criminality' are also implicitly political in the sense that such discussions are articulated with policies that sustain the marginalisation of black people and guarantee the continuation of imperialist exploitation in different forms.

'Black criminality' has been historically represented in various ways corresponding to the ideological orientations of the person(s) making the classification. As a matter of fact, black people have not always been closely identified with criminality as much as recent moral panics about 'black crime' would suggest. According to Gilroy (1987b: 75) 'The changing patterns of their portrayal as law-breakers and criminals, as a dangerous class or underclass, offer an opportunity to trace the development of the new racism for which the link between crime and blackness has become absolutely integral.'

The argument of Gilroy is that if black people embody the problems that are ordinarily attributed to them, then such problems would essentially remain the same and would be manifested by all black people but 'the precise shape and dimension of these problems have constantly changed, reflecting a shifting balance of political forces in the struggles between black settlers and both institutional and popular racisms' (Gilroy. 1987a: 75). Contrary to the claims of self-professed left realists that black people were identified with crime because of their marginalisation, which supposedly made it more difficult for them not to commit crimes in order to survive, Gilroy and many others have convincingly argued that the identification of black people with criminality derives from the age-old tendency to view serious criminal acts as being alien, for example, during the garrotting panic of 1862. In 1878, the 'Jack the Ripper' panic surfaced to reinforce the assumption that heinous crimes were un-English in conception and perpetration. It was widely suggested that the Jews of Spitalfields in East London were the likely source of inspiration for the Ripper and a spate of anti-Semitism followed.

When Parliament debated the issue of alien criminality, Russian, Rumanian, Polish and Jewish immigrants who settled in the East End of London were the focus of the debate. Furthermore, 'Jewish crime' was said to have one speciality of its own - the so-called 'white slave traffic' which allegedly involved the recruitment of respectable white ladies for prostitution around the world. The 1912 Criminal Law Amendment Act introduced flogging as part of the punishment for the men of 'almost entirely foreign origin who were engaged in this vile trade ...' (Gilroy, 1987a: 78). This shows that black people were not the first to be singled out and collectively victimised or criminalised. It also shows that the association of foreigners with criminality is also vaguely linked to a eugenic concern about the purity of the dominant racial category.

Garland (1985: 196) argues that the association of crime with concerns about the nation and the quality of the white race can be found in 'the images and metaphors of "efficiency", "degeneracy", and "fitness"' which were constantly combined with the evolutionary analogy of social Darwinism to link 'criminological proposals with the future of the race and the empire.' This suggests that the foreignness of crime is not reserved for foreigners but is also applied to citizens whose crimes or abject poverty caused them to be collectively seen as a 'blot' or 'stain' on an otherwise immaculate national conscience. Hence, criminals and the poor from the same dominant race and nationality were frequently categorised 'as "savages" or "semi-savages" with a "very low order of intellect and a degradation of the natural affections to something little better than animal instincts".'

The identification of black people with criminality started in the late 1940s and early 1950s with emphasis on issues of sexuality and miscegenation. This gave way to concerns about a 'flood' of 'illegal' immigrants in the 1960s. In the 1970s, the dominant label of 'black criminality' was that of the 'mugger.' This was quickly replaced in the 1980s with the image of the rioter and in the 1990s the emphasis is on gang warfare or the so-called 'Yardies' (Keith, 1993). Hence, newspaper reports that black pimps were living off the immoral earnings of white women were cited in a secret memo to the cabinet on 30 January 1954 by the then Home Secretary, Sir David Maxwell Fyfe. He carried this propaganda forward to a cabinet meeting during which he argued that popular opinion on immigration was highly negative because of increased crime which was linked to unrestricted immigration.

This was ambivalently supported by Sir Harold Scott, the London Commissioner of Police between 1945 and 1953 who linked Cypriots, Maltese and coloured British subjects with disproportionate numbers of people gambling, living on immoral earnings, and drugs dealing. This was ambivalent because he specifically disagreed with the assumption that increases in criminality were caused by increasing immigration. As far as he was concerned, 'Most of our criminals are home-grown' (Gilroy, 1987a: 79-80).

The home-grown thesis became the focus of widespread attack during the next decade and culminated in the infamous 'River of Blood' speech by Enoch Powell who predicted that in the 1980s 'the black man will hold the whip hand over the white man', causing blood to flow like a river. During the 1970s, the Home Affairs Select Committee on Race Relations and Immigration investigated 'police/immigrant relations' and arrived at the ambiguous finding that black people were either less criminal than white people or that they were just as criminal as the latter but not more. The Chief Officer from Leeds reported a 'special difficulty' with the high number of 'West Indian girls leaving home and sleeping rough for one or two days at a time' but concluded that, in spite of this, prostitution among white women was far more widespread than among black women in Leeds (Gilroy, 1987a: 89).

The immigrant, as immigrant, is very rarely the focus of criminological research in the United Kingdom and elsewhere even though theoretical assumptions of the 'alien' are not all together uncommon in criminological literature and policy statements. Building on the sparse evidence provided by McClintock and others who pioneered research on the subject of immigrant criminality in the United Kingdom, Professor Tony Bottoms (1967), the Director of the Cambridge Institute of Criminology, whilst still a research officer at the institute, noted that relevant research had a 'natural tendency to concentrate upon criminal acts arising out of racial conflicts ... rather than on the general level of criminality among the various immigrant groups ...' which was the main concern of his paper.

This book does not focus on racial conflict-related criminality or on the general criminality of immigrants but on the politics of the racialisation of the war on drugs as part of the politicisation of immigration and the victimisation of the innocent which are too often ignored by those who focus on taken-for-granted general levels of criminality with little or no scepticism about what is crime and what is penalty.

Compared to the Irish, according to Bottoms (1967: 365), 'Discussions about crime among (New) Commonwealth (read black) immigrants tend to become much more emotional'. Bottoms did not say exactly why such discussions were counter-theoretically emotional but this is probably because of the additional significance of the specificity of the racialisation of blackness or the double consciousness that (some of) the Irish belonged and also did not belong to the United Kingdom at the same time. According to Bottoms, 'assertions and counter-assertions on this topic are indeed part and parcel of many arguments about whether the flow of immigration from these (Commonwealth) countries should be stopped, slowed down or encouraged' even though crime among this group is not 'excessive' compared to the Irish.

The only type of criminality among black immigrants as reported by McClintock (1963) was increasing 'violence' which was made up of almost exclusively 'domestic violence', the discounting of which would have resulted in a decline in violent offences by Commonwealth immigrants in the relevant period of 1957-1960. Yet this was easily generalised in a good deal of moral panic-type of attention 'with the conjunction of the terms "immigrant" and "violence" arousing some expected responses' (Bottoms, 1967: 366). According to Bottoms, about half the coloured populations in prisons in those days were 'convicted of possessing drugs or offences related to prostitution' (1967: 368).

It was necessary for Bottoms to emphasise the low involvement of black people in criminality in those days because the opposite was xenophobically emphasised by politicians of all parties and some scholars. He concluded that 'there is no "general immigrant crime problem" in this country, at least relative to other criminal problems' and went on to add that, 'As for the Commonwealth immigrants, they seem to be almost remarkably crime-free except in relation to' (domestic) violence which he curiously saw as not being very threatening to the public (Bottoms, 1967: 370).

Theoretically, what Bottoms was suggesting is that the political racialisation of crime-immigration-blackness lacks any systematic evidence in research and therefore should not be upheld by theorists. He is sceptical about American findings that second generation immigrants are almost universally more crime-prone than the first generation, given that the rates for the Irish immigrants were relatively stable from generation to generation and the rate for the first generation of black people was almost negligible in Britain.

Recent research shows that, before the 1980s, drug trafficking was dominated by white people and that drugs intelligence units have since been conflated with immigration intelligence units with stereotypes of the Jamaican Yardie (Keith, 1993) as the folk devil (Cohen, 1972) of such campaigns (Dorn, Murji and South, 1992). The almost negligible involvement of black immigrants in the 1960s has since changed into their over-representation in criminal justice statistics in the United Kingdom. It has been repeatedly reported by the Home Office (Home Office Statistical Bulletin, 12/89, 'The Prison Population in 1988' p.10, see table 5.3 below for detailed trends) that black people make up more than 10% of the prison population while black women make up more than 20% of all female prisoners. This compares with 57% of all women in US prisons being from ethnic minorities (Chambliss, 1995).

This is out of line with black proportional representation in the total population of Britain and the US. It is also out of tune with the relative lack of criminological interest in the crimes of black women (Rice, 1990). The call by Rice for the criminality of black women to be studied alongside that of their white sisters is defective given that such criminological interests are growing with the predictable demonisation of the black female drug courier who is unfairly labelled the typical courier. Richard Clutterbuck (1995), for instance, baselessly claims that most couriers are women even while the Home Office reports that most of them are men (see also, Wilmot, 1989; Home Office Statistical Bulletin, 'Statistics of Drugs Seizures and Offenders Dealt with, United Kingdom, 1994' Issue 24/95, 1 December 1995). The Home Office does not always break down its figures by race and nationality, but many criminologists and administrators interpret these statistics to mean that black people are disproportionately involved in criminality.

Smith (1994) reviewed what he called the 'unsatisfactory and incomplete' evidence for racial prejudice in criminal justice administration and came out with a number of thought-provoking statements. Contrary to the conclusion of Reiner (1992) that bias has been demonstrated at every stage of the criminal justice system, Smith substituted 'various stages' for 'every stage'. He suggests that bias remains in the system because of the exemption of certain criminal justice officials from the provisions of the 1976 Race Relations Act. Smith also stated that proven bias against black people at every stage is small in magnitude compared to the statistical evidence that black people are more highly involved in criminality compared to Asians and whites.

This book differs from the summary of Smith in two important respects. First, this is not a book about bias as such but about problems that confront black women, black men and children in the war against drugs. Some of such problems would result from bias or prejudice but, as Jefferson (1991) suggests, a focus on bias alone (such as the attempt by Hood, 1992, to 'isolate specific race effects' as if racism is ever experienced in isolation from sexism and other forms of exclusion) would miss out the institutionalised political problems that do not depend on the attitudes of individual officials. Secondly, this book is not concerned with the magnitude of bias because such measures do not tell us anything about the legally imposed difficulty in proving allegations of racism or the ways that people who perceive injustice deal with it. This book is more interested in explaining the forms that the problems facing black people take in the criminal justice system and in society and how black people are coping with such problems.

These views about the overwhelming law-abiding nature of black people were fast giving way to increasing demonisation of black people even before the 1980s of Thatcherism. Hall et al (1978) have argued that the demonisation of black people was already peaking in the late 1970s, following the mugging panic. The moral panic of the 1970s legitimised the 'law and order' campaign that contributed to the electoral success of Thatcherism. As the 'Party of Law and Order' consolidated its power, the Metropolitan Police Force came out with unusual statistics to prove that 'mugging' was a predominantly black crime suffered by predominantly white 'victims'. This came in the wake of the widespread criticism against the police for provoking the street protests of the early 1980s through discriminatory policing against black people. The counter offensive by the police and the popular press found unusual allies in the new left who took black poverty as evidence of black crime-proneness and thereby reinforced the image of black people as criminals and of black women as whores.

Pryce (1986: 85-94) shows that some black men help to perpetuate this abusive image of the black woman. Some black men find black women too demanding and unhelpful. They prefer white women who are in better positions to help them financially. Black women have many tales of woe about how black men exploit them sexually and abandon them, how they keep chains of women at a time, and how black women admire white men because they are more faithful to white women. But this picture is not representative of the relationships between black women and black men since it seems to characterise only those that Pryce called the hustlers.

Moreover, Pryce confessed that he did not attempt to study how black women were coping with conditions of internal colonialism because he felt that a black woman would study that better. His generalisation on the nature of the relationships between black men and black women is contradicted by such a study by black women (Bryan, et al, 1985) which shows that black men and black women struggle together against the oppressive conditions of internal colonialism, a 'survival' technique which Pryce ignored by not looking critically at the criminal justice system. My position is also a generalisation like that of Pryce but, whereas the generalisation here derives from a conscious effort to study black women in comparison with black men. Pryce studied only black men and apologised in his appendix for not covering black women and yet he made very serious claims about them.

Pryce argues that 'the exploitative element of "survival", so integral to the psychology of hustling, has come to be the dominant trait characterising the relationships' between black pimps and white women, but he did not say whether there are white pimps too and, if so, how they relate with black women and white women. He simply states that some hustlers pimp white women to earn money with which to maintain their black lovers in 'relative idleness.' Such black women do not seem to question the morality of being supported on money earned by white women. But when the pimp associates with a black prostitute, they feel threatened and attack her violently, resulting in arrests and court appearances (Pryce, 1986: 80-81).

This helps to promote the myth that crimes committed by blacks against other blacks (and in this case, by black women against other black women) are the greatest threat to the black community. Reacting to official statistics published by *Ebony* magazine to demonstrate that more blacks are killed by other blacks in one year in America than were killed in the nine years of the Vietnam war, Headley (1983: 51) argues that, if this is compared with

58

institutionalised violence against blacks, it will become insignificant and also be understandable as a consequence of the latter.

Such institutional violence is conducted through the colonial practice of collective victimisation of poor black men and women by which the crime problem becomes localised in the inner-city 'colonies' of sizeable black settlement. For example, the Institute of Race Relations (IRR, 1987) documents evidence of special police operations which hold poor black residents of the inner cities suspect. This originated from a 'moral panic' in Britain as early as the 1950s; the 'colony' came 'to be identified with a particular range of petty crimes, of which the most common were brothel-keeping, living off immoral earnings, and drug-pushing' (Hall et al, 1978: 352).

It is clear from this policing focus that black women were still seen as bad women who must be policed to check them from mixing with white people, illegitimacy, prostitution, and drug trafficking. The failure of special police squads, targeted at the internal colonies, to stamp out the unwanted activities goes to show that '... it is not a policing problem; soaring street crime is caused by widespread alienation of West Indian youth from white society' (Hall et al, 1978: 331). This sounds like the simplistic positivism of left realists but unlike them, Hall et al critically analysed the 'amplification' techniques by which 'crime' figures are used by the police to justify their special focus on black youth, resulting in the victimisation of innocent people. The policing of prostitution also affects poor white women who inhabit the inner cities but the policing of street crimes, which is focused on poor young black men, also expose black women to indirect surveillance due to their proximity to black men.

This shows that the problems of black women are similar in some ways but different in many respects compared to the problems facing white women and black men. Hall et al (1978: 369) loosely compared the struggles of blacks and women and found that they are both sectors of the general class struggle. By so doing, they made the familiar mistake of defining black women out of existence. Either you are in the black sector or you are in the women's sector of the working class. The fact that black women are struggling in both sectors at once was not worth mentioning by Hall et al in their comparison of struggles, but it is crucial in understanding what they saw as 'aligning sectoral struggles with a more general class struggle' (Ibid.).

The struggles of black women who resist racial discrimination and demand justice and fair play have been documented in Bryan et al (1985). It contains records of resistance against discrimination in workplaces and collective agitation by organisations like the Black Women's Group which picketed police stations to demand fair treatment for detained black men and women.

Conclusion

This chapter has tried to argue that, in some cases, black women are treated differently from black men and white women and in some other cases, they are treated similarly. The problems facing black women appear different because they are relatively affected by the special police focus on the black community as well as by the predatory survival strategies of black hustlers. White women are relatively safe from the former, but share the latter to some extent. Black men are relatively free from the latter but are more closely affected by the former. Although the informal victimisation of black women (by hustlers and employers, for example) does not seem to involve the criminal justice system, the formal/informal dichotomy of victimisation breaks down when it is recognised that the informal victimisation of black women sometimes exposes them to encounters with the formal criminal justice system as 'victims' or as suspects and defendants.

The next three chapters provide empirical evidence of the problems facing black women in the criminal justice system and how organisations of black women are tackling such problems. There is no attempt to measure the extent of the problems that face black women compared to black men and white women. What has been done in the following chapters is an attempt to understand the nature of such problems with a view to clarifying the features of Victimisation-As-Mere-Punishment (VAMP) and Victimisation-In-Punishment (VIP). However, such theoretical clarifications are not explored fully until chapter six.

3. Black Women and Policing

Introduction

The previous chapter ended with a focus on the internal colonies of England and the present chapter takes off from there by looking more closely at the problems posed for black women and people like them by the criminal justice system in the internal colonies of London. The evidence is mainly from London but analogous evidence from other internal colonies is brought in where necessary.

The sources of the evidence were both documentary and observational. The documentary sources included official and unofficial reports and publications. The observational evidence was information provided by individuals and groups and the personal observations of this author during the fieldwork.

During the fieldwork, there was no attempt to directly observe police behaviour towards black people in the same way that court appearances of defendants were observed because a lot more is known about police behaviour than about problems facing defendants and how they cope with such. An indirect approach was adopted for the assessment of the impact of policing on black women. This involved participant observation at the meetings of the Hackney Community Defence Association and the meetings of the 'Policing and Sentencing' committee of the Society of Black Lawyers. Those meetings indirectly provided insights into the problems that faced black people in the criminal justice system in general and policing in particular.

However, given that these groups were interest groups and therefore might not be expected to give a balanced or impartial view of the issues, the observations and pieces of information that they provided were examined against the background of existing relevant research and publications. What is presented in this chapter is the reconstruction of the observations and available information to give a general idea of how the construction of 'evidence' and 'suspects' by the police is linked with the victimisation of innocent people in the name of law and order (Leng, et al, 1992; McConville et al, 1991; Keith, 1993 and Gilroy. 1987a, 1987b).

The Construction of Criminal Categories

> 'Black people are ... on the wrong end of the rough/respectable, non-deserving continuum of the working class. They are identified as the new "dangerous classes". A false link has been made in the mind of the public, between crime and ethnicity. This clearly has its roots in the tradition of white, mainland British xenophobia. The effect of this is felt by the black population, and is often left out of crime surveys' (Brake and Hale, 1992: 91).

This section attempts to affirm the above statement by identifying the key elements in the mythical mental linkages between crime and the politics of race, gender and class which Mike Brake and many others have struggled to demystify. This is a critical tribute to Brake who died of cancer in 1992 shortly after completing the above-cited work with Hale as a tribute to another critical criminologist, Steven Box (1983), who also died of cancer.

A possible criticism to be levelled against Brake is that while he made connections between conservative criminology and the conservative policies of Thatcherism, he tended to lump black people together with the 'working classes' as if black people do not have variable class relations. However, such a criticism would not be fair especially since the above epigraph, taken from his posthumously published book, refers to a 'false link' being made by the public and therefore recognises that black people are more complex than popular stereotypes would presume. A proper tribute to Brake would be the deepening of his class-race-gender awareness in theory and in practice.

The aim of this section is to illustrate a small part of Brake's critiques of both left and right 'realist' positions around individual responsibility for crime and psycho-biological determinism versus authoritarian welfare populism and socio-economic determinism. This section will demonstrate that the self-professed realists of the right are not realistic enough for advocating individual responsibility while encouraging the victimisation of whole groups and categories of people, many of who happen to be innocent. Similarly, the section will demonstrate to what extent the self-styled left realists have left realism by focusing almost exclusively on street crimes contrary to the defence of the poor by Brake. Box and many others on the critical left who wonder why the majority of the poor are overwhelmingly law-abiding while many of the rich get away with murder and most prisoners are poor.

The self-professed left realists could retort that they too are committed to the defence of the poor but from the point of view of taking the crimes of poor people against poor people seriously at the level of working class politics. This is a valid concern that Brake would share for, while he highlighted what was left out of crime surveys, he never implied that such surveys were false. He only emphasised that such surveys - upon which left realism draws in the form of local crime surveys - are inadequate to the extent that they leave out the politics of oppressive racialisation in the criminal justice system and society, and thereby ignore both the crimes of the powerful against the poor and the resistance of the poor against oppression in their ahistorical accounts of 'processes which take place at no place, always in the present' (Keith, 1993: 17). For a critical account of the possible links between the new left and the new right, see Gilroy (1987b) and Gilroy and Sim (1987). See also Scraton (1990) for a critique of left-realists' exaggerations of the differences between themselves and those they style left idealists.

By focusing on what Stuart Hall (1980b) would call the dialectical process of 'encoding/decoding' of a specific policy statement, the present section does not assume that crime is a fiction constructed by the authoritarian state for the oppression of the marginalised or that crime can only be deconstructed in order to be solved. As Hall (1980b: 134) rightly argued, what is being offered here is a 'dominant, not determined' interpretation of a historical event, bearing in mind that 'it is always possible to order, classify, assign and decode an event within more than one "mapping".' Moreover, like Hall, this writer believes that the interpretations being offered here are 'preferred' or hegemonic interpretations because they 'have the institutional/political/ideological order imprinted in them and have themselves become institutionalised'. Readers are invited to draw their own conclusions or to read the following message in different ways, some of which are anticipated and responded to in passing within the present reading.

The notice that is reconstructed below is an 'URGENT NEIGHBOURHOOD WATCH MESSAGE' issued by the Redland Police of Bristol, dated 27 August 1991 which was received by this author through the Society of Black Lawyers who claim that the police have since apologised for the message. It is essential to reconstruct the leaflet as much as possible because it was received in the form of a photocopy that cannot be reproduced photographically in a book of this quality. The iconography of Neighbourhood Watch could not be reproduced here but the reader can interpret the text independently with the help of the original emphases.

Figure 3.1: Neighbourhood Watch Message

MESSAGE FROM REDLAND POLICE   **URGENT**

THE 'THREE MINUTE GANG' ARE OPERATING AGAIN ALL OVER THE AREA. THEY ARE A TEAM OF AFRO CARIBBEAN MALES AND ARE VERY WELL ORGANISED. THERE COULD BE SIX OR MORE IN THE TEAM, BUT THEY WORK IN TWOS & THREES, SWOPPING (sic) PARTNERS REGULARLY. IF YOU SEE:-

1   AFRO CARIBBEANS SITTING IN A VEHICLE WATCHING PROPERTY

2   AIMLESSLY WANDERING AROUND LOOKING AT HOUSES

3   KNOCKING ON DOORS

4   SHOULD AN AFRO CARIBBEAN KNOCK ON YOUR DOOR, AND THEN MAKE SOME EXCUSE WHEN YOU ANSWER, THAT HE IS LOOKING FOR SOMEONE.

5   IN FACT IF YOU FEEL UNEASY ABOUT THE WAY EITHER ONE OR A GROUP OF AFRO CARIBBEANS ARE BEHAVING

DIAL   999   IMMEDIATELY

CRIME

TOGETHER WE'LL CRACK IT

Please take the registration number of any vehicle concerned, and equally important as good a description of the people involved paying particular attention to the clothing they are wearing. Clothing is important because as previously mentioned they regularly swop partners.

This notice appears to be an openly racist stereotyping and discriminatory targeting of black people by the police. Note how the focus of the Message becomes increasingly generalised from the 'Three Minute Gang' to 'Afro Caribbean Males' and then to any 'Afro Caribbean' or any 'group of Afro Caribbeans'. The fact that the gang was said to be operating

'AGAIN' suggests that they have operated before. In that case, the members might be known if some of them had been arrested before.

More probably, however, the members were not known at all and, perhaps, that was why the fifth message is so all-embracing; it could be anybody who is black. This collective targeting and its assumption of guilt by association suggest a special policing of black people because item five cannot be read in isolation from the earlier four and also because it is strategically or emphatically located both at the line in front of which the panicky word 'crime' is gigantically printed and at the point of the call to dial 999. The suspect group seems to be the whole of black people in the area who may be driving, walking, or making white people uneasy, even because of their appearance or clothing.

This writer has never seen any evidence that the police target groups of white males with similar notices that could make anybody 'feel uneasy about the way either one or a group of (white people) are behaving.' The only such policing that affects mainly white people is the policing of travellers and joy-riding, but the fact that travellers and joy-riders are mostly white is never mentioned in anti-traveller or anti-joy-riding propaganda in England and Wales, even when efforts are made to distinguish new age travellers from the more respectable Gypsies (see 'United We're Nicked' - the critical supplement on the 1994 Criminal Justice and Public Order Bill co-published by the *New Statesman & Society*, 24 June 1994, and Civil Liberties Organisations opposing the bill).

Since the leaflet was a Neighbourhood Watch message, there is no doubt that it was issued or authorised by the police. It even carried the police seal of authority and stated that it is a 'message from Redland Police'. Neighbourhood Watch schemes are relatively autonomous from the police but, like any other aspect of multi-agency policing, they were initiated by top police officers in mainly white middle class neighbourhoods in Britain, as in the old South Africa, and they are expected to be under the control of the police (Brogden and Shearing, 1993). The colonisation of Neighbourhood Watch schemes by the police is especially true because, while the police generally look at the public as allies in the fight against crime, 'in the police view the public's judgement cannot be relied upon' (McConville and Shepherd, 1992: 161-162). Indeed, a book co-published by the Croom Helm press and the Police Foundation claims that 'Neighbourhood Watch schemes provide a convenient and economical way for police to disseminate crime prevention propaganda ...' (Weatheritt, 1986: 82).

It is likely that propaganda pieces such as the one above could contribute to racism against black people and result in false alarms, malicious prosecution, and unlawful imprisonment. It is also possible that such criminalisation of a defined group could provoke black resistance against being officially stigmatised by the police as members of a 'subculture' with a 'substantial criminal fringe', as Joshua, Wallace, and Booth (1983: 54) demonstrate in the case of the 1980 Bristol 'riots'.

This suggestion of racialised difference is strong because the image of community policing which the lithograph representing Neighbourhood Watch on the leaflet appears to show is that of a white police officer and a white family consisting of a man, a woman and a girl, indicating that the 'community' is gendered and racialised in the threatening 'we and them' tones of the editorial of *Daily Mail*, 8 October 1985:

> Either they obey the laws of this land where they have taken up residence and accepted both full rights and responsibilities of citizenship, or they must expect the fascist street agitators to call ever more boldly and with ever louder approval for them to 'go back whence they came'.

This was written in the wake of the killing of PC Keith Blakelock but one of the Tottenham three wrongly convicted of the killing turned out to be a white man, an indication that the racialisation of black people would also affect poor white people adversely to some extent. The tone of this editorial is comparable to that of *The Sun*, 30 September 1985, following what the paper called 'The Shame of Brixton': 'If decent men and women of West Indian origin do not maintain peace then there is a real danger that their communities will be permanently alienated.' Van Dijk (1993: 268) has correctly pointed out that, 'The main ideological point of "riot" coverage is their explanation in terms of the alleged criminal character and violence of blacks, and the exoneration of white institutions (government, police, and so on) from blame for the black revolt. This point is embedded in a broader ideological structure of nationalist racism in which minorities, immigrants, immigration and the multicultural society are associated with negative qualifications, and white British people, society, and culture are presented as positive and "under attack" by the aliens.'

Such discourses tend to exclude or marginalise black people. Certainly, the police leaflet was not meant for the gaze or consumption of the black community and it may have been designed to be hidden from black people in order to maximise its effectiveness. However, in 1995, Police Commissioner Paul Condon of the London Metropolitan Police directed similar propaganda specifically at the black community or those he called 'leaders of the black community' whom he warned through the mass media, after writing to them individually, that he was about to launch 'Operation Eagle Eye' against black youth because his statistics suggested that they commit 80% of the muggings in London.

This Neighbourhood Watch leaflet is similar to what Chigwada (1991: 136) saw as, 'A glaring example of the racist stereotyping and assumptions made about black people by the police ....' She was referring to the leaflet that was distributed in 1987 to Neighbourhood Watch schemes and post offices in Wombourne, Staffordshire. Like the leaflet referred to above, it was written on police note paper and the message was reported by *The Times*, (13 October 1987) as follows: 'I would like sightings of blacks and coloured and their vehicle numbers. No prejudice. Intelligence gained that they are coming out of the city and committing crime (namely, house burglary)'. The local Labour Party denounced the leaflet as being 'overtly racist' and the Staffordshire police apologised, saying that the leaflet should never have been distributed (ibid) and that it 'was never intended to be racist' (*The Guardian*, 13 October 1987).

Notice that the police emphasised that there was 'no prejudice' in the offensive leaflet and stated in their apology that it was never intended to be racist. Notice also that their apology relates to the distribution of the leaflet and not to the holding of the underlying assumption that black people are more likely to commit certain crimes. 'Intelligence' has been troubling scholars, some of whom have devised controversial scales for the measurement of individual intelligence. When the individual ability to organise information, understand correlations and make predictions is abstracted and applied to a legal personality like the state or some of its agencies, the assumption remains that intelligence activities are essentially made up of intelligent actions by intelligent professionals. In this propagandist sense, it is all too easy to overlook the fact that 'intelligence failures', according to Hastedt (1991: 3-4), 'which students of strategic surprise stress are inevitable and which critics of covert action constantly warn against, bring forward charges of betrayal, incompetence, and rogue elephants on the loose'.

This view is advanced further by Gill (1994: 235-240) who, following Robert Mandel, discussed four "clusters of distortions" that could be found in the intelligence process: these are (1) the difficulties of targeting and evaluation, (2) 'proficiency and personality limitations of individual officials', (3) bureaucratic bottle-necks in the compartmentalisation of related tasks and duties, and (4) the development of oversights or the absence of effective autonomous regulation of the intelligence community by the government and non-governmental agencies.

These 'distortions' of intelligence are not always clear to members of the public when the police make claims on 'what intelligence gained'. The claim being suggested to the public in such propaganda is the claim to objectivity similar to the claim to scientificity made by many scholars for the expert knowledge that grants them relative access to power resources. The warning in this book is that the intelligence community is not necessarily the intelligent community. Once upon a time, police intelligence used to be referred to as criminal investigation. The replacement of investigation with intelligence arose probably after the second imperialist World War, perhaps, following the emergence of military intelligence as a science and technology more sophisticated than mere spying. However, we must not forget that 'what intelligence gained' could still be plainly silly.

As far as the police were concerned, the leaflet was based on what police 'intelligence gained' and, presumably, there would have been nothing wrong with the information if it had not been publicised as the guiding assumption of a specific police surveillance. In other words, when the Chief of Scotland's largest police force, Mr Leslie Sharp, 'joked' that if a robot cricket umpire was painted black, it would 'be no good because it would start smoking pot, mugging old ladies and robbing shops' (*The Voice*, 24 March 1992), he was saying something that seemed to be a principle of 'internal colonial policing' (Cashmore and Mclaughlin, 1991) or what the Institute of Race Relations (1987) called Policing Against Black People. Moreover, if senior police officers could hold such views, the attitudes of the beat officers can be expected to be even worse, given their greater discretionary powers, an expectation confirmed by numerous researchers (see McConville and Shepherd, 1992; IRR, 1987; Keith, 1993, for example).

Ian Taylor (1994) is critical of 'critically-minded social scientists' (with the exception of Betsy Stanko) for what he called their 'dismissive deconstruction' of the fear of crime revealed by opinion polls and local newspaper crime reports 'as contemporary instances of "moral panics".' Such a critique would be unfair to Mike Brake, Maureen Cain, Steve Box, Penny Green, Paul Gilroy, Phil Scraton, Stuart Hall, Sandra Walklate and most critical criminologists who realistically emphasise, like Ian Taylor himself, that the (Tory) Party of Law and Order is losing the fight against crime while successfully marginalising further those who are relatively powerless in society.

To say that leaflets like the one being 'deconstructed' here could lead to false accusations of innocent black people is not to deny that crime is on the rise or to say that the fear of crime is baseless. The claim being made here is that the fear of crime has been falsely conflated with the fear of black people and that this link is unfair to most people of whatever 'race'. This point is supported by Taylor (1994) when he demonstrated that the demonisation of Moss Side (which is 30% Afro-Caribbean) as the source of the crime problem in Manchester is largely false given the generalisability of what former Metropolitan Police Commissioner, Kenneth Newman, called 'symbolic locations' (see Gilroy and Sim, 1987: 100) to 'definitions placed on particular buildings and territorial spaces in the local neighbourhood, and also in the wider conurbation of Greater Manchester'. However, the generalisability of 'symbolic locations' should not result in the reduction of racialisation to deprivation in a way that could conceal or distort the special history of black people and the politics of law and order.

Besides, given the extensive use of publicity by the police with the active support of the mass media, some public concerns would obviously be constructions or reconstructions of problems already identified, magnified, and publicised by the police. Apart from the morality of such commercial games, it may be asked if they yield the desired results. Weatheritt (1986: 82) indirectly pointed out an aspect of the commercialisation of policing by noting that 'Neighbourhood Watch is ... a good way of increasing the market for the standard products of physical crime prevention.' A good way of increasing the consumption of security gadgets is not necessarily a good way to increase the prevention of crime. In other words, it is possible for the market in such gadgets to boom at times of high crime waves.

This book will not go into the debate around privatisation. It is sufficient to note that the analogy with commercialisation suggests to this author that the targeting of black people by the police does not have to develop from an anti black world view, but that an anti black world view could and often does develop from such institutionally discriminatory practices that are found in major social institutions. This idea is more aptly captured by Hall et al (1978) with the concept of the amplification of deviance by the police and the mass media. To say that black crime is amplified is not to say that all black people are innocent saints who are unjustly criminalised, but to point out that black people are no more and no less criminal than other categories of people in an authoritarian state like Britain. It is in this sense that Gilroy (1987b: 118) talks about 'The Myth of Black Criminality'. Brake and Hale (1992: 91) agree with Gilroy by stating that black people are now unfairly 'identified as the new "dangerous classes".'

It is important to note here that the 'monetization' of justice which Young (1987) observed goes beyond the reliance on fines as means of punishment and the buying and selling of legal and judicial services which Adam Smith traced (MacCormick, 1981), to include the buying and selling of the idea of what categories of people are criminal or respectable. This is similar to the moral pictures exhibited in 'the gallery of folk types - heroes and saints, as well as fools, villains and devils' which, according to Cohen (1972: 17), are 'publicised not just in oral-tradition and face-to-face contact but to much larger audiences and with much greater dramatic resources.' What this suggests is that the publicity materials for policing that at first sight appear to portray overt racism could indeed be part of normal police work as well. If this is the case, and Leng et al (1992:119) argue that it is widely so, then racism could be said to be institutionalised in the normal ways the police do their work.

For instance, the Institute of Race Relations has argued that one of the reasons why black people are over-represented in the arrest figures of the police is that: 'Clearly, there has been a shift in policy in the 1980s which selects out inner-city areas, with their high concentration of unemployed black youth, for a particular form of policing - with its own policing assumptions, special tactics and specialist squads' (IRR, 1987: 1-2). The Institute referred to the tactic of 'targeting' which was applied to terrorists in Northern Ireland. It operates by isolating certain areas for closer police operational focus by means of surveillance, through paid informants, on 'selected individuals and groups' and on what were termed 'symbolic locations' (Ibid, p. 2).

What the Institute of Race Relations did not indicate is that such a tactic was not always tacit but was also colourfully advertised for mass appeal that could render the paying of informants more or less redundant. The marketing techniques of publicity could be used by the police to manipulate the desire for individual security and encourage people to look for what the police have already constructed as clues to suspects. It should be pointed out here that, like most marketing techniques, police publicity does not appeal to all sections of the public in similar ways. Some members of the public show more support for the police than others. The Institute of Race Relations details ways by which sections of the press serve the police with what Mr Justice Thomas of the US Supreme Court opportunistically popularised as 'hi-tech lynching' of black people in their campaign for more stringent surveillance on the black community (IRR, 1987: 51-55).

Similarly, Ericson, et al (1989: 79) have argued that in Canada, 'For the accused publicity can be a form of punishment, with lingering stigmatic effects, even if she is found not guilty.' Two observations that could be made about 'the punishment of publicity' are that it is not punishment but what Brake and Hale (1992: 16) call 'invisible victimisation' or what this writer called Victimisation-As-Punishment (Agozino, 1991). This is because it is not only the accused that are subjected to such negative publicity, and the punishment of publicity is not punishment but Victimisation-As-Mere-Punishment when the targets are innocent. Large groups of people are often stigmatised as suspects long before some of their members become accused. Moreover, even for those who are eventually found guilty, punitive publicity before conviction is a form of what we have called Victimisation-In-Punishment.

It is likely that the more closely any group of people are watched, the greater the chances of innocent members of that group being proceeded against mistakenly or maliciously. Apart from people who are released after wrongful conviction, the high proportion of black people released from detention without proceedings or discharged and acquitted shows that black people are more readily arrested when there is little ground for suspicion. A high arrest rate does not necessarily mean a high crime rate since it is not the case that all those arrested are necessarily criminal or that those not arrested are necessarily law-abiding. However, discharge and acquittal are not proofs of innocence but also rely on the adequacy of evidence and of the benefit of the doubt, a benefit that cannot be expected to be enjoyed equally by the mainstream and by demonised minorities.

It could also be said that criminal justice personnel favour black people and that that is the reason why many black people are discharged or acquitted, but such a suggestion would be wrong because it is not a favour to be arrested and then discharged without conviction and also because closer police surveillance is not a way to demonstrate fairness to black people. Moreover, to say that black people have relatively higher acquittal rates because the criminal justice system is relatively fair to them is to ignore the struggles in the black community and in courts against what could be called victimisation-as-policing.

The concern of the black community is very real and increasingly so given the provision under Clause 55 of the 1994 Criminal Justice and Public Order Act to revive the racist SUS law by authorising the police to stop and search all vehicles and pedestrians in certain localities without giving or having any reason or justification to do so. The Act also provided for prisons for 12-14 year olds, restricted the right to bail, virtually abolished the right to silence, empowered the police to take body samples without consent, and increased the fine for the possession of cannabis from £500 to £2,500, among other Leviathan measures (*New Statesman & Society*, June 1994).

The conclusion that could be drawn in this section is that Brake and Hale (1992) were right in pointing out that there are links between conservative economic policies of privatisation and the rise of the law and order society. They rightly pointed out that the concern of conservative politicians shifted from crime-reduction to plain retributivism or punishment for the sake of punishment. What this section has tried to demonstrate is that the conservative philosophy of individual freedom in a hypothetical market-place has not always been put into practice by law and order officials because it is groups and categories, rather than individuals, who are targeted by the control culture. As a result of the continuation of the assumption of guilt by association or collective responsibility, which is an essential element of moral panics, the legal ethic of innocence until proven otherwise seems to have been reversed especially for people marginalised on the bases of race-class-gender relations.

What this means is that the conservative propaganda that poverty does not necessarily cause crime could be true in the critical sense that 'the rich get richer and the poor get prison' (as Steve Box would say), not necessarily because they are more criminal but also because they are too poor to effectively challenge their visible and 'invisible victimisation' by the agents of the law and order society. Given the adoption of the law and order ideology by Tony Blair as a Labour Party key electoral issue, Brake and Hale are right in pointing out how naive the self-styled left realists are in believing that the next Labour government would necessarily be the answer to the deepening crises of hegemony (Hall, 1988) which gave rise to the law and order society.

However, it must be said that Blair's concern with law and order is completely different from that of Thatcher because he also emphasises the need to take the causes of crime seriously. Moreover, this is not the first time that the Labour Party prioritised crime as a policy issue. In 1964, the party published the report of a study group chaired by Lord Longford, *Crime: A Challenge to Us All*, which again differs both from Tory claims that only the Conservatives are the Law and Order Party and from Blair's anti-consensus claim that only Labour can call itself a party of law and order with any conviction because Labour is committed to taking the causes of crime as seriously as it takes crime. The problem is that Blair agrees with left realism that social deprivation causes crime. This indicates that he is not taking the crimes of the privileged seriously enough. Secondly, he seems to evade the issue that social deprivation needs to be tackled, not just because it causes crime but, more importantly, because it is criminally negligent to socially deprive people in the midst of plenty and turn round to criminalise or victimise the deprived innocents. Blair soon widened his focus by calling for moral regeneration and strong family discipline but, historically, it is always the poor who are assumed to lack good breeding whereas rich boys (the public reaction would have been different if they were girls) are protected in public schools where they could expose their bums to parents during a sports day without being expelled for being 'unteachable' (see The Independent on Sunday, 'Prince's fellow pupils "moon" parents' 9 September 1996). In connection with this, Tony Giddens warns that

> Tony Blair isn't right to say that strong families bring about a more cohesive society. Anyone who knows southern Italy can see the essential falsity of this idea. The strength of families drains away any sustained sense of public life. In deprived neighbourhoods the strongest families are often the most criminalised. It isn't strong families as such that we should be after, but ones that are egalitarian and communicative. In a democratic family, work is shared out equally, whether the work be paid or unpaid (Giddens, 1996: 19).

Victimisation as Policing

The police could argue that they do not have the resources with which to watch everywhere as intensively as they do the inner city 'colonies'. They could even argue that they saturate the inner cities in order to protect black people against racist attacks as Kinsey, Lea and Young (1986: 123) assumed for the sake of argument. I will not go into the debate around the adequacy of the police response to racist attacks although cases like that of Stephen Lawrence, the 18 years old black youth who was murdered on 22 April 1993 'by five white youth', according to the Inquest, 'for no other reason than the colour of his skin', suggest otherwise. The inquest agreed that there was 'a lost opportunity' to find the evidence for the conviction of the killers and the family accused the police of investigating possible drugs links to the murder instead of concentrating on finding enough evidence to allow prosecution to proceed. The family unsuccessfully attempted a private prosecution due to the lack of effectiveness in the ways that the police investigated the alleged killers who were 'accused' by the *Daily Mail* (14 February 1997) in an unprecendented media campaign for 'justice to be done'. The police are expected by the public and by the State to operate reactively on information and complaints from concerned members of the public and to act proactively, using their own discretion.

Contrary to the definition of 'targeting' by Kinsey, Lea and Young (1986: 151) as 'the observation and tracking of particular known offenders', available evidence shows that individual offenders are not always known and that targeting usually focuses on groups and categories, most members of which may be innocent, while certain known offenders may not even be targeted at all. The police fail to restrict their special operations to individuals whom they have reason to suspect and they also proactively construct some of the concerns that the public later bring as complaints.

The Handsworth 'riot' Review Panel set up by the West Midlands County Council saw the maltreatment of black women by the police as the immediate precipitating factor for the 9 September 1985 uprising. The panel concluded that, 'large numbers of the people of Handsworth have a view of the police which accepts that the assault and intimidation of black women is consistent (with) general police practice' (IRR, 1987: 20). This conclusion was supported by Solomos and Rackett (1991: 48) who reported the allegation that the assault on a black woman by the police during an argument with a black man over a parking ticket was the 'spark' for the 'tinder ... of deteriorating relations between young people, especially blacks, and the police ...' in Handsworth.

Similarly, the death of a black woman, see case 2 below, during a police raid at her house precipitated the Broadwater Farms uprising during which PC Keith Blakelock was killed and following which two black men and one white man were convicted of murder. Although the inquest into the death of Mrs Jarett returned a verdict of accidental death, Chadwick and Scraton (1987) claimed that the verdict was part of the discourse that they identified as speaking ill of the dead. The 'Tottenham Three' have now been cleared of the charges of murdering Blakelock although the second black man involved remained in jail for an earlier conviction of murder for which he was serving a death sentence. What these cases illustrate is that attacks on black women by the police could have implications for black men (and for poor white people who share some of the problems facing black people) and vice versa.

The allegation of police victimisation of innocent black women can be illustrated with the following cases documented by the Institute of Race Relations. Note that what these cases show is a series of accusations or allegations from the point of view of the victimised. They do not prove that these accusations are true. In fact, some of the allegations were rejected as false by juries. However, juries are politicised and often racialised in the criminal justice system (see Gordon, 1992 for an analysis of black struggles to be tried by juries that are truly their peers and the establishment view that black people are unfit to be jury members in cases involving black defendants). Thus the rejection of the complaints and allegations by juries, as in the case of the acquittal of the police officers who savagely beat Rodney King with clubs and shot him twice with a stun gun in Los Angeles, is more of a cause for concern than a reason to pat the police on the back. The differences between American politics of race and jury trials and those of England, not withstanding, a brief comment on the Rodney King trials, is in order here because any similarities between the two systems of politicisation would help us to understand better what is specifically English politics.

Smith (1994) used this case to illustrate a hypothetical scenario which starts with black people committing an offence, followed by police attempts to arrest, a possible resistance by black offenders who fear police partiality, and then by police brutality, black riots and more police arrests. This is supposed to be part of the explanation for the over-representation of black people in the criminal justice system. However, Smith's hypothetical scenario is faulty in two important respects. First of all, it is not true that Rodney King committed any traffic offence; he was not tried for any such offence and the officers maintained that they simply suspected him of over-speeding on drugs. Similarly, most black people or any other category of people arrested are not offenders but suspects who must be assumed to be innocent until proven otherwise.

Secondly, it is not true that uprisings like the Los Angeles 'riots' are simply cases of 'a huge number of offences (being) committed by black people in protest at the verdict' (Smith, 1994: 1048). The uprising was by people who were black and people who were not black even though it was predominantly black. The protest against police brutality took mainly non-criminal forms like prayers in black churches and speeches or newspaper articles by political activists. In other words, it is important to distinguish between protests against police criminality and jury complacency from crimes that might be committed by a few opportunists under the cover of such protests. This writer believes that the majority of the people who 'riot' do not engage in criminal activities except in so far as 'rioting' itself is a criminalised activity.

The four police officers who were unambiguously captured on amateur video beating Rodney King were initially acquitted by an all-white jury. The subsequent trial of the same officers for civil rights violations at the Federal level resulted in the jury acquitting two of them and finding the Sergeant in charge of the operation and the officer who delivered most of the fifty-six blows guilty of violating the civil rights of Rodney King. The two officers appealed against their convictions and the court of appeal upheld the conviction and also ruled that they should be given more serious sentences. By making it a civil rights case, the Federal court emphasised a widely shared belief that the officers discriminated against Rodney King on the basis of his race, but such a presentation ignored the gender and minimised the class aspects of the actions of the police officers. This writer believes that the gender of Rodney King operated in the trivialisation of the police brutality by the all-white jury that acquitted the aggressors and by the Federal court that acquitted two of them and gave light sentences to the other two. Gender discrimination is not something that happens only to women.

There is little doubt that if Rodney King had been a woman, he might not have been given so many blows and stun gun shots just to be arrested for suspected overspeeding. No female member of the jury would attempt to defend the indefensible with the excuse that the victimised was in control of the beating. The ideology of masculinity makes it possible for black men to be seen as strong and macho, able to fight their way through and absorb hard knocks with the deadly smile of a Tyson. To quote Jesse Jackson (*The Guardian*, 5 May 1992), 'their primary offence was to be young, strong and black.'

This is not to suggest that black women, in particular, and poor women, in general, face less difficult problems than black men from the police. The gender of Rodney King is not just his sex as a man but, as the defence lawyers argued in favour of the policemen, the fact that he was seen as 'a drug crazed giant'. This view articulates the macho strength of a giant with the drug culture which police officers closely identify with blackness. These were most likely also articulated with the working class or 'underclass' nature of the neighbourhood of South Central Los Angeles to produce the brutality for which the victimised was later to be awarded nearly four million dollars in damages.

The differences in the problems facing black men and black women are not only in terms of the degree of oppression but also in terms of the kinds of oppression that they are subjected to. This suggests that while a black woman might not be subdued with 56 blows from the police club, she might suffer the humiliation of being insulted as a sex object. Again, this is not to say that stereotypically 'strong' black women have not been beaten and even killed by the police. The point is simply that gender discrimination affects black men too, but in very specific ways that are not identical with gender discrimination against black women.

All the same, I will use cases like that of Rodney King and the ones to be itemised shortly merely as illustrations of victimisation as perceived by those who have suffered it rather than as evidence against the police. This is because very few of the narratives reflect the points of view of the police and also because this is not a court trial. In a sense, the whole book should be seen as a study of perceptions of the problems that face black women and comparable groups in the criminal justice system. It is true that some of the illustrations provided refer to black men and not to black women, but the following cases will demonstrate that, even when black men are the focus of action by the police, black women are often directly affected as well. Except for a few lines that are paraphrases, these are direct quotes of the descriptions offered by the victimised as published by the IRR:

1 In February 1984 Linda Williams Lodged an official complaint after the police arrived at her Peckham home and demanded to see her son, Errol. Mrs Williams says that when she asked to see their search warrant, she was dragged downstairs by the hair and, while she was on the floor, she was repeatedly kicked in the back by one police officer while another stood on her legs. Mrs Williams was pregnant at that time.

2 On 5 October 1985, Floyd Jarrett was stopped on suspicion that he stole his own car. While in detention, the police took his key to go and search his Tottenham home for stolen goods. They entered the room without permission and when Floyds's mother asked how they got in, they said that the door was open. She asked for a search warrant and one of them pushed her aside. She fell and broke a table and lay unconscious. The four police men ignored her and conducted the search but found nothing. Her daughter called the ambulance but Mrs Jarrett died on reaching the hospital. The inquest returned a verdict of accidental death and the officers were not even charged. This death ignited the Tottenham rebellion during which a police officer was killed.

3 On 28 September 1985 a team of officers went to the home of Mrs Cherry Groce in Brixton, South London, to arrest her son, Michael, who was wanted for armed robbery. In fact, Michael Groce no longer lived there. The officers smashed down the door with a sledge-hammer and then an inspector rushed in shouting 'armed police'. With his finger on the trigger, Mrs Groce said, the officer suddenly rushed at her, pointing a gun at her. She tried to run back but he shot her. She is now paralysed and confined to a wheelchair. This shooting initiated the Brixton rebellion that followed.

4 In April 1983 an Instant Response Unit of the police arrested a black youth, Emile Foakes, and accused him of taunting a group of white youths. According to him, the police grabbed him and called him a 'black nigger'. When his mother, Mrs Esme Baker, attempted to intervene, she was forced into the van, her dress was torn open and her breasts exposed. An officer prodded her in the breasts with a truncheon and said; 'I didn't know a nigger woman

had breasts.' Both Emile and his mother were acquitted of the charges of threatening behaviour and of assaulting the police.

5 North Kensington Law Centre (1982) documented this case in their report, *Police and the Nottinghill Community*. At a bus stop, the police were said to have accused a black man of loitering with intent to pick pockets. When he objected, the police accused him of stealing his own trousers because they looked too big for him. A black woman who was present called out that she would be a witness for him even though she did not know him. At that point, the police called for reinforcement and both the man and the woman were charged with assault. On the way to the van, according to the woman, she was deliberately tripped to the ground and one of the officers stamped on her groin.

6 In June 1986, two police officers tricked their way into Mrs Sheila Maddix's flat in West Norwood, South London, by claiming that they were council estate officers. Then they admitted that they were police officers without showing any identification or search warrant. They said they had come to question her 21 year-old son, Paul, about a rape. The family was prepared to co-operate and Paul went into his room to get dressed. Then 25 more officers stormed the house, pushed Mrs Maddix out of the way and handled her so roughly that she had to go to hospital for treatment. Paul was taken away, questioned for four hours and released without any charge (IRR, 1987: 16-26).

Furthermore, while reconstructing an attack on the Pembury estate of Hackney, *The Sun*, Thursday, 4 July 1991, published a statement that, 'A suspected crack factory was busted in a commando-style raid, by nearly a hundred police ...' But what did the police find in the suspected crack factory? Out of the 13 people arrested, none was charged with manufacturing or selling drugs, four were charged with public order offences just for being present during the raid, one man was charged with driving without insurance and another was handed over to immigration officials. One other man was charged with stealing and illegal use of a library card! Only six people were charged with the possession of small quantities of drugs (*Panther*, Summer 1991, No 4).

The way these arrest statistics were constructed by the police was narrated by one affected black woman, Lucille Lawrence, aged 49. According to Mrs Lawrence, the officers sprayed gas into her face as she tried to close her windows. Then they smashed through her door with a sledge hammer. They pushed her and, as she fell back, they ran into the sitting room, into the bedroom, and into the bathroom. Then they took her family, including a toddler, into the kitchen with one policeman at the door and a policewoman guarding the sink. They were refused entry into the bedroom, sitting room, or the toilet which Mrs Lawrence specifically demanded to use. According to her, 'They closed the doors - we don't know what they planted inside there.' After ripping the whole flat apart, they strip searched her daughter and her son's girlfriend in the toilet. Then five of the officers fell on her son, Trevor, boxed him and sprawled him on the floor just to handcuff him (*Panther*, Summer 1991).

This raid was the subject of a campaign by the Hackney Community Defence Association during the fieldwork for this book. It involved a black man who returned to the estate where he lived and was arrested by the police who had earlier raided the estate for drugs and fire arms. His daughter came out to ask why he was being arrested and she too was arrested. His granddaughter came to find out what her grandfather and her aunt had done and she too was arrested. The granddaughter was later released without charge, then re-arrested and charged with common assault against the police, and finally, all the charges against her were dropped. She now appeared scared to go forward to the police and testify for her grandfather and her aunt who were charged with causing grievous bodily harm and actual bodily harm, respectively. Both charges were later reduced to actual bodily harm and common assault, respectively.

According to the man's daughter, 19 year old Claudia McCalla who received bruises on her face and arms, her father had told the officers that he was just returning from a course, that he was tired and that he was eager to enter his flat because he was worried about his family. The officers reportedly said that he was not going anywhere and started to hurt him. That was when Claudia told them, 'Leave him, he's my dad. He lives at number 2, we all live there.' Their response was to push and grab her by the neck and by the legs. People were shouting, 'Stop holding her by the neck, you're going to kill her.' They put her on the ground and cuffed her hands behind her back. While still on the ground, one kneeled on her back and another pushed his knuckles into her head, pushing her face against the ground. In the van, they continued pushing her head against the wall. She protested saying, 'You can take your hands off me now. I'm hand-cuffed, I'm not going anywhere, I'm not a dog.' They replied, 'You are a dog 'cause you're acting like one .... Don't think we're going to treat you any different because you're a girl.' Treating her like a man, perhaps, included charging her with assaulting four police officers at once!

The HCDA condemned this raid on the estate as an instance of 'fire brigade policing'. They protested that black people were specially targeted during the raid with the result that many innocent people were victimised and brutalised by the police. On 10 September 1991, the Mayor of Hackney wrote to the HCDA to warn them never to send their newsletter, Community Defence, to him again because, 'Like 99% of the residents', he was fully in support of the police in their efforts to rid the community of drug dealers and armed robbers. He also threatened that an association like theirs that received council funding should not specialise in attacking the police.

The association resolved to send an open reply to the Mayor through the press and through posters, saying that even if it was only one per cent of the community that were being unjustly harassed and criminalised by the police, they deserved support and defence. They pointed out that the police had even written a letter to every flat on the estate apologising for '... any inconvenience this evening's police operation may have caused .... We have used a large number of police officers in order to protect...the residents of the estate ...' However, the HCDA believed that the residents appeared to need more protection against the police, given the provocative ways that they operated.

Illustrations are not strong proofs because they could be challenged by different illustrations, especially from the police, to show that these instances are fabricated, or that they are not racist, or that they are not only racist because they are also shared by white women and by poor men of all racial groups. These illustrations serve to indicate the nature of the problem as it affects black women and as they and their organisations perceive the problems rather than as proof of the extent of the problem. However, there is reason to believe that these instances of perceived Victimisation-As-Mere-Punishment (VAMP) are only a tip of the iceberg even as they affect black women. The informants claimed that such incidents were common but that many of them were not publicised because many people are glad if the police drop charges against them and would not turn round to accuse the police.

This was implicitly denied, however, by Mr Benard Taffs, the Chief Superintendent of Hackney and City Road Police Stations, who claimed that his division dealt with about 10,000 custody cases in 1991 and 'only a small percentage resulted in complaints' (*The Guardian*, 6 April 1992). Mr Taffs wrote this to express regrets over the 1989 assault on the 73 year old great grandmother, Marie Burke. It was reported that WPC Tina Martin, a martial arts expert, violently pushed the St. Lucian-born Marie Burke to the ground when she brought medicine to her bed-ridden 79 year old husband, Mr Edgar Burke, who was being dragged away, half-naked, by the police. Mrs Burke was initially charged with assaulting four police officers and, when the charges were dropped, she struggled and won fifty thousand pounds worth of damages awarded by a jury against the Metropolitan Police.

Mr Taffs seemed to be saying that those who did not make formal complaints had nothing to complain about. This was disputed by those who offered information for this book. They claimed that the fear of further victimisation and limitations of access to legal representation were the main reasons why many 'victims' did not make formal complaints against the police. Mr Taffs also asserted that the assault on Mrs Burke was not racist because the jury threw out any suggestions that that was the case. But instead of alleging that the proportion of race-related complaints was small and that such complaints were not usually against racism as such, it will be more informative to monitor the rate of success of complaints by race, gender, and class.

Such monitoring could come from the Police Complaints Authority but in their 1990 annual report (PCA, 1991: 22), they stated that they have deliberately kept quiet on racism since they were founded. They said that they now wished to respond to the widespread demand for ethnic monitoring of complaints. Their response was in the form of an excuse that they could not keep such statistics partly because they lacked the necessary facilities and partly because they were 'totally impartial' and so race and gender were completely irrelevant to their assessment of cases. They also reported that cases that concerned racist behaviour by police officers were few probably because the accusation of racism is very difficult to prove. It requires proof beyond all reasonable doubt at the PCA because racism is a disciplinary offence. This is the only example where proof in a civil case is required beyond the usual standard of a balance of probabilities. Racism, like sexism, is a disciplinary offence in the police force but it is not necessarily a criminal offence unless it is manifested as perjury, an example of which was Mark Furhman's lie under oath during the O.J. Simpson trial. It seems, therefore, that the higher level of proof in allegations of racism against police officers was designed to discourage complainants from coming forward. However, racism and sexism are not even disciplinary offences among judges and magistrates who enjoy absolute judicial immunity against prosecution.

After series of complaints from the Hackney Community Defence Association and from affected individuals, the Police Complaints Authority launched 'Operation Jackpot' in 1991 into allegations of corruption at Stoke Newington police station, Northeast London. Three officers were suspended during the investigation, eight officers have been transferred to other stations since. The only officer named was Detective Constable Roy Lewandowski who was jailed for 18 months for stealing from the home of a dead man. Crown Counsel Kenneth Aylett told the appeal court that, in the light of the material gathered during Operation Jackpot, the Crown did not wish to sustain the convictions of one black woman and three black men who claimed that drugs were planted on them by officers from Stoke Newington station.

The Crown Counsel expected more appeals as the PCA released more material from Operation Jackpot. Earlier, the Crown Prosecution Service offered no evidence in 17 drug cases, and 17 defendants were acquitted in 17 other cases. Four more cases were waiting to be heard, seven cases - including the four successful ones - had gone to appeal while 12 civil actions were pending (*The Scotsman*, 3 March 1993). This suggests that some of the black women and black men who were in prison for drugs offences and who still protested their innocence may actually be suffering Victimisation-As-

Mere-Punishment. It is noteworthy that the success of a civil suit against the police does not increase the chances of successful criminal proceedings against the officers concerned.

Judges often strike out such criminal proceedings on the ground that the defendants could no longer face a fair trial given the difficulty in recollecting events that took place a long time ago and given the fact that the prosecution witness would reveal to the jury that he or she had already won a civil suit with damages awarded against the police. This happened in the case of PC David Judd who was charged with perjury and perverting the course of justice after Rupert Taylor of the Notting Hill Carnival Committee was awarded 60,000 pounds worth of damages for being wrongly accused of possessing drugs that PC Judd allegedly planted on him (*The Guardian*, 24 November 1993).

The extent to which the problem of victimisation-as-policing was shared by categories other than black women would indicate the extent to which social relations apart from those of race are also operative in such encounters. In the absence of comprehensive data on all such cases, ordinal and interval measures of the extent, rates and ratios of victimisation appear impossible. I am not suggesting that the most important social relations in these encounters of Victimisation-As-Mere-Punishment are either those of race, gender or those of class relations. The suggestion of class as the most crucial social relation in this context is tempting because all the black women who were affected happen to be poor and all the white women, white men and black men likely to be similarly affected are also poor. And given also that '... London's black communities, especially their youth, the latest heirs to London's run-down, "high crime" areas (are the) prime targets (of) "saturation policing"' (Jefferson 1990: 5), it is likely that poor black women would be victimised in different ways compared to poor white women because of their closer proximity to poor black men. However, this author believes that the poverty of the people affected cannot be understood without reference to the race and gender relations that affect them.

While these cases do not prove that all black women who get into contact with the police are innocent, they demonstrate that black women could become targets of special policing through their association with or mere proximity to suspected black men. This is the familiar colonial police tactic of collective responsibility for crime and guilt by association. Whole communities could be bombarded for attacks on colonial officers by a few individuals or groups (whether or not such attacks were excusable as self-defence by the colonised).

It is difficult to say whether victimisation-as-policing was a simple case of transference of colonial policing techniques to the 'internal colonies' of London, just as such techniques were said to have been originally transferred to the colonies from the militarised policing of Ireland. For example, Ahire (1991: 53) states that,

The training and orientation of the British police was deemed to be unsuitable for services in the colonies. The only appointments made from Britain were of persons who could 'show that they have had military training in the armed forces of the Crown', or that they were ex-officers of the Royal Irish Constabulary (RIC).

The argument of a reverse transference from the colonies to the internal colonies has been forcefully put by John Rex (1987: 103) who states that

... Handsworth is a purpose-built ghetto .... Around the year 1960 it was becoming clear that the population of Birmingham's inner-city wards was becoming increasingly black .... The Labour-led Birmingham City Council decided therefore to appoint a Liaison Officer for Coloured People - not, it should be noted, a Race Relations Officer to ensure that no citizen had his rights diminished on grounds of race, but a Liaison Officer to maintain liaison with an 'alien element' in the population. To this post it appointed a former colonial policeman, thereby making it clear that the task envisaged was a colonial one, and a policing one.

This dramatic evidence appears persuasive but it can be challenged on two grounds. First, a retired colonial police officer could take another job without turning it into a colonial or a policing one. Such an officer could become a bus driver, for example, and nothing would make it 'clear' that the duties of such a driver involved colonial and policing tasks. Secondly, it could be argued that not all colonial police officers were racist until their retirement and beyond. As Memmi (1990: 85) put it in his 1957 classic statement: 'every colonizer does not necessarily become a colonialist.' Some police officers may have been anti-racist in colonial service or they may have acquired the consciousness of anti-racism as a result of their colonial tasks. Even the legendary Fanon was once a colonial psychiatrist before committing class suicide by joining the Algerian revolutionaries in the war of independence.

Rex could respond to these doubts by stating that the duty of a bus driver is not the same as those of a race liaison officer. The latter is unlike any other job in the sense that the experience of colonial police service might cause the black community to have little or no trust in the designated officer. There is no doubt that policing of the internal colonies could copy one or two techniques from the 'external colonies.' However, it would have made little or no difference if the designation of the officer was what Rex wished for - if the appointee was a race relations researcher and not a retired police officer - while the policy remained the same in practice. Perhaps the policy would not have been the same, but the 'internal colonies' had since got Race

Relations Officers who had neither colonial nor policing experience and yet the only thing that changed was the increasing number of black people who were being over-represented in criminal justice statistics.

To argue for direct colonial links would imply that, if there had been no colonies, such tactics might not have developed. However, guilt by association and collective responsibility are not peculiar to colonial situations. They appear to be a feature of the policing of marginalised groups in most capitalist societies. The targeting of poor black people appears to be a continuation of the special policing of poor people dating back to the rise of capitalism and public policing (Thompson, 1977). It appears to be safer to conclude, with Jefferson (1990: 9), that the tactics may not have been re-imported from the colonies directly but that they were all similar to the '... planned aggression of the arrest and dispersal tactics ...' of colonial policing that were applied to the industrial disputes of the 1980s in Britain.

It is likely that the victimisation of black women that results from collective targeting and the assumption of guilt by association also affect black men who may try to protect their women from police brutality as in Broadwater Farms. It is possible that poor white women who also live in the internal colonies, and especially those who associate with black men as wives, friends, or mothers, are sometimes victimised by the police but this is not likely to be identical with the policing of black women. This is because, as the above illustrations and references have suggested, the target of such special squads is particularly the black population.

The above illustrations are consistent with gender analysis which suggests that the way black women who have committed no offences are affected by the encounters between black men and the police should be examined even when the subjects are men (Gelsthorpe, 1990). As we shall see, the evidence is also consistent with class and race analysis in the sense that the affected women might have escaped victimisation if they were rich enough to afford residence in the suburbs, outside the internal colonies, or if they were white and were associated with white men instead of black men. There was no evidence of black men being victimised because they were related to suspected black women, except in the case of pimps who lived with prostitutes and were therefore not as innocent as the victimised black women referred to above, or in the case of black men who confronted the police as in Handsworth and Broadwater Farms when the police victimised black women.

There were many similar cases of white women who were victimised by the police in much the same way as black women (see Hillyard, 1993). They were the Irish women who were arrested each time there was an IRA bomb blast in an area. Many such women became victimised because they happened to be the girlfriends, sisters, mothers, or wives of jailed or wanted IRA men. However, the specificity of the 'racism' against the Irish, who were virtually in a state of war with the British, demands a separate analysis that could not be fully tackled here.

This author came across only two cases of the victimisation of white women by the police just because they happened to be associated with suspected black men. The first case occurred in November 1982 when a disabled Rasta man, Mr Patrick Wilson, was stopped by the police shortly after driving his white girlfriend, Miss Susan Farbridge, to the mini-cab office where she worked. Patrick said that when the police became abusive, he drove back to the mini-cab office so that people could witness their abusiveness. The police followed him there and arrested him for reckless driving. When Susan came out to confirm that Patrick was disabled and that whilst he could drive, he could not walk, she too was arrested. They were both strip-searched at the Tower Bridge police station in London. Susan was further humiliated by being forced to jump up and down whilst naked. They were both awarded damages later but the police officers were not prosecuted (IRR, 1987: 13, 19, 41).

Similarly, the HCDA informed this author that a white woman was harassed because of encounters between the police and a black man. The black man in question happened to be her son and she was pulled by her hair when she went to ask the police why they were dragging him away in handcuffs. She reported to the HCDA that her son's solicitors advised him to ensure that his witnesses were not black, otherwise the court might doubt their sincerity. Members of the HCDA present at that meeting said that that was an outrageous thing for a solicitor to say and she modified her statement by saying that it was not put as clearly as that, but that there was no mistake about the meaning. As it turned out, the HCDA had got eight people who were willing to testify and they were all white.

Perhaps some of the women who were harassed during the arrest of black men could not bear to watch their loved ones being taken away by the police whom they had little reason to trust. Perhaps their emotions ran high and they did not only ask what was the matter but also verbally protested or hauled insults at the officers. For such 'threatening behaviour' they could be arrested and charged. However, the charges of actual bodily harm and of common assault initially brought against some of the women suggest an unusual scenario where women (including a 73 year-old grandmother) physically take on groups of policemen.

It could be claimed that black people were over-represented in the criminal justice system because they actually commit more crimes. Ian Taylor (1982), for example, asserted that, 'In Britain, "mugging" is, indeed a form of self-employment (and maybe a primitive form of street-level anti-white politics) that is disproportionately practised by unemployed West Indians.' This is supposed to be a left realist position that was supported by Lea and Young (1984: 165) who confidently asserted that 'black people have a higher crime rate than would be expected from their numbers as a proportion of the population.' The main bases for claims like these are official statistics, local crime surveys and structuralist claims about black family life and black culture as a criminal subculture (see Reiner, 1992, for the key models of interpretation).

Official statistics, as McClintock (1974) convincingly argued, are better measures of the political accountability of the criminal justice system. Similarly, victimisation surveys more accurately measure attitudes to crime and to black people than what Gilroy (1987b) calls the 'mythical' high level of black criminality. Gilroy (1987b) has argued that this so-called realism of the new left exemplifies 'how radical and conservative, socialist and openly racist theories and explanations of "race" have been able to converge dramatically.' By placing the assertion of Taylor against that of Kenneth Newman, Commissioner of the Metropolitan Police and former commander of the Royal Ulster Constabulary (who alleged in 1983 that, 'In the Jamaican, you have a people who are constitutionally disorderly ... It's simply in their make up, they're constitutionally disposed to be anti-authority'), Gilroy (1987a: 72) demonstrated that such assertions are ahistorical. They tend to ignore the fact that black people in Britain were not originally seen primarily as a crime problem and that their construction as such was closely related to immigration control and the law-and-order government of the Tories as was revealed in the discussion of internal colonialism (see section 2.4). Gilroy clarified his critique of the left realist position on the 'race and crime debate' as follows:

> The argument against it should not be read as a denial of the fact that blacks engage in criminal acts, though there are a number of unresolved questions around the extent of black participation - in particular around the role of official statistics in verifying their involvement. It is no betrayal of black interests to say that blacks commit crime or that black law-breaking may be related to black poverty as law-breaking is always related to poverty. The possibility of a direct relationship between ethnicity, black culture and crime is an altogether different and complex issue (Gilroy, 1987b: 99).

It could be said that Gilroy overstated his case by conceding that 'law-breaking is always related to poverty.' This is an overstatement that could be used to justify police surveillance of black communities that are relatively poor, whereas the majority of the poor, be they black, brown or white, manage to be overwhelmingly law-abiding while many of the rich and powerful get away with murder. The convergence drawn between left realism and the nonsensical biologism of Newman also seems to be overstated. However, this second apparent overstatement is more justifiable in the sense that it sharply illustrates a common preoccupation among left and right realists with working class criminality - a point that Lea and

Young (1992) indirectly confirm while trying to distance themselves from the right realists in other respects. Gilroy's critique of the empirical bases of such claims is both convincing and important as a critique of the over-policing of black communities.

It would be unwise to assume that all black people who were convicted of offences were innocent 'victims' of selective policing. Jefferson (1991: 178) made a slightly similar point when he stated that 'when all is said and done, most commentators conclude that at least part of the explanation for higher black arrests has to do with higher offending behaviour'. He warned that such approaches that rely on the comparison of statistics tend to be atomistic by obscuring 'the more general point about the police focus on deprived areas' (Jefferson, 1991: 182). Moreover, it would be a case of blaming the victimised if 'black over-offending' is held responsible for black 'over-representation' in arrests rather than for some criminal activities like every other category of people. Furthermore, it would be even more incorrect to suppose that all black people are crime-prone or that whoever was targeted or arrested in the partial and selective ways that black people are policed was necessarily being 'criminalised' rather than being victimised as this book suggests.

For example, the Policy Studies Institute has documented relevant examples to show that the policy of stopping people may appear superficially discretionary but it 'is inseparable from a tendency to assume that black people have committed crimes and that whoever has committed a crime must be black' (Smith and Gray, 1983: 130, 137). This sounds like an overstatement but the observations of the authors during their research, indicated a strong tendency to assume that certain criminals must be black until reported otherwise. However, the authors warn that, 'There is no proof that the race of the suspects was a reason for the bad behaviour (of the police), but this seems likely.'

The Question of Attitudes

The fact that the two white women mentioned above were harassed because of their association with suspected black men suggests that they may have been victimised partly for crossing the racial frontier. There was no case of a black woman similarly affected by actions originally targeted at a white man. During the fieldwork, Stuart Hall personally observed that white women who were married to black men were often subjected to ridicule and harassment by wide sections of the public and that he would not be surprised to find that such a racist ideology was shared by sections of the police force. However, Hall (1979: 13) warned against the 'utterly cynical and quite unacceptable proposition' aimed at the mitigation of police racism with 'the police inevitably reflect the society' sort of argument. According to Hall, the argument of inevitability suggests that the police cannot do anything about racist officers, whereas they give a high profile to their campaign to weed out the so called 'bad eggs' or criminal elements in the force without taking racism equally seriously.

Hall has been frequently criticised for 'placing too much emphasis on the role of ideology in the social process' (Hall, 1988: 9). His argument that ideologies are not class-specific but are 'discursive' in the sense that they are articulated, disarticulated, and rearticulated from different elements in society is persuasive. Yet it could be doubted because ideology cannot be given primacy over social relations in social analysis since ideological beliefs, no matter how widely shared in the society, affect different categories of people differently relative to their class, race, and gender.

Hall (1988) insists that ideology, culture, race, gender, and class are all central to the analysis of the contemporary crisis in Britain. This is the relevance of his formulation of the theory of articulation to . The question of how many centres there are in the present analysis could be answered by stating that there are as many centres of analysis as there are issues to be analysed. When two or more issues are articulated, as is often the case in social relations, some issues are likely to be more central than others. This is especially the case with the analysis of the specificity of the crisis in criminal justice where the vast majority of the people involved were poor even though they differ ideologically, sexually, and racially. However, this book is interested in how these social relations are articulated and the implications of their articulation especially for black women, rather than in the ranking of race, class, and gender relations. Such a hierarchy of social relations is hypothetically impossible within the perspective of articulation that presupposes the integration of the different social relations while recognising their differences.

Far from being critical of Hall for emphasising the role of culture and ideology, I recognise the relevance of such an emphasis to the arguments presented. Such an emphasis is similar to the very important call by Cabral (1972) for revolutionaries to take 'the weapon of theory' seriously by going back to the cultural roots of the resistance against domination and oppression. According to Cabral and also according to Ngugi wa Thiong'o (1986), culture is not just what Cultural Studies theorise as 'popular culture'. According to these cultural activists, culture is part of the struggle in the sense that it is produced in the struggle and employed either for domination or liberation (Agozino, 1996b). While this writer agrees with Hall's 'discursive' defence against the critique of the prioritisation of culture, this book does not wish to leave the impression that there is no doubt about Hall's claim that ideology, class, race and gender are all central to every analysis.

The doubt about the centrality of everything makes allowance for the alternative interpretation that there could be as many centres to any analysis as there are issues or analysts, even though some issues could be seen to be more central than others. The reformulation here is that social relations appear more central than the ideological considerations behind them. It is true that race-class-gender are ideological, but it is also true that they are more than ideological, they are also materialist. In this connection, Pashukanis (1989: 74-75) states: 'Having established the ideological nature of particular concepts in no way exempts us from the obligation of seeking their objective reality, in other words the reality which exists in the outside world, that is, external, and not merely subjective reality.' The slight difference between the application of the theory of articulation here and that of Hall is that the latter regards the theory as 'emergent' or 'brand new' whereas the former regards it as good old historical materialism.

What Hall (1988) tries to avoid is a reductionist discussion of 'law and order' that is based exclusively on policing strategies. He emphasises the overall ideological crisis of hegemony without making the mistake of what Shaw (1984: 186) calls the 'minimising (of) the concrete effects of repressive police tactics.' Similarly, Hall could not be said to be reducing the problem to individual attitudes because he emphasises that 'Racism is seen and experienced by black people as having much more to do with the way in which institutions work towards them than with the particular attitude of this or that individual' (Hall, 1987: 48). This view is correct because marginalised individuals and groups do have negative attitudes towards those who oppress them but to the extent that they lack power over institutional arrangements for actualising their prejudices, their attitudes cannot be translated into oppressive practices like racism, sexism or class exploitation.

In spite of the gravity of the problems facing black women because of the policing strategies targeted at black communities, and in spite of the greater readiness of black women than black men and white women to organise self-help, it is surprising to find that some black women believe that the police were fair to all in the ways they did their work. One black woman asked the author whether he had 'chips on (his) shoulders' when she was asked if she experienced any problems at the hands of the police. She was further asked whether she believed that the problems would go away if people did not talk about them. She said that she had not noticed any problems and that if she had problems in the criminal justice system, it had nothing to do with the fact that she was a woman or a black person. It depended, according to her, on her personal conduct. Another woman present quickly disagreed with her and they launched into a long debate in which the first one maintained that black people were not the only ones who had problems and the second one insisted that the problems facing black people were special in many ways. The debate was deviating from my central concern and so they were asked about their personal experiences with the police.

The first woman praised the police for treating her very well. She said that she was even treated better than a white friend of hers whose car had been similarly stolen and who had to wait much longer to recover it even after the police had found it. She said that the police treated her very well because she was very polite to them, but it seemed that she suspected that her car was stolen by a black person. She said repeatedly that a black person was more likely to hurt a black person than a non-black person would be. Empirically valid as this claim may be, it neither proves that black people are more criminal than white people nor that the black people who are treated unfairly by the police are only those who are not fair to the police. The same thing could be said of white people because 'most interpersonal crime is intra-racial' (Harris, 1992: 108). The favourable perception of policing by this woman seems to support the conclusion of the Policy Studies Institute that

> Where West Indians were victims of crime in specific instances, they give a favourable assessment of the services provided by the police ... and there is evidence that the police tend to make more efforts on behalf of West Indian victims than on behalf of white victims (Smith and Gray, 1983:333).

Less surprisingly, given the long history of discriminatory policing that black people have had to resist, the second woman was sure that she was being prosecuted for reckless driving because she was a black woman. However, she admitted that she was wrongly driving along a one-way street when a white man jammed his car into hers as if deliberately. She said that it was during a heavy rainstorm and that the man was able to get witnesses from the white people around while she was too shocked to move from her car. She believed that the man was drunk because of the melodramatic way he went about recruiting witnesses to the accident, but the police did not give him a breath test and paid her little attention. The man had reported that his car had been kept off the road in order to claim more damages, but she saw him driving in it and wrote to inform the police. That was when they decided to charge her.

These two contrasting opinions show that some black women might not be aware of the problems that face black women in the criminal justice system and that some black women may believe that the police were discriminatory in a specific instance where they might not be. Listening to them made this author resolve more strongly not to ask people whether they felt that they were being treated unjustly or fairly. It was more useful to ask them what kinds of problems they faced and how these differed from the problems faced by other people. But no matter how hard the author tried to avoid asking about attitudes, the informants returned to them time and time again.

For example, another black woman said that a lot depended on the officer making the arrest and a lot depended on how polite the arrested person was. This sounds very sensible except that it ignores the institutionalised ways that the police interact with black people, as Hall (1987: 48) pointed out above. The woman seemed to see the problems entirely in terms of the attitudes of this or that individual. Her emphasis on the attitudes of black people appears to be contradicted by her personal experience because she said that she was shocked into silence and did not try to resist arrest. Yet one of the police officers who arrested her was mocking her in the van and telling her to take a last look at the sun because she would go down for a long time. The woman was happy that the black officer present tried to comfort her, telling her not to take any notice of what the white officer was saying. She said that she would have been happier if he had done or said something to call the white officer to order since they were both of the same rank.

The woman believed that such comments, which assumed that the suspect was guilty even before being charged, could drive someone into a frenzy. She claimed that this might have been the case with the two women with whom she was detained. One was suspected of being mentally ill and the other was remanded in custody for obtaining property by deception. She claimed that she was given access to facilities to wash in the morning, probably because she was very polite or because she was treated as a colleague, being a social worker, whereas the two women who talked back to the officers did not wash, according to the woman, probably because they did not ask to.

She also claimed that the drug found on her was given to her by 'a very close friend', meaning the man who was charged with her and who was remanded in custody while she was given bail. This seems to illustrate that, even when the institutionalised ways that the police work against black people are overlooked, even when only the attitudes of individual officers and particular suspects are being considered, it is not proper to treat the attitudes of officers and those of the suspects as if they have equal potential impacts on the outcome of cases. This is because officers are in positions of power which they could abuse in a way that could cause individual suspects to become indignant or abusive. If the two women mentioned above did not wash, it could be because they were not told that they had the right to wash or that there were facilities for such. The point is that, even if the women were abusive without provocation, the police had the duty to inform them what their entitlements were. Carlen (1988: 123) found that

> A few women admitted that they had always taken a confrontational stance towards all 'authority' figures and that they themselves provoked the police into violent retaliatory measures. But it was police harassment of black people that was mentioned most frequently as being both unprovoked and provocative.

One black woman believed that if she was white, the police would not have doubted her when she told them that she was living alone in her housing association flat. They could have phoned the housing association to confirm this but they detained her and went to her house and returned to say that they did not find anybody there. They only released her on bail when her sister came to confirm that that was indeed her flat.

When the informants were asked if it would have made any difference to have more black women as police officers or to treat black women like white women, most of them reported that it would not have made any difference if such black officers did nothing to challenge discrimination and if they started practising repression against black people. Moreover, they said, white women were also being repressed by the police even though black women were more strongly repressed.

Organising Community Self-Defence

The suggestion that the police and the public share some racist ideologies about black people and that such ideologies have class, gender, and race-specific outcomes for individuals and groups was made by one case brought to the notice of the Hackney Community Defence Association in the presence of this author. A light-complexioned man reported to the HCDA that he had a 'slight misunderstanding' with his wife and that 'being a black woman, she was naive enough to go to the police' with a complaint that he threatened her life. The police arrived, kicked down the door and beat him up. They took him to the station and later charged him with public order offences for which he was bound over to keep the peace. He intended to bring a civil action against the police for maltreating him, saying that neither his drinking problem nor his past offences, which he said he had clearly left behind him, entitled the police to treat him brutally.

One of the black women present challenged him for saying that his wife was naive because she was a black woman. Everybody wanted to speak on this at once and some thought that it was a diversionary issue on which those who were interested could organise a separate seminar. The woman who raised it was reminded that she rarely came to meetings and that, in any case, the said wife had admitted that she was mistaken. The black man chairing the meeting ruled that the issue should be shelved and returned to at the end of the meeting. Unfortunately, the man at the centre of the controversy had left, like most other people who came to solicit the support of the association, soon after getting such assurances.

When the group returned to the matter, most people were tired and most had left. But those still remaining agreed that it was too serious a matter to be fully discussed at that particular meeting. Some suspected that if it was a case of a black man married to a white woman, he would not have got off so lightly. The woman who raised the matter suggested that HCDA should choose and pick cases to avoid supporting common criminals. Others said that even common criminals deserved to be defended if the police went out of their way to brutalise them because no offences committed or alleged to have been committed by them deserved such treatment.

They suggested that since it raised the serious problem of the inadequacy of police protection for black women who suffer domestic violence, it should be the subject of a seminar or conference in the future. This issue was touched upon at the 8 September 1991 meeting of 'Black Community Against Women's Oppression' that focused on the subject of Black Women and Housing (*Black Voice*, Vol. 23, No. 1, 1992).

The meeting highlighted racism, sexism, and class exploitation as the main foundations of various forms of oppression that manifest in various ways, including inequalities in housing. The meeting noted that black people have been historically concentrated in the poorest quality housing in the private market and, when they applied for council housing, they seemed to be treated as if they were seeking favours rather than demanding their legal rights.

It was also argued that the belief that black women were favoured compared with black men in the allocation of council housing was an under-estimation of the delays and discrimination that black women face in accommodation, compared with white women who seemed to get allocations more quickly, a fact that has been confirmed by MacEwan (1991). The meeting agreed that a black man might move in with a woman without allowing their relationship to develop and afford the woman the time for a free choice in the relationship. The premature cohabitation usually led to strains in the relationship and this could result in domestic violence. The observations at the meeting point to the belief that domestic violence was not a simple matter for the police to resolve, but a complex issue that could only be faced by also tackling the problems of racism, sexism, and class exploitation. This conclusion is supported by the findings of MacEwen (1991: 21) according to whom 'ethnic minority women are ... more likely than women generally to be poor and to encounter difficulties in obtaining suitable housing and employment.'

Even a campaign group that fights against police harassment might not always focus attention on the gender implications of cases that apparently affect only black men. One of the recent campaigns of the HCDA was captioned, 'Self Defence is no Offence' and it concerned a black man who was referred to in an earlier leaflet of theirs as a 'mixed race man in his late twenties.' He was a recreation attendant for Hackney Council and a sculptor. On 25 October 1990, he was driving along Kingsland Road in Hackney when he was attacked at a red light by two men on a motor bike. They called him a 'Paki bastard' and punched him in the face. He sped away from them and thought that he had escaped but they caught up with him at a garage. One of them attacked him with a heavy chain and he was wounded. He pulled out a small clay-modelling knife with which to defend himself. He fought back in self-defence and wounded the bike rider.

The police charged him with wounding and intent to cause grievous bodily harm. In court the bike riders admitted to abusing him racially and to assaulting him. When asked why, one of them answered, 'It's obvious isn't it?' Many witnesses testified to the fight and gave contradictory accounts but none of them saw the chase. The defendant had good character references and no previous convictions, but the jury found him guilty of actual bodily harm and the judge gave him an 18 months jail sentence.

Even before his conviction, he was suspended from work by the council which reasoned that the mere fact of being arrested and released on bail disqualified him from working with the leisure services. After his conviction on 4 September 1991, a disciplinary hearing was held in his absence and, without being represented by his union as he was entitled to be, he was officially sacked on 13 September. The HCDA concluded that he 'was attacked on the street, attacked in court, and has now been attacked by Hackney Council, a Council that claims to be anti-racist!...We uphold the right of black people to defend themselves against racist attacks. We condemn the empty words of Councils' anti-racist policies when in reality they reinforce the racism of police and courts.' This echoes the call by Gilroy (1990) for an end to trendy anti-racism by organisations like Rock Against Racism that were out of touch with the reality of the situation of black people.

This man decided to appeal against his sentence and HCDA members picketed his place of work to demand his reinstatement and his release from prison. It seems striking that the association centred the campaign around the man without highlighting how his imprisonment may have affected his family. One of the women present was said to be his 'partner' and that she was obviously feeling the crunch of his loss of income and the psychological strain of the harassment. His appeal was being handled by a black solicitor who was said to be 'incompetent'. The group was reluctant to approach a new solicitor and start new briefings because the sentence was fast running out. They suggested approaching other black lawyers to ask the one handling the appeal to act fast. But they had yet to raise 200 pounds to pay for the transcripts of the case without which the solicitor could hardly prepare grounds for appeal. The idea that the black solicitor was incompetent happened to be a stereotype held by even white solicitors and judges (see Kennedy, 1992). According to a black QC, Roberts (1991), black barristers, including Queen's Counsels, are still struggling against such misconceptions.

All these indicate that the politics of gender, race, and class were also played out within groups that were dedicated to the defence of individuals on these bases. Perhaps this was one of the reasons why women try to organise separately and autonomously, but it would be too simplistic to assume that women did not treat women on gendered, racialised, or classified bases. This is not the place to go into the internal politics of campaign groups but that could be an interesting project for future research.

If the readiness to organise collective self-help is taken as a partial indication of the extent of perceived problems facing a category of people, the problems facing black women could be said to be more urgent compared with those facing black men and white women. This observation was taken up with the Hackney Community Defence Association that was set up following the shooting of Colin Roach in a police station where he had gone for protection because he feared for his life. The police said that he had shot himself and calls for a public enquiry were refused (RFSC, 1989). If black men were the most frequent targets of police harassment, why then did they not organise most constantly and separately for collective defence? One of the leaders of the HCDA, a white man, told the author that black men appeared to be very macho and tended to have a mistaken belief in their ability to defend themselves individually in any conflict situation. Black women seemed to recognise their vulnerability in conflicts with predominantly white male officials and so tended to be more willing to organise separately for collective strength.

This opinion seems to reflect contemporary feminist organisation and consciousness as well as the historical tendencies in colonial Nigeria, for example, where women rose, almost exclusively, to resist the imposition of taxes on women whereas such had already been imposed on the men with relative success. It also echoes the puzzle of why it was possible for the apartheid regime to impose the pass laws on men but faced an uprising when it tried to extend this to black women. Less remotely, the greater readiness of black women to organise for self-help was seen in the fact that most voluntary organisations that care for black people in the criminal justice system were for and by black women.

However, this apparent reluctance of black men to organise resistance is misleading because all it shows is that the organisations of black women are more issue-specific whereas the organisations founded by black men tend to be more-embracing. In other words, it would be nonsense to assume that only women resisted the pass laws, for example, since the Sharpeville massacre arose from the mass demonstrations called by the Pan African Congress against such laws.

A close look at the HCDA showed that more black men participated in its activities than black women. Two black men turned up to support two white men who appeared in court, charged with assaulting police officers and were later found innocent of the charges. No black woman turned up in court to support those men and, at the group discussions of the association that were observed, there were more black men than black women. There were more white women and white men in the association and the only Asian who was noticed was there to complain about wrongful imprisonment.

The relative absence of black women from the meetings was probably because of the late evening to midnight timing when many mothers cannot afford to leave young ones by themselves.

To ask why there was nothing like a 'Black Male Prisoner's Scheme' is like asking why there is nothing like male groups in political parties and men's editors in newspapers. It could be argued that the interests of more men were reflected in the structures of social institutions and this is what made the organisation of specialist interests by women appear to be complementary. Such a complementarity seemed to be reflected in the fact that the organisations set up by black women did not tend to be separatist. Groups set up and run by black women also campaigned on behalf of black men and black organisations that were male-dominated, like the African Research and Information Bureau which seriously addressed the issues of gender and class inequalities in society.

A more likely explanation of gendered organisational patterns would be that of the relative exclusion and the relative invisibility of the specific concerns of black women in organisations of black people. It is noteworthy that this was one of the reasons given by the only organisation run by black men for black men to justify their existence. According to Mercer and Julien (1988: 98), 'One of the many reasons why the Gay Black Group came into existence was that we found our specific concerns were excluded and invisible in the agendas of the white left and gay organisations and the black organisations that many of us had also participated in.' A similar justification was offered by Cockburn (1988) for 'much more separatism in socialist feminism.'

The Gay Black Group was not contacted during the fieldwork because their specific interest in sexuality is outside the focus of this book. Perhaps this justifies their claim that their interests tend to be invisible in issues tackled by the black community. However, it is possible that the policing of sexuality and the ideology of homophobia may affect black gays and lesbians more adversely than their white counterparts. Such issues could be investigated by researchers who are interested in the politics of sexuality.

The white women and the black men who provided information for this book agreed with the view that the police and racist attackers target black men most often for victimisation. The informers also agreed that such attackers pick on black women more frequently than on white women. The difference is not only in terms of frequency, but it also has to do with the nature of such attacks. Attacks on black women and on black men by neo-fascists may not be only racist but also sexist in character. Black men were said to be picked on for daring to go out with white women and black women were often stereotyped as whores. Some of the informants suggested that black people were being attacked more frequently by the police probably because black men and black women were less likely to sue the police for wrongful treatment than white women. This does not appear to be true because the level of complaints against the police and the number of civil actions brought against the police by black people is proportionately higher than would be expected from passive 'victims'.

For example, more than half of the five hundred thousand pounds worth of damages paid out by the police in 1989 alone went to black complainants (*The Voice*, 6 March 1990). Nevertheless, the suggestion that black people were not challenging police injustice as much as they should appears to be true. Although a 'proper' level of complaints can never be ascertained for any category of people, no black person should perceive police or racist victimisation without challenging it for fear of further victimisation or because of lack of access to legal representation.

In what was described as a 'landmark victory', a Nigerian woman was recently awarded $215,000 as compensation following her humiliation by US customs officials who strip-searched her for drugs, found nothing, and sent her to a clinic for more intimate search and x-ray but still found nothing (*West Africa*, November 11-17 1991). That such a victory could be hailed as a landmark when the humiliation of black men and women is almost routine in international airports is an indication that much more could be done to challenge undue victimisation.

Conclusion

This chapter is based upon the interpretation of documents, opinions and perceptions received from a small and selected set of informants. It is therefore not safe to make general quantitative claims from the above interpretations because the method and data seem inappropriate for the measurement of the extent of victimisation. The limited claim made by this chapter in particular, and this book in general, concerns the nature of the victimisation as perceived by those who suffer it and by those who were working to counter it. It could be said that the perceptions of these groups and individuals and those of this author do not represent proof of the facts of victimisation, but they suggest the nature or pattern of the perceived victimisation. When these perceptions appear to support findings by other researchers, this author was persuaded that such perceptions were not isolated or unique to the perceivers. It is only in such cases that this author was persuaded to generalise beyond the particular perception, while recognising that the same perception might be interpreted differently by a different author.

4. Black Women and the Courts

Introduction

The previous chapter has tried to present the problems that face black women in particular and poor people in general. The picture presented above is incomplete because the police do not work in isolation from other agencies and also because the focus of the discussion was primarily on black women and incidentally on black men and white women as well. Poor white men and Asians were left out of the analysis because they were not as comparable with black women as black men and white women were. In this chapter, the discussion will go beyond the police and consider the impacts of the courts on black women, black men, and white women. The focus will still not be extended to white men and Asians for the above reason. Wherever possible, statistical figures for white men, Asians and 'others' will be tabulated along with figures for the focal groups. This would give a fair sense of the general distribution and permit the comparison of white women with white men in the same way that black women and black men are compared.

Since the focal interest of the book was the differences and similarities between black women and black men, and between the former and white women, the field observations of the author were restricted to these three categories. By so doing, something was lost in the sense that the observations were not comprehensive. However, something was also gained in terms of time and material resources.

Disparity and Discrimination

It is the disproportionate representation of black people in the penal institutions that gives the impression that the courts were not completely free from the ideology that informs the policing of black people. However, in order for the courts to deal fairly with the people appearing before them, the Commission For Racial Equality insisted that 'the criminal justice system must now make a concerted effort to ensure that its decisions are not only fair but (are) seen to be fair' (CRE, 1989: 5).

Studies of discrimination and substantive inequality in the politics of race by the courts are inconclusive. Mair (1986), McCoville and Baldwin (1982), and Crow and Cove (1984) all concluded that there was no significant difference in the treatment of people of different races in the courts when the circumstances were similar. These findings differ from those of Walker (1988) who stated that 'More blacks tended to receive custodial sentences, this difference being partly attributable to the higher proportion of violence and robbery offences sentenced which tend to receive harsher sentences; but even within this group they received more custodial sentences.' This is supported by Hudson (1989), Gordon and Shallice (1990) and Hood (1992).

According to Thomas (1970: 64), 'Disparity of sentences is frequently considered the fundamental problem of sentencing.' This problem is even more serious in cases where two or more people are charged with a common offence but receive sentences or bail conditions that do not relate to one another. According to Thomas, the principles that make such 'discrimination' justifiable are the respective responsibility for the offences by each defendant. A mitigating factor like age might apply to one and not to the other, and the previous offences of one might justify the use of individualised measures for one and a tariff sentence for the other, based also on the sentencing options available to the courts rather than entirely on respective culpability. The convincing inference here is that some forms of discrimination (in the sense of discretion) are justifiable and so discretion could also be discriminatory when unjustifiable. What is interesting in Thomas' argument is that even discretion could be biased if unjustified. The question is not whether or not discrimination exists, but the nature and the extent of discrimination.

However, this book is limited to the discussion of the nature of perceived discrimination and leaves the measurement of the extent out of the analysis. A more urgent task is to show that the kinds of disparities Thomas tried to justify as principled do not surface only at the stage of sentencing. In the preliminary hearings of the application for bail, such details as respective responsibilities, offending history, and mitigating factors were not supposed to be known to the courts, and yet the courts granted and refused such applications in ways that suggest discriminatory assumptions about re-offending and possibilities of surrendering. The barristers who provided research information emphasised that black people in particular and foreign defendants in general were perceived to be greater threats. The following observations of cases will illustrate that black women were perceived as more (or less) threatening in some specific instances than black men and white women (see Table 4.1).

Much of the controversy over the nature and extent of discrimination in the criminal justice system derives from the fact that researchers focus too much attention on whether discrimination exists (especially in sentencing) as if it is the only problem facing black people in the criminal justice system. It is suggested here that it is appropriate to broaden the focus to include other problems of disparity that may or may not be the consequence of direct discrimination but which might (at the least) be indicative of serious problems deserving attention. Let us start with prosecution rates, an area where the overlap of criminal justice agencies is most profound.

The group 'other' in Table 4.1 includes non-British Europeans, Arabs and people of mixed racial parentage where one parent was not black. It also includes those who refused to declare their ethnic origin. Asians and 'others' were left out of the comparison by ratio but they were represented on the table to give a general impression of what the distributions were.

This table shows that the average black man in London was four times more likely to be proceeded against than the average white man. The average black woman was also five times more likely to be proceeded against than the average white woman in London and six times less likely to be proceeded against than the average black man. This can be interpreted to mean that black women faced different problems compared to black men and white women in the criminal justice system.

Table 4.1: Persons proceeded against per 100,000 of the population of Greater London MPD 1984 and 1985 by sex, age, and race

Ages	Whites	Blacks	W:B Ratio	Asians	Others
MALES					
10-13	1,000	2,000	1:2	500	800
14-16	9,000	37,000	1:4	3,900	5,500
17-20	19,30	53,100	1:3	11,000	16,700
21 +	3,500	14,800	1:4	3,100	6,900
10 +	4,700	20,200	1:4	3,500	7,200
FEMALES					
10-13	100	400	1:4	40	160
14-16	1,000	3,800	1:4	200	400
17-20	2,400	9,400	1:4	1,300	4,000
21 Plus	600	2,600	1:4	700	2,900
10 Plus	700	3,300	1:5	700	2,500

SOURCE: H.O.S.B. 6/89, 10 March 1989: 'The ethnic group of those proceeded against or sentenced by courts in the Metropolitan Police District in 1984 and 1985' Table 2.

A different interpretation would be that, in comparing black men with white men and black women with white women, the one point ratio difference between black women and white women is not significant. This suggests that all women faced different problems compared to all men in the criminal justice system. This suggestion is doubtful because the ratio of black women to white women is higher than that of black men to white men in all age cohorts except in the 14-16 years and the 21 and over age groups. Juvenile and young black women have a 1:4 ratio in comparison with their white counterparts, and juvenile and young black men have the higher ratio of 1:2 at the ages of 10-13 and 1:3 at the ages of 17-20 compared with young and juvenile white males of similar ages.

Table 4.2: Proportions per 100,000 of the total population of persons tried at the Crown courts and at the Magistrates' courts who were acquitted of all indictable offences by sex and race in 1984 and 1985

Sex	White	Black	Asian	O	Not.	Total
Magistrates Court						
14	7	Male	7	8	8	7
22	7	Fem	7	7	6	5
Crown Court						
Male	24	25	27	29	24	25
Fem	28	24	34	29	26	27

SOURCE: *H.O.S.B.* 6/8910 March 1989: 'The ethnic group of those proceeded against...in 1984 and 1985' Tables 5 and 6 (note that O = Others, Not = Not Recorded).

Statistics conceal as much as they reveal about the problems that face black women. That is why they should be read as indicators of the likelihood of officials acting against individuals from different backgrounds rather than as evidence of the criminality of those concerned (McClintock, 1974; Kitsuse and Cicourel, 1963). This is evident from Table 4.2 above which shows that not everyone proceeded against who was necessarily guilty of any offence. This table was collated from tables 5 and 6 in the original in order to make the differences and similarities of outcomes for the focal groups in the two courts easy to grasp.

The table shows that, whereas black women were more likely to be proceeded against than white women, as we saw in Table 4.1, black women stood fewer chances of being acquitted at the Crown Courts (with proportions of 24% compared with 28%) and an equal chance of being acquitted at the Magistrates' Courts (equal proportions of 7%) with white women. This relationship appears to be reversed between black men and white men. Black men had slightly higher proportionate acquittals in both courts, or 8 and 25 per cent compared with 7 and 24 per cent for black men and white men in Magistrates' and Crown courts, respectively.

However, when black women are compared with black men, the former stood fewer chances of being acquitted at both courts, implying that they faced different problems. It is interesting that black women were the only category of women who had lower acquittal rates compared to men of the same racial category in the Crown courts. With these figures, it is not surprising that black women were over-represented in penal institutions given their much lower proportion in the total population. However, it could be argued that the acquittal rates of women suggest that only women with cast-iron evidence against them were tried, while some men were tried on weaker evidence.

The above table does not bring out the differences in the seriousness of the problems facing black people as clearly as the written parliamentary answer from John Patten, Minister of State at the Home Office, to Alex Carlile MP, 30 October 1987. He reported that the percentages of those remanded in custody who were later acquitted or not proceeded against were four per cent for whites, seven per cent for blacks, six per cent for Asians, and six per cent for other in 1985.

The percentage discharge and acquittal rates are higher for black people than court acquittal rates for black people precisely because the table for acquittals only (4.2 above) does not include the proportion of people detained and released or cautioned without trial. What the figures reported by Alex Carlile show, according to NACRO (1988: 5), is 'that black people may be more likely to be inappropriately remanded in custody.' However, released or acquitted black people may have been appropriately remanded if the police officers dealing with them believed that they were likely to commit more crimes or unlikely to turn up for proceedings. Their high discharge rate suggests that the police were prejudiced against black people who are seen as being too crime-prone and unreliable to deserve bail.

This is supported by Voakes and Fowler (1989) who maintained 'that more black people find themselves in prison than whites who have committed the same type of offences and who are likely to have worse criminal records.' Similarly, Smith (1994) argues that 'Afro-Caribbeans may tend to be remanded in custody rather than bailed because their family circumstances tend not to meet criteria commonly used in making decisions about awarding bail.'

Smith concludes that this might affect conviction rates 'probably' because it is more difficult to prepare a defence in custody. He suggested that a recognition of Afro-Caribbean family patterns and traditions as normal would ease the difficulty of obtaining bail and moderate the ways that the laws in England and Wales traditionally 'express national identity' by excluding or marginalising 'present-day ethnic minorities' (Smith, 1994). What is not clear here is what Smith regards as Afro-Caribbean family traditions and identities. However, if this is a reference to single-parenthood, it must be emphasised that there is nothing that makes single-parent families traditional to Afro-Caribbeans.

This suggestion of racialised prosecutions of black women and black men is supported by Chigwada (1991: 149) who cited the National Association for Mental Health as saying that 'a large number of black women sanctioned by police action (Under section 136 of the 1983 Mental Health Act which gave individual constables wide discretionary powers to detain people suspected to be mentally disturbed for 72 hours of compulsory psychiatric observation without authorisation from any court and with no right to a solicitor or to redress if diagnosed normal) were later diagnosed "not mentally ill" at the hospital.' This claim has been empirically supported by Dunn and Fahy (1987) and by Faulkner (1989). Hilary Allen missed this point even though her book started with a case study of a black woman and a black man who were sentenced to psychiatric hospitalisation and prison respectively. According to Allen, the man should have gone to hospital and the woman should have gone to prison because the psychiatric reports showed that the woman seemed more normal than the man. Allen (1987) saw differential sentencing simply in terms of gender discrimination without raising the question of race-class-gender articulation and disarticulation.

Support and Isolation

One hundred and thirty (130) appearances at the Magistrates' courts were observed by this author during the fieldwork. Most of these appearances were at the Camberwell Green Magistrates' court. Some of the defendants appeared more than once, following adjournments and remands. Not all the appearances at the courts were observed because the author missed some that were called while he was having discussions with people who had earlier appeared and also because he often kept the afternoons free for discussions with individuals and groups.

The greater number of proceedings initiated against men may explain why women appeared to be relatively more likely to appear as supporters of men in court than the reverse. It was observed that black women and white women were much more likely to accompany their male friends or relatives to the courts to give them support than the reverse. Most women were supported by fellow women, usually of the same race. This appears to support the assumption of Gilligan (1982) that women were more likely to give support to people in trouble. This pattern of support appears less surprising because men dominate the number of defendants appearing in court. However, such predominance of men should have brought more men to court to stand sureties for fellow men or just to give them support, but the reverse seems to be the case.

One of the women who discussed the problems facing her with this author said that she did not inform her husband about her appearance because she did not want her family to be involved in any way. She would prefer to get it over and done with as quickly as possible and maybe tell him afterwards. However, she accepted that her husband would have told her if he was the one in her situation, and that she would have made time to go and give him support. She was grateful to this author for sitting with her most of the day and discussing with her, suggesting that she would have been more confident if she had friends or family to support her. Some of the barristers told this author that many men might refuse to go to court to support their women probably because they were involved in the alleged offences and might be scared of being identified and arrested in court.

This is different from Victimisation-As-Mere-Punishment as far as the elusive men are concerned. However, it may be suggestive of Victimisation-As-Mere-Punishment if the women were not involved in the first place but were pressurised under patriarchal domination to take the 'rap' for their men. It could also be suggestive of Victimisation-In-Punishment if the women were actually involved, but the fact that they were standing trial alone would make them fully responsible for acts that they may have been only partially responsible for.

Members of the Hackney Community Defence Association told this author that the larger the turnout of supporters at a trial, the greater the likelihood of the defendant getting fair consideration from the court that takes such support as a measure of public interest in the case. This suggestion is worth investigating in future research. A female probation officer was of the view that many women accompany their men to court because they did not want them to be tempted and 'snatched' by young female court officials. This appears to be simply what the probation officer suspected, but a similar problem was slightly experienced by this author when he tried to discuss with a woman who practically fled to her boyfriend. When the author tried to explain, he was told to find someone else to chat up because the woman was not the only beautiful woman in the world. The author apologised for the inconvenience he caused and told them why he wanted to talk. The author was told that everyone had his or her own problem and that the author should just get lost. This suggests that the woman felt threatened or isolated in court and would have felt more vulnerable to manipulation if she had no one to run to at that moment of doubt.

The probation officers who provided research information emphasised that race was a factor in establishing rapport with probationers. They were of the view that black defendants tended to trust black probation officers more and black officers tended to be more sympathetic with black clients. The officers told the author that they were aware of the inequalities that disadvantage black defendants in the criminal justice system and that they try to balance these a bit by being more supportive of black clients.

The probation officers reported that when a probation officer recommended supervision as a form of sentence, such an officer would invariably be the supervisor. The tendency, therefore, was for officers to recommend other sentences or to make a 'null report' when they were not comfortable with the prospect of supervising a given client. The probation officers were also of the view that the courts did not regard probation supervision as a serious sentence whereas it was more serious than absolute or conditional discharge. They said that they now try to recommend conditional or absolute discharge more often but the courts did not always follow their recommendations.

This was supported by Voakes and Fowler (1989) who concluded that the social enquiry reports produced by probation officers were not responsible for the more frequent use of custody for black defendants. Although they observed that the higher number of 'null reports' on Asians in SER requires improvement in the practice of probation officers, they maintain that 'such improvements will be wasted without alterations in the practice of magistrates and judges.'

Jefferson and Walker (1992: 90), in a study of Leeds courts, found that 'a "cocky" demeanour' was one possible explanation for harsher treatment, but it was only rarely observed, more often with white than black youths.' No evidence of the mythical defiance by black women in courts was found by this author. This view was recently popularised by the play, 24% by the Jamaican-born playwright, Paulette Randall. This play recently toured High Security Prisons probably because it was written from a perspective that blamed the high proportion of black women in prisons on their supposed defiant postures in courts. According to the author: 'Black women don't (say sorry) because that's not part of our culture' (*The Guardian*, 29 April 1991).

The closest evidence of demeanour that this author found was that nearly half the white women who were observed in court during the fieldwork pleaded guilty compared to few black women and even fewer (proportionately) black men who pleaded guilty. Such pleas do not indicate defiance but are more understandable in the light of discriminatory policing and the greater likelihood of victimisation that could result from the special targeting of black people in crime control excesses. Such pleas do not reflect only perceptions of guilt and calculations of bargaining for less severe sentences, they also reflect perceptions of innocence and expressions of rightful indignation.

Even in the public gallery, the black women were very quiet and did not try to heckle the magistrates and the police witnesses like the white women and men. When one of the black women shouted, it was to correct her address because the court had got it wrong and they were going to give her son bail on the condition of residence. There was only one case of a white woman who was cursing loudly in the dock and she was remanded in custody 'for her own good' pending a psychiatric report. The same happened to the black man who was frequently leaping up to interrupt the proceedings and give instructions to his counsel.

There was some evidence that the defendants were discouraged from speaking in court. Those defendants who were not represented or who wanted to conduct their own defence had their cases adjourned again and again with the usual advice that they should get a solicitor for their own good. It seemed that the defendants did not trust the barristers adequately because most of them had never seen their legal representatives before the morning of the hearing. Some of the defendants who insisted on representing themselves against the advice of the magistrates said that legal aid barristers were not likely to be sympathetic enough to their cause and they were not rich enough to hire trusted barristers.

The barristers also criticised the provision of legal aid for being so inadequate that there appeared to be one justice for the poor and another for the rich. This brings to mind the theme of the reification and commercialisation of criminal justice which was mentioned earlier. This commercialisation was probably why many of the defendants saw the judicial process as a financial transaction in which the poor got the worst deal. As one of the probation officers put it, 'If they are middle class, they tend to be business-like about it; they pay money to get good solicitors or pay the fine and get off.'

The extent to which gender relations were taken into consideration in cases involving black men was significant. One was said to be a 'family man living with his girlfriend and children.' The sentencer saw a child whom the defendant was sitting with a moment earlier in the public gallery and asked if that was his child. He said yes and he was told in a non-threatening tone that he was not supposed to bring a child into the court. Women who brought children into the public gallery were always ordered out of the court by the attendants. Many of the men got bail because their mothers came to stand surety or to guarantee bail on condition of residence.

A very interesting case was that of a man charged with abusing his two step-daughters aged 11 and 15. The prosecution said that the step-daughters were reluctant to testify against him but that they maintained that their allegations were true. He had been refused bail on two previous appearances and the social worker reported that it would be in the interest of the family to give him bail. The police officer asked whether the safety of the children could be guaranteed and the social worker gave assurances. It was a three-women bench and the sentencing magistrate addressed the man without asking him to stand up as usual. He was given unconditional bail and his wife hugged him outside. This appears to have been an instance of what is known as family paternalism which is supposed to aim at protecting the whole family rather than protecting only women (Daly, 1987). The support from the wife and the emphasis of the probation officer on the interest of the family may have persuaded the court to grant him unconditional bail even though he had been refused bail on two previous occasions.

Throughout the observational visits to the courts, the focus of attention was not on the legal arguments and counter arguments advanced in courts though these could not be ignored. The focus was the language of the court room 'business' and how it borrowed from ambiguous conventional symbols of commerce and how such 'loose talk' affected the outcomes for different categories of people. Too much attention to procedure could result in such paradoxical views like the assertion that, 'Racial discrimination was not observable (in courts), though proportionately slightly more Blacks and Asians were subject to harsh treatment' (Jefferson and Walker, 1992: 90).

This is paradoxical because it claims that discrimination 'was not observable' and at the same time claims that the 'harsh treatment' of blacks and Asians was observed. The harshness suggests roughness, as Roger Hood (1992) found in a comparative study of Crown courts in Dudley and Birmingham - black defendants in Dudley were given more severe sentences than the ones in Birmingham even though the seriousness of the offences they were charged with was similar. According to Hood, 'The evidence strongly suggests that black offenders at the Dudley courts, especially those with black co-defendants, did not get the benefit of mitigating factors as frequently as did whites, nor as did blacks dealt with at Birmingham.' This suggests that 'harshness' is a function of particular benches rather than that of defendants, but this suggestion ignores the evidence that such harshness is often institutionalised and widespread rather than being subjective and localised (see Cook and Hudson, 1993).

A look at the symbolic language and rituals of presentation could indicate that the commercialisation of criminal justice had greater impact on black people as a whole and on black women in particular, given the higher level of unemployment and deprivation among black people. At a conceptual level, the concepts of charging suspects and making convicts pay in cash and/or kind suggest the increasing process of 'monetization' which Young (1987) analysed with specific reference to the fine or the 'commodification' that Pashukanis (1989) explained more broadly. Moreover, beyond this semantic evidence for commercialisation, this book will now attempt an interpretation of the symbolic ways black women, black men and white women are presented in court. For a detailed analysis of the use of language in this way by the courts, see Carlen (1976) and Eaton (1993).

The Hierarchy of Discreditability

The perception of 'dependency' appeared to be conveyed by the order in which men and women were mentioned in cases where men and women were jointly charged. There were seven such cases and in all of them, the cases of the women were called only after those of the men were mentioned. In one of them a white woman was alleged to have fled with a white man after he allegedly committed an aggravated robbery at a post office. The prosecution argued that mere presence could be aiding the offender, but the magistrate said that there was 'not much of a case against her'. The man was remanded in custody for three weeks and the woman was granted bail on condition of residence.

The outcome was different when a black man and a black woman were charged with the obtaining of property by deceit, including many claims of social security benefits for which they were not qualified. The defendants were French-speaking Africans who needed an interpreter. However, the interpretation was whispered to the defendants and the court did not slow down the proceedings to allow the interpreter enough time. The prosecution asked for an adjournment to enable them to get forensic reports. The defendants were committed to trial at the Crown Court and remanded in custody for one week. Although they were charged with the same offences, the woman's case was still called after that of the man had been called and he was asked to sit down in the dock as if the two cases were separate.

In a slightly similar appearance, a black man and a black woman were charged with the possession of, with intent to supply, substances analysed to be 'crack' cocaine. The prosecution did not hesitate to magnify the detail that 'they were found in bed together', probably to present the woman as a whore and partly to establish the closeness of their relationship as evidence of their conspiracy. Items suspected to be used for the manufacture of crack were said to have been found in the house. The man was found with two hundred pounds and the woman with five hundred pounds in cash whereas they were both unemployed. The man was said to have been deported from the US to Jamaica and he later came to Britain with a forged passport. The woman had lived at that address for seven years and had only known the man for three months but claimed that she did not know about the drugs.

The prosecution objected to bail on the grounds that they had connections with drug dealers abroad and were likely to interfere with witnesses. The defence counsel stated that the said international connections were family members and not drug dealers, that the woman was married and only recently separated from her husband, and that she had a two-year old son to look after. The court remanded them both in custody because of the seriousness of the offences, the irregularity in the man's identity, and the likelihood of re-offending.

One magistrate sentenced a black woman to fifty hours of community service for her role in a burglary with two black men. The 1991 Criminal Justice Act made community service orders conditional on the convict accepting that form of penalty. Probably in keeping with this provision, the sentencer felt that it was necessary to ask the black woman whether she thought that she was being discriminated against when each of the men 'seemed to walk away' with fines of one hundred and eighty pounds and three months imprisonment suspended for two years. She said that she did not mind. This is interesting in that it was the only time the court was observed asking a defendant if the sentence was too severe. It is also noteworthy that part of the reasons why the men were fined rather than given community service was because they had both just secured employment from which to earn money and from which they might find it difficult to make out time for community service.

This seems similar to the case of a black woman and a black man charged with theft and with resisting arrest. The woman was given bail on condition of residence and the man was remanded in custody pending the provision of a surety to the tune of two hundred pounds to ensure that he would attend in two week's time. The same thing happened in the case of the woman who was detained overnight and then given bail by the court while the man with whom she was charged was remanded in custody to await the results of the analysis of the substances found on them which were suspected to be drugs. She stated that she was treated well by the court because the man accepted that he was the one who gave her the substances that were found on her, but such a confession was not supposed to have been known to the magistrate at that stage. It was more likely that she faced qualitatively different problems because she had been working with some of the court officials as a social worker investigating child abuse.

In another case, three black men and one black woman were charged with theft. The prosecution asked for a two week's adjournment to enable them to complete an identification parade on the men. The first man was granted bail on the condition of two sureties and curfew at his mother's residence. The second man was granted bail on the condition that he returned to the court in one week for the identification parade. The third man and the woman were then given unconditional bail. Apparently the linking of curfew with mother's residence could result from the fact that the mother was the one who came to court to support her son and stand surety. However, it is likely that by coming forward with such guarantees, women who had committed no offences may become directly or indirectly exposed to control by the criminal justice system.

The last case of a man appearing with a woman that was observed involved two white people accused of possessing cannabis. The prosecution applied for the case against the man to be adjourned to enable the court to take it with another case pending against him that had to do with possession as well. The man was granted bail and the woman was then tried for possessing 25 grams of cannabis. She pleaded guilty and it was revealed that she had previous convictions. Her counsel argued that she suffered from asthma and that she used cannabis medicinally. The court learnt that she had four children to bring up on a social security benefit of one hundred pounds a week. She was fined sixty pounds in addition to twenty-five pounds cost to the prosecution. She was given six weeks to pay.

Some of the black women who were facing drugs charges said that a black woman could not have got off so lightly. This was supported by the barristers who spoke with the author. They were of the view that there appeared to be a shift in policy against women in general and against black women in particular. They said that offences for which women without previous convictions could have been given probation now attracted higher tariffs probably because the courts were sensitive to allegations that they were paternalistic. Such shifts in policy were likely to affect black women differently. The systematic data that seem to support this claim are presented in Table 5.1 which shows that the proportion of black women in prison was rising much faster than that of black men in prison. This may suggest that black women are becoming increasingly involved in criminality but, if we make allowance for the fact that all prisoners are not necessarily criminals, then it is more likely that prison statistics suggest increasing surveillance on black women in particular and the black community in general. Although most crimes are 'solved' through reactive policing, the imprisonment of most black women is drugs-related and this category of offence is 'solved' mainly through proactive policing.

There were no cases of black men standing trial with white women nor of black women standing trial with white men and no black women appeared together with white women. There were a few appearances by black men and white men but those were not the immediate concern here. What can be inferred from the cases of women being charged with men of their race for similar offences is that the women appeared to be seen as less responsible for their acts than the men. The only cases where the women were assumed to have equal responsibility with the men were the two cases of the black women who were remanded in custody with black men. However, even then, they were mentioned after the men, not before. It seems that the order in which men and women were mentioned suggests a hierarchy of discreditability. This seems to be a reversal of Becker's hierarchy of credibility in such a way that men were seen to be more discreditable than women and so the disposal of cases depended more on discrediting the defence of the men than on testing the reliability of the accounts provided by the women. It suggests that the discredibility of the women was dependent on that of the men and not vice versa. If the man pleaded guilty, it could be taken for granted that the woman with whom he was charged would also plead guilty. Such an assumption could not easily be held in a patriarchal society if the order of mentioning were reversed.

This order of mentioning is ironical for a Western society like England that traditionally believes that it is courteous to mention ladies before gentlemen. Heidensohn (1985: 101) referred to the symbolic ranking of gender statuses and roles as 'sexual dimorphism', but there are also racial

110

and class dimensions to it that make it a 'trimorphism' of social relations. Goffman (1979) analysed 'function ranking' of gender roles in the family and found that this was reflected in the representation of gender in advertising, resulting in 'the ritualisation of subordination.' Eaton (1986) would argue that the presentation of defendants in courts and in official records also contributes to the affirmation of existing hierarchies.

The suggestion of an informal hierarchy was also reflected in the order by which men and women were presented on the case lists. It was startling to find that the case lists each day usually began with the cases involving men, while women usually came in nearer the bottom of the lists. This might be related to the apparent presentation of women as secondary actors (Allen, 1987). If this was the case, then it could be expected that the name of the woman would be listed immediately after that of the man when they were charged together, but this was not the case probably because, even when people are charged for the same offence, they are presented as if they are involved in two separate offences. Moreover, the names were not listed alphabetically. The court officials were not asked why this was the pattern until the final week of the fieldwork. The clerks at the 'listings' office said that the whole thing was computerised and that the rule was to list the older cases first. The clerks searched through old lists until they found a list that was topped by a woman. This suggests that men might have been topping the list because they were greater in number and therefore had a greater probability of being listed first.

However, from the day this author called the attention of the clerks to the case 'league tables', it was observed that at least one list was topped by a woman each day. This might be by chance or because the clerks were not comfortable with the earlier observation and wanted to grant women some formal equality; or it might mean that women got shorter adjournments because they were usually involved in minor offences. The second suggestion was partially corroborated by the probation officer on court duty who explained that the tendency was to try minor offences immediately except where the defendant pleaded not guilty, whereas serious offences took longer for both prosecution and the defence to prepare their cases. No matter who topped the lists, anyway, the attendants did not follow them systematically in calling cases. One of them told the author that they usually checked to see which defendants were present with their counsel and then call them up accordingly.

As far as this author knows, the only cases in which women were mentioned first while being tried with men were not English cases, but they further illustrate the suggestion that the order of mentioning was hierarchical. This was the case of Winnie Mandela who was charged with being an accessory to assault 'after the fact' and with kidnapping. Mrs Mandela was mentioned before her driver who was charged along with her and who was in turn mentioned before Mrs Mandela's less prominent female friend, Xoliswa Falati (London Times, 4 June 1993). It is likely that Mrs Mandela's class relatively disarticulated her gender - even though her victimisation could be linked to that of her husband (Mandela, 1984) - just as the class of her driver relatively disarticulated his gender in the rearticulation of the hierarchy of discredibility. For a fuller commentary on this case and how it exemplifies Victimisation-As-Mere-Punishment, see Agozino (1991).

A similar articulation of class, race and gender was obvious during the trial of Angela Davis. The press observed a break with the court tradition according to which the cases of women were called only after those of the men with whom they were charged together had been called. Moreover, when this informal hierarchy of male and female defendants was reversed, as in the cases of Angela Davis and Winnie Mandela, it goes to suggest that class is articulated with race and gender in the ranking of individual defendants. For example, Angela was always mentioned before Ruchell Magee who was '... "the other defendant" in the Angela Davis case ... overshadowed by the newly acclaimed heroine of black revolutionaries' *(San Francisco Chronicle,* 18 January 1971). The press made a big issue of the different class backgrounds of the two defendants, emphasised their blackness and stressed their gender differences, forcing them to separate their cases and pursue the same issues in different courts.

Perhaps the cases of these two women were called before those of the men with whom they were charged because the women were celebrities and because they were black women who are frequently assumed to be macho. If that was the case, then the suggestion that the order of mentioning was hierarchical would seem to be supported. There might be similar cases in which some women in England were called first when standing trial along with men, but the limited coverage of the observation for this book did not reveal any. This suggestion of the operation of a gender, class, and race hierarchicisation of defendants needs to be studied further to see how generalisable it could be. The only thing that has been demonstrated here is that many women were mentioned after their male co-defendants and it is being suggested here that this might be a reflection or a reinforcement of conventional societal hierarchies.

The suspected hierarchies of race, gender and class (though still only a suspicion yet to be proved) appear so consistent in the presentation of research reports that it is no longer persuasive to call them informal or chance occurrences. They appear to be the formal ways of doing things to reinforce conventional ideologies of superiority and inferiority. This may be as a result of the political nature of criminal justice and criminology. However, even within the discipline of Statistics that prides itself with being the apolitical (and therefore 'mature') social science (Garland, 1985), the presentation of categories of people is not simply nominal but also ordinal in the hierarchical sense. Many official statistics begin with the category of 'white', then go on to that of 'black', from 'males' to 'females', and from 'adults' to 'children'. This order ensured that white people usually came first in official statistics and in most research report tables.

A notable exception is that of South Africa's annual Race Relations Survey in which the order of presentation was 'African', 'Asian', 'Coloured', and 'White'. This appears to be an innocent obedience to an alphabetical order but the choices of group labels curiously correspond to the racial hierarchy of apartheid in an ascending order. If the government had chosen to classify 'Africans' as 'blacks' at least to emphasise that all South Africans are Africans, then the ascending order of presentation would have collapsed alphabetically. See Cooper, et al, 1990, who reported that the South African Government chose to retain the racial classifications provided by the Population Registration Act upon which most apartheid laws were based. The government intended to retain the classifications, even though the PRA was repealed in 1991, until the tricameral parliament that was based on the population register was replaced after a democratic election.

Similarly, women usually came after men and so on in statistical tables. This 'order' seems to be obeyed uncritically by researchers even when their focus dictated otherwise. Another notable exception was Jefferson and Walker (1992) who start with the category 'Black' followed by 'Asian' and then by 'White'. However, because they did not theorise this arrangement, it is capable of being interpreted as an ascending order resembling the superficially alphabetical hierarchy of South African official statistics. That Walker and Jefferson did not theorise the order of their presentation suggests that the hierarchicisation of statistical presentations is a taken for granted practice among researchers rather than a deliberate attempt to uphold conventional statuses. However, to say that this order of presentation is not necessarily conspiratorial is not the same thing as saying that statistical hierarchies are of no consequence in the perception of categories of people and practices directed at these categories. This is probably an over-interpretation of the facts but it goes to warn that a mere alteration in the order of mentioning would not result in greater justice if the unjust hierarchies in the wider society are not removed.

Such an apparently dubious hierarchy was deliberately rejected in the tabulation of the field observation, not because of the wish to reverse the hierarchies, but, because the primary focus of this book was on black women. Hence black women were listed in the tables before black men and white women followed. The official statistics have been left in the 'order' in which they were received just to show how much is taken for granted when statisticians claim to allow facts to speak for themselves. This might be what Hacking (1991:194) had in mind when he wrote that, 'The bureaucracy of statistics imposes (order) not just by creating administrative rulings but by determining classifications within which people must think of themselves and of the actions that are open to them.'

Observations on Procedure

In this sub-section, the field observations will be presented with specific reference to the problems that faced black women compared with black men and white women. The comparisons were based on observable differences and similarities in the procedures and outcomes for similar cases. Only appearances by black women, black men and white women were recorded because they were the critical groups of interest. Some of the issues already discussed above may come up again in the tables for further discussion.

The interesting thing here is that the fine was the single most frequent disposition relied on by the courts, as Young (1987) and Bottoms (1983) have demonstrated. Of the two black women who were fined, one was immediately discharged because she had the option of spending one day in prison whereas she had spent four days in detention. On the contrary, one of the four white women was fined four times on four charges of loitering and another reminded the court that she had a second matter pending but the court discounted it, saying that it must have been entered in error. One of the black men who was fined was eligible to have the money refunded if he kept the peace during the time he was to be bound over.

It is also noteworthy that none of the black women was remanded for a social enquiry report. This might be because very few of them pleaded guilty or because those of them that pleaded guilty happened to be involved in relatively minor offences that could be disposed of without any need for a report. The second possibility appears to be supported by the fact that two of the black women were given conditional discharge while no white woman was given this. However, severity of the offences alone could not explain this since all the organisations and professionals who provided research information highlighted the lack of social enquiry reports for foreign defendants as a major problem facing many black women who were sentenced, especially for drugs-related offences. This is not a problem of selective perception by the organisations but a practical problem that has been the subject-matter of their campaigns for some time now. The category of foreign women will be discussed later in chapter six but it is not desirable to separate them from black women who are British citizens in this chapter because, as Bryan et al (1985) argued, all black people are perceived as foreigners by most white people in England.

One of the organisations that provided information, Akina Mama wa Africa, stated that one of the prisoners they were working with complained that an official from her country's embassy brought a character reference written on her behalf by a top government official but the judge ruled it inadmissible on the ground that he believed that everything could be bought with money in her corrupt country. Another organisation, Women In Prison, was experimenting with the possibility of providing Home Circumstances

Reports to enable foreign women to qualify for parole. WIP were running a Female Prisoners' Welfare Project named Hibiscus in Nigeria. The Criminal Justice Act 1991 specified the requirement of Social Enquiry Reports in all cases for which custodial sentence was being considered, but it was not clear how this would be applied to foreign nationals in general and black women in particular.

Table 4.3: The disposition of defendants pleading guilty by race and sex

Disposition Type	Black Women	Black Men	White Women	Total
Cond. D	2	2	-	4
Fine	2	7	4	13
Sus. Sent	-	4	1	5
Custody	-	1	-	1
Report	-	3	5	8
Comm.S.	1	-	-	1
Total	5	17	10	32

SOURCE: Fieldwork, London, summer, 1991.

Notes: Cond. D = Conditional Discharge, Sus.Sent = Suspended sentence; Custody = remanded in custody or given custodial sentence; Report = remanded for probation or psychiatric report; and Comm.S. = Community Service.

As we have seen, only one black woman was given community service and the magistrate asked her if she thought that the sentence was too severe. One of the white women remanded for a social enquiry report had appeared because she was missing appointments with probation officers who said that they were willing to give her another chance. She was advised to 'take advantage of their generosity' or she would be sentenced without the report. This seems to confirm the information from probation officers according to whom women appeared more embarrassed than men and tended to conceal their cases from relatives. Women were said to be more likely to evade appointments for a SER even when sentencers required it.

Once again, the numbers are small but the greater number of black women being given unconditional bail suggests that their alleged offences were not serious. One of such cases concerned a black woman who was accused by another black woman of damaging her car. The defendant told the author that she was provoked into inflicting the damage. Another observation worth noting is that two of the black women who were remanded in custody were remanded along with black men whereas no white woman was remanded with a man. The fact that three out of 11 white women were remanded in custody compared to 3 out of 17 black women suggests that the white women had a higher remand rate, but this could also be interpreted to support the earlier suggestion that the black women were charged with minor offences for which white women could have been cautioned. The smallness of the sample would not permit a wider generalisation of these results, but when viewed in the wider context of how policing affects black women and that of their over-representation in the criminal justice system, the cases might be indicative of serious problems of victimisation and injustice that could be uncovered through research focusing specifically on remand decisions.

The black man and the white woman who were remanded for psychiatric reports had been shouting and cursing in the dock. One of the white women who was remanded happened to be four months pregnant and her aunt came to testify that she would provide her with accommodation and make sure that she did not fail to appear if she was given bail on the condition of residence. The magistrate turned down the application for bail on the ground that the defendant appeared 'to be living what social workers would call a loose life.'

This author observed that women were more likely to appear as witnesses for men than vice versa. Similarly, all the instances of people being given bail on the condition of surety had women as the providers. In one instance, the amount was 20,000 pounds and it was guaranteed by the mother of the accused. This same pattern was followed in the cases of the condition of residence - defendants were usually required to live at their mothers' addresses.

Table 4.4: Conditions of bail by race and sex

Conditi	B.Wom	B.Men	W.Wo	Total
R. in C.	3	12	3	18
Uncon.	11	19	4	34
Reside.	3	8	2	13
Curfew	-	8	1	9
Surety	-	3	-	3
Passpo.	-	1	1	2
PsychR	-	1	1	2
Total	17	53	11	61

SOURCE: Fieldwork, London, summer, 1991.
Note that Conditi = Condition of bail; B. Wom = Black Women; B. Men = Black men; W.Wo = White Women; R in C = Remanded in Custody; Uncon = Unconditional Bail; Reside = condition of Residence; Passpo. = Surrender of Passport; and PsychR = Psychiatric Report.

On the whole, it was rare for a foreign defendant to be granted bail and when this was granted, the magistrate explained that the conditions had to be stiff because the defendant was a foreign national. Even a defence counsel said in a plea of mitigation that his client was 'a Ghanaian born in this country.' It is possible that the extra precautions taken with the foreign defendant were discretionary, but this was likely to affect black women more adversely than white women. Two of the black women who were remanded in custody with black men were foreign nationals and one of them needed the services of an interpreter. Tarzi and Hedges (1990) have shown that, out of 150 sentenced foreign prisoners, 46 were refused bail, 64 did not apply for bail because they had no fixed address or lacked sureties, and only 17 were granted bail on the condition of high sureties that they could not afford.

Table 4.5: Outcomes of contested cases by race and sex

Outcome	B.Wo	B.Men	W.Wo	Total
Fine	-	4	-	4
Crown C.	2	10	2	14
Custody	-	2	-	2
Dismiss	-	4	-	4
Drivers	-	2	-	2
Total	2	22	2	26

SOURCE: Fieldwork, London, summer, 1991.

Note that Crown C. = cases sent to the Crown Court for hearing; Custody = Custodial Sentence; Dismiss = cases dismissed or withdrawn; and Drivers = those who were disqualified from driving.

The importance of Table 4.5 lies in the indication of the number of black men who had the cases against them withdrawn or dismissed (4). This seems to suggest that proceedings were initiated against black men more quickly and without adequate grounds, as NACRO (1988) observed. It is probable that black women who were close to such men would also be affected unnecessarily. This picture will become clearer if linked back to the statistics for the trial and acquittal of men and women at the Crown and the Magistrates' courts in London (Tables 4.1 and 4.2). The suggestion that black men were more likely to be acquitted than black women is further illustrated by those tables.

The statistics on the ethnic origin of the people given probation supervision are not very reliable because the Home Office reports that the officers in the inner city district where blacks predominate refused to participate in the survey. However, the returns from those who did respond suggest that black women were disadvantaged compared with both black men and white women (Table 4.6).

Black women were one per cent higher than black men in the most serious type of supervision - criminal court orders. This appears insignificant when viewed against their equal overall percentage representation in 'all types' of supervision. However, this difference is noteworthy because white women were proportionately fewer than white men by the same percentage except in domestic supervision and 'all types' where, like black women in the earlier types, they were one per cent higher than white men. When this is compared with the high proportion of black women in prison, the relative uniqueness of the problems facing black women is further suggested.

These variations may be as a result of the error of coverage because the number of women asked questions increased disproportionately in the after-care category. Moreover, when the number of men not asked almost equalled that of women not asked questions (in domestic supervision), black men and black women recorded equal percentages. It is interesting that domestic supervision is the only category in which the representation of black people is proportionately lower than their overall proportion in the population. This is probably because, unlike criminal court orders, domestic supervision is voluntary aftercare and so not many black people volunteer for further supervision if given the choice.

Mair and Brockington (1988: 124-25) concluded that female offenders were generally more frequently given non-custodial sentences because they are more likely to be subjected to social enquiry reports. They stated that this may be a sign of leniency to female offenders but also argued that, 'if women are being subjected unfairly to what might be perceived as wide-ranging intrusion into their private lives ... then women are being treated neither equally nor justly.' One response could be that equality or justice for women does not lie in their being given as much imprisonment or as few probation orders as men because men are neither the standard bearers of justice nor a homogeneous group against which women could be measured for equality. Probation orders are preferable to immediate custody but what Mair and Brockington suggested is that the view of probation as a soft option could result in women who deserve absolute or conditional discharge being given probation. Garland (1985) and Young (1976), among others, have also argued that, although probation orders were formulated as 'welfare sanctions', they are actually intrusive.

Table 4.6: Probation service clients by type, sex and race of those supervised, 31 March 1987

Type Sex	White	Black	Asian	Other	Refused	Total	Not Ask
CRIMINAL COURT ORDERS							
Male	93%	3%	1%	1%	2%	56,060	6,900
Fem	92	4	1	1	2	141,540	1,390
AFTER-CARE							
Male	88	5	3	1	3	33,220	6,400
Fem	87	6	2	2	3	1,150	260
DOMESTIC SUPERVISION							
Male	93	1	3	1	3	2,570	370
Fem	94	1	2	1	-	32,480	330
ALL TYPES OF PROBATION SUPERVISION							
Male	91	4	2	1	2	91,850	13,670
Fem	92	4	1	1	2	17,790	1,980

SOURCE: H.O.S.B. 1/89, 31 JANUARY 1989: 'The ethnic origin of persons supervised by the Probation Service, March 1987', TABLE 4.

Black women are more likely to be given criminal court orders and after-care supervision than black men or white women. If the argument of Mair and Brockington is right, it suggests that black women are more closely supervised probably because they face qualitatively different problems compared to white women and black men. This suggests that the black woman still wears the tag of the 'bad' woman (Davis, 1981; Bryan et al, 1985; Wilson, 1985) which makes her the target of closer surveillance by the criminal justice system than those who are given conditional or absolute discharge.

Conclusion

This chapter has tried to present the observations of this author along with some information from individuals and groups with whom discussions were held during the fieldwork. The evidence of race-class-gender discrimination in the criminal justice system is not strong in this chapter. This is probably because I am not seeking to test whether there is any such discrimination. I assume that such forms of discrimination exist and attempted to find out the possible forms that they would take and how those affected have tried to deal with them.

The observations on disparity and discrimination, support and isolation, the hierarchy of discreditability and observations on procedure together suggest the forms that discrimination could take in the courts. It is true that observations about the relative isolation of the female defendant in court and those about a possible hierarchy of discredibility do not directly reflect discrimination. However, they serve to point out how the problems that face black women in courts reflect or affect problems that are faced by black women and people like them in society.

Similarly, although this chapter talks about the greater likelihood of black women being affected adversely by race-class-gender politics in the courts, this should not be interpreted in quantitative terms only. Given the limited size of the observations and the small sizes of the statistical difference, the importance of the differences in frequency should be seen more qualitatively. Such differences are seen here as suggestive of the qualitative differences in the race-class-gender relations that affect black women compared to black men and to white women. The smallness of the quantitative differences suggests the similarities in the social relations that affect these three categories of people and thereby justifies the comparative approach adopted here. However, the smallness of the quantitative differences suggests important qualitative differences among the three categories that cannot be fully explored in the present chapter or book. The next chapter will throw more light on the qualitative significance of quantitative differences especially when related to the methods and findings of Hood (1992) and others.

5. Black Women in Prison

Introduction

This chapter concludes the presentation of evidence for the uniqueness or otherwise of the problems that face black women in the criminal justice system. Chapters three and four analysed the problems that faced black women, in particular, in the ways and means that they were policed in the community and processed through the courts. This chapter analyses problems facing black women in prison service establishments.

Much of the evidence presented in this chapter is from the voluntary organisations that work with black women in prison and also from documents and publications. As in chapters three and four, the method of comparison between black women, black men and white women involves the use of triangulation of different sources of data (Jupp, 1989). This helped the author to evaluate the claims of one source against evidence from other sources.

The Gender and Race of Prison Populations

At the time of writing, the prisons in Britain were mainly male institutions: women comprised less than four per cent of the total prison population in 1989. However, the population of women in prison was growing faster than that of men. This is supported by the Prison Reform Trust (PRT, 1996) in a report which opened as follows:

> Just four years ago (1992/93), the average number of women in prison was 1,374. On July 26, 1996, there were no less than 2,313 women prisoners. This represents an increase over the period of 68 per cent, a rate of growth with no precedent in the modern era.

According to NACRO (1991) the average daily population of women in prison was 1,767 out of a total daily average of 48,610 in 1989. In the same year, 37% of imprisoned women (including fine defaulters) were sentenced for less serious offences like theft, handling, fraud and forgery. This compares with 23% of men imprisoned for similar and less serious offences. The percentages for serious offences were reversed for women; 12% of women and 19% of men were sentenced for serious offences. Moreover, the women tended to be imprisoned for first offences. For example, available data on 30 June 1989 show that 30% of women imprisoned had no previous convictions compared with 9% of men.

This picture is even more gloomy for black women because, according to the voluntary associations that provided information for this book, many black women in prison were not only first offenders but also recent immigrants to an unfamiliar culture, and many of them still protested their innocence. Their experience is that of being inside 'a prison within a prison' - a phrase attributed to a foreign white male prisoner but generalised by Tarzi and Hedges (1990). They suffer from isolation and inadequate communication with more distant relations as well as from the prison regime that all prisoners experience in different ways. According to NACRO (1991), black women were 26% of all women prisoners on 30 June 1990, whereas they were less than 3% of the total population of women in Britain.

The Prison Reform Trust (PRT, 1996) argues that 'the use of prison ... for all these women' is 'highly questionable'. This is because, according to the Trust, a 1993/94 survey of Holloway Prison, the largest women's prison in Western Europe, found that 'two-thirds of the prisoners had never been in prison before' and they were facing trial for less serious offences compared to male prisoners in Britain. Moreover, 29% of the prisoners in Holloway were connected with drugs offences and this matches the proportion of foreigners in the prison, although not all drugs related prisoners in Holloway were foreigners. The Prison Reform Trust is of the opinion that, although drugs offences are serious, the women who are exploited by drugs barons as couriers did not 'personally constitute a grave danger to the public'.

Maden, Swinton and Gunn (1992) have attempted to explain the over-representation of black women in prison populations, but concluded that black women were not over-represented among the women in their sample who were serving sentences for drugs offences. Their claim is that, when only UK residents were considered, 83% of drug offenders sampled were white and 13% were black. The conclusion that 13% representation of black women among UK residents is normal seems to distort the fact that black women make up only about 3% of the general population. To say that 13% representation of black women is normal is to suggest that black women are relatively more criminal, and so their apparent over-representation is actually normal, given their 'mythical crime rate'. However, it is impossible to measure crime rates of categories of people in the general population from prison statistics or from samples drawn from prison populations. Thus, the over-representation of black women must always be related to their proportion in the total population and to the accountability of criminal justice officials rather than to an attributed crime-proneness.

There is also the question of the 'inferential fallacy' (Hood, 1992) which concludes that there is discrimination from the disparities apparent in statistics of prison populations. However, it is surprising that Hood did not extend this logic to the hegemonic inferential fallacy shared by both the new left and the new right (see Gilroy, 1987b; Agozino, 1997 for a detailed critique) that black people must be more crime-prone simply because they are over-represented in criminal statistics. A version of this argument readily points to the low representation of Asians in the official crime statistics as evidence that if it was all down to racism, then Asians would be over-represented like black people (Hood, 1992, Jefferson, 1992). This version collapses immediately it is extendended to all Asians and all black people given that the jails in Nigeria or Jamaica are not more congested than the jails in India or Pakistan. If Asians are essentially more law-abiding, then this would be evident in Asia as well but the disparity in Asian representation warns us to avoid seeing racism in isolation from class and gender relations. The fact that Asians in Britain are relatively well-off compared to Asians at home and black people abroad suggests that their class relations have relatively disarticulated their race relations in Britain, making them relatively above suspicion and providing them with relatively more resources for self-defence when falsely accused, although they might be more readily attacked in envy over their enterpreneurial skills.

Hood (1992: 6) has argued strongly that discrimination may 'be the result of a cumulation of small "race effects"' at different stages of the criminal justice process. He found that about 80% of the over-representation of black men in prison populations 'was due to their over-representation among those convicted at the Crown Court and to the type and circumstances of the offences of which black men were convicted.' The remaining 20%, according to Hood, are due to 'differential treatment and other factors (like not pleading guilty) which influence the nature and length of the sentences imposed' (Hood, 1992: 179). As for black women, Hood concluded that there is no discrimination against them when compared to white women and that, when compared to black men, the 'chivalry thesis' that women are generally treated more leniently than men is confirmed.

This book is not interested in the treatment of black women in the criminal justice system as such but in the problems facing them as perceived by affected individuals and voluntary associations that are working with them. However, the findings of Hood regarding the treatment of black women calls for at least three responses that are relevant here. First, to say that chivalry applies to all women irrespective of race is to assume that chivalry would have the same impact on black women as on white women, whereas chivalry is historically a white patriarchal practice that claims to be protective of white women.

In this connection, bell hooks (1994: 57) argues that

> During slavery in the United States, white men in government who supported the idea of sending black folks back to Africa gathered petitions warning of the danger of sexual relations between decent white men and licentious black females, asking specifically that the government 'remove this temptation from us'.

This could be interpreted as evidence of chivalry in the indirect sense that those lustful white men were not only interested in being saved from sin through the banishment of Eve from Paradise; it also represented their race-class-gender discrimination against African Americans as a missionary, if not humanitarian, agenda for the encouragement of chastity among black women. This 'chivalry' (if that is what it was) proved dubious enough to force Sojourner Truth to ask pastors who preached that gender inequality was according to God's plan, 'Ain't I a woman?' (see Hooks, 1981). The chivalrous protection of white women did not demand their repatriation to Europe to keep them away from the seductive gaze of black men, not to mention the dishonourable intentions of some poor white 'trash'. The sexual abuse of enslaved black women and their torture along with black men were being blamed on the victimised, and the issue was not that the crimes of rape and torture should be punishable, but that the purity of the master race was being 'polluted' through miscegenation. Was that chivalry? (see also, Agozino, 1997).

This reference to the historical origins of chivalry is relevant here because of the ahistorical empiricist methods through which Hood arrived at his conclusions. He reviewed seven methodological inadequacies found in previous sentencing research, especially sampling, inferential, and comparative errors, but he did not mention their ahistoricity which his own research shares. Reference to the well-documented history of the discriminatory policing of black women should have warned Hood to look beyond the isolated cities that he observed in one single year before making generalisations about the truth of the chivalry thesis. Although Hood proved beyond doubt that some of the disparities in the treatment of black people in courts cannot be accounted for without reference to discrimination, he tried to localise the problem of discrimination as if it is something that happens only at the courts in Dudley and only to 20% of the black men.

Although Hood found that 36% of black women received custodial sentences at Dudley courts where they had a probability of custody measure of 26%, he concluded that, overall, their probability of custody measure was similar to their observed rate of custody just as in the case of white women.

This conclusion does not say anything about the fact that Coventry courts were included in the comparisons whereas 41 white women (or 39% of them, the highest in any of the other courts) were sentenced to custody there and no black woman was sentenced to custody there. This fact may have contributed to the evening out of the differences between the overall observed rates of custody for black women and white women. In other words, if nearly 40% of white women were found to have been sentenced to custody in Coventry whereas no black woman was sentenced to custody there, to compare the overall custody rate of black women and white women without calling attention to this empirical difference would have the effect of giving white women an additional 40% frequencies of custody or that of subtracting the same proportion from the black women, given that Coventry does not seem to be representative of the sentencing rate of black women.

Again, by talking about the seriousness of the danger and distress suffered by 'victims' of 'mugging' with which black defendants were disproportionately charged, and without mentioning the seminal analysis of the 'amplification' of this kind of crime through colonialist strategies of control and communication (Hall, et al, 1978), Hood makes the questionable suggestion that those who are convicted of such crimes were necessarily the actual offenders. He and his colleague studied sentencing in some criminal courts but, as soon as the defendants were sentenced, they started calling them offenders instead of convicts. This conventional way of describing convicts conceals the fact that not all prisoners are offenders of any sort.

Secondly, the sophisticated methods of Hood and his colleague were designed to 'isolate' the effects of race on sentencing. For this purpose and due to 'the sensitivity of the subject' they required difference at a high level of statistical significance (Hood, 1992: 21). This suggests that the problem of racism is entirely or even mainly quantitative and not also, or even mainly, qualitative. Furthermore, the attempt to isolate race as a factor seems inappropriate for the purpose of understanding racism which is never experienced in isolation but in articulation with gender and class discrimination (Hall, 1980, 1988, 1996). Jefferson (1992) may have been referring to this methodological fallacy when he contended that the 'dominant approach' of using 'sophisticated techniques' to reveal 'the purely "racial" dimension' to criminalisation 'is a bit like sieving flour with ever finer meshes: eventually there is too little getting through to enable anything to be made' from the final results.

Analysis of the differences between men and women should be sensitive to the extent to which black women were affected by actions that were originally directed specifically at black men, as the Institute of Race Relations has documented (IRR, 1987). Hood found that many of the black women received custodial sentences partly because they were charged with other defendants who were black, but he did not say whether the co-defendants of black women were male or female. If they were male, it could be the case that the women were charged along with the men when they may not have been accomplices, and this may be the reason why many more black women pleaded not guilty and ended up receiving longer sentences. This reluctance to plead guilty should not have been too easily written off as evidence of a confrontational demeanour because it could actually be suggestive of Victimisation-As-Mere-Punishment by which innocent people are included as targets of actions taken against individuals who are close to them. However, the concept of Victimisation-As-Mere-Punishment or that of criminalisation does not assume that all black women who end up in prison were innocent or wrongly convicted.

Thirdly, to say that 'disparities are not the same thing as discrimination' (Hood, 1992: 48) is different from implying that disparities are irrelevant to the understanding of the problems that face black women in the criminal justice system. Section 95 (1) (b) of the Criminal Justice Act 1991 which Hood cited does not make racial discrimination by judges a criminal offence, given their judicial immunity against prosecution, but it urges the Home Secretary to

> publish such information as he considers expedient for the purpose of ... facilitating the performance ... (by persons engaged in the administration of criminal justice) ... of their duty to avoid discriminating against any person on the grounds of race or sex or any other improper ground (Hood, 1992: 191).

The implementation of this section is seen by the former Chair of the Commission for Racial Equality, Michael Day, in a foreword to Hood (1992), as being capable of helping to check discrimination. However, the provision is not an innovation but a confirmation of the view of McClintock (1974) that criminal justice statistics are provided primarily for the purpose of accountability and, while inadequate for the purpose of accountability, they are completely inappropriate for the purpose of studying criminal propensities. This book is therefore using these figures as a rough guide to the accountability of criminal justice officials.

Table 5.1 shows that the proportion of all black people in prison service establishments was more than twice their proportion in the total population of England and Wales. Moreover, while the percentage for black men in prison was consistently equal to or slightly lower than the overall proportion of black people in prisons, that of black women was consistently nearly twice that of the overall percentage of black people in prisons. For example, in 1994 the percentage of black people in the provisional prison population figures was 11%, that of black men compared with the total number of males was 11% and, that of black women to all females was 21%.

The Home Office reported that on 30 June 1989, 7,600 or nearly 16% of all prisoners were known to be from 'the ethnic minority communities.' This was one per cent proportionately higher than figures for June 1988, continuing the increase from 12.5% in 1985. On 30 June 1989, 10.53 per cent of male prisoners were known to be black in origin, compared with 9.46% in mid-1988 and 7.98% in mid-1985. For females, the proportion was 19.31% which is similar to the 19.36% of mid-1988 and therefore breaking the almost consistent increase from 12.17% in mid-1985 (H.O.S.B., 12/90. 'The Prison Population in 1989' 1 April, 1990). No matter how one looks at it, the proportion of black people in prison is not in line with their proportion in the total population of less than 3%.

The higher proportion of black women (compared with black men) and white women (compared with white men) suggests that black women faced significantly different problems in the criminal justice system. It might be argued that the seriousness of the offences committed by blacks and their previous records explain their disproportionate presence in the prisons. However, this is not an entirely convincing argument because, when compared on offences of similar seriousness, white people appear to have more previous convictions. The Home Office (H.O.S.B., 8/88, 'The prison population in 1987', 30 March 1988) reported that when the seriousness of the offence was controlled for, whites had more previous convictions than blacks. In the offence of burglary, for example, 74 per cent of whites and 59 per cent of blacks had six or more previous convictions. For drug offences, 42 per cent of whites and 24 per cent of blacks had six or more previous convictions. This is further evidenced by the significantly larger proportions of black people who were in prison on remand and those being detained for non-criminal matters (Table 5.2 below). According to Vivian Stern (1987: 18) non-criminal populations of prison establishments, or those she called 'civil prisoners', are who have defaulted on maintenance payments, are in contempt of court or are those held under the Immigration Act.

Table 5.2 was a Written Parliamentary Answer to Mr Birmingham, MP, by the Secretary of State in the Home Office, Mrs Rumbold, on 4 February 1991 (holding answer to question asked on 25 January 1991). The table does not require much comment. The central point is the now familiar higher proportions of black people who are in prison for non-criminal offences despite the small number of black people in the population. It is interesting that it is only in this category and in the convicted but unsentenced group that black men and women have nearly equal proportions. More than thirty-three per cent (33.33%) of non-criminal women were black and 32.19% of the non-criminal men were black. Also 8.73% and 8.98% of convicted but unsentenced men and women, respectively, were black. This might be further evidence of the higher use of remand in custody for black defendants and the higher use of immediate custodial sentences for convicted black people. This was especially the case with foreign prisoners who were not referred for social enquiry reports and who were rarely given bail or non-custodial sentences.

Table 5.1: Population in prison service establishments on 30 June by percentages, sex and ethnic origin (census classification) in England and Wales 1990-1995

All Prisoners	Total	White	Black	South Asian	Chinese/Other	Unrecorded
1990	44,523	36,400 (82%)	5,002 (11%)	1,275 (3%)	897 (2%)	949 (2%)
1991	44,754	37,130 (83%)	4,822 (11%)	1323 (3%)	952 (2%)	527 (1%)
1992	45,486	37,705 (83%)	4,773 (10%)	1,388 (3%)	1,043 (2%)	577 (1%)
1993	44,246	36,855 (83%)	5,013 (11%)	1,356 (3%)	926 (2%)	96
1994	48,879	40,803 (83%)	5,595 (11%)	1,345 (3%)	996 (2%)	140
1995 (P)	51,084	42,207 (83%)	5,982 (12%)	1,497 (3%)	1,318 (3%)	80

Table 5.1: Continued, Population in prison service establishments on 30 June by percentages, sex and ethnic origin (census classification) in England and Wales 1990-1995

Males						
1990	42,910	35,323 (82%)	4,633 (11%)	1,248 (3%)	843 (2%)	863 (2%)
1991	43,210	36,081 (84%)	4,470 (10%)	1,296 (3%)	885 (2%)	478 (1%)
1992	43,950	36,616 (83%)	4,464 (10%)	1,363 (3%)	981 (2%)	526 (1%)
1993	42,666	35,691 (84%)	4,690 (11%)	1,335 (3%)	854 (2%)	96
1994	47,075	39,450 (84%)	5,225 (11%)	1,318 (3%)	944 (2%)	138
1995 (p)	49,086	40,697 (83%)	5,592 (11%)	1,470 (3%)	1,247 (3%)	80
Females						
1990	1,613	1,077 (67%)	393 (23%)	27 (2%)	54 (3%)	86 (5%)
1991	1,544	1,049 (68%)	352 (23%)	27 (2%)	67 (4%)	49 (3%)
1992	1,536	1,089 (71%)	309 (20%)	25 (2%)	62 (4%)	51 (3%)
1993	1,580	1,164 (74%)	323 (20%)	21 (1%)	72 (5%)	-
1994	1,804	1,353 (75%)	370 (21%)	27 (1%)	52 (3%)	2
1995(p)	1,998	1,510 (76%)	390 (20%)	27 (1%)	71 (3%)	-

SOURCE: H.O.S.B., 'The Prison Population in 1995', Issue 14/96, 3 July 1996, Table 7.

The high proportion of black people among the non-criminals in prison also reinforces the view that there is disproportionate criminalisation and victimisation of black people. 32.19% of non-criminal men compared to 10.80% of all men and 33.33% of non-criminal women compared to 22.92% of all women; however, the original figures were too small to make this percentage difference statistically significant. The vulnerability of black people who were relatively poor or more recent immigrants might contribute to the high proportions of black people yet untried and those convicted or sentenced for other offences. Since the poor and the recent immigrant might not be able to afford the amounts demanded by courts for bail or might not have people in England who are ready to stand surety for bail, they are more likely to be found among prison populations on remand. Although many black people were born in Britain or have lived here long enough not to be called recent immigrants, racialised immigration policies have continued to keep the families of most of those who are already here away. The result is that the recent immigrant and the first generation immigrant may be similarly isolated from family support in times of need. Besides, all black people are often assumed to be foreigners or descendants of immigrants in Britain even when they are citizens of the United Kingdom (see Hood, 1992; Cook and Hudson, 1993; Fitzpatrick, 1995). Note that the proportion of all black people in Table 5.2 (10.80%) is similar to that in Table 5.1 for 1992 (10%) while that of black women fell slightly by 3% from 23% in 1990 to 20% in 1992. This higher over-representation of black women may be indicative of the greater likelihood for black women to be collectively victimised along with the black men in their lives, as we saw in chapter three, even when they might be innocent. However, Fitzgerald and Marshall (1996: 151) concluded that 'there is no effective difference in the proportion of black British male and female prisoners' but they failed to point out that black British women were still more over-represented compared to black British men, whereas no other category of women had a higher proportion than their men in prison as Table 5.3 demonstrates (10% compared to 11% among the men and women respectively).

A striking difference between the figures in Table 5.3 and those of the USA is that black women made up more than 50 per cent of the prison populations of women in some states (French, 1981: 380). This proportion is only approximated in England at some institutions like Cookham Wood Prison where 40% of the inmates were black women (Mama, 1989). Chambliss (1995) reports that the over 50% representation of ethnic minority women is now a nation-wide phenomenon in the USA and he links this to the war on drugs. French (1981) compared prison populations in North Carolina by race and sex and found that there were proportionately more blacks in the female population than in the male population, that the females tended to be lowly educated, that this was even lower for black women, and that more black women were imprisoned for drugs offences.

Table 5.2: Provisional population of prison service establishments in England and Wales on 30 September, 1990: by type of prisoner, sex and ethnic origin

Status	White	Black	%Black	Asian	Mixed	Other	Total
MALES							
Untried	5,633	923	12.86	192	176	251	7,174
Convicted	1,532	158	8.73	36	33	49	1,808
Sentenced	27,915	3,485	10.34	973	616	702	33,691
Non-Crim	92	66	32.19	19	13	15	205
All	35,171	4,632	10.80	1,220	838	1,017	42,878
FEMALES							
Untried	208	53	17.32	7	21	17	306
Convicted	73	8	8.98	2	4	2	89
Sentenced	777	303	25.31	26	40	51	1,197
Non-Crim	5	3	33.33	-	1	-	9
All	1,063	367	22.92	35	66	70	1,601

SOURCE: House of Commons, 1991, Hansard, 185, 4-15 FEB, PP33-36W. Note that Untried = remand prisoners who were awaiting trial; Convicted = convicted prisoners who were awaiting sentence; Sentenced = Sentenced inmates of prisons; Non-Crim = non-criminal populations in prisons.

Table 5.3: Population in prison service establishment on 30 June 1995 (provisional figures) by ethnic origin, sex and nationality in England and Wales

Type	Total	White	Black	S.Asian	Chi/Oth	Unrecord
ALL	51,084	42,207	5,982	1,497	1,318	80
British	46,607	40,565	4,542	849	637	14
Foreign	4,089	1,376	1,414	636	659	4
Unrecord	388	266	26	12	22	62
MALES	49,086	40,697	5,592	1,470	1,247	80
British	44,945	39,134	4,360	834	603	14
Foreign	3,771	1,313	1,207	625	622	4
Unrecord	370	250	25	11	22	62
FEMALES	1,998	1,510	390	27	71	-
British	1,662	1,431	182	15	34	-
Foreign	318	63	207	11	37	-
Unrecord	18	16	1	1	-	-

SOURCE: H.O.S.B., 14/96, 'The Prison Population in 1995', 3 July 1996 Table C.

Racist Relations in Prison

Inside the prisons, according to one black woman who served thirty months, 'There is a lot of racism from prison officers, teachers, the lot, but mainly from prison officers .... If you're black you get more pressure, because you are not only fighting for your prisoner's rights, you're fighting for your black rights' (Mars, 1985). This issue can be illustrated with specimens of complaints against racist abuse by a black woman in prison and the characteristic responses that she received. The specimens were received by this author from NACRO's Women Prisoners' Resource Centre during the fieldwork.

The official complaint form advised prisoners to try to resolve their request/complaint informally if they could. Failing that, they should make a written request/complaint on the form provided within three months of the facts coming to their notice. Request or complaint should be limited to one issue at a time and separate forms should be used to raise separate issues. The complaint should be clearly written without insulting language and it should be written in English or Welsh because other languages may lead to delays. The language requirement has been noted by voluntary organisations and probation officers as one of the problems facing black women in prison. Many of them are not proficient in English and some are not literate in their mother tongues. They also claim that some of the complaints of the prisoners could not be followed up because the prisoners were frightened that a formal complaint would expose them to further discrimination from the officials.

The complaint to be considered here came from a black female prisoner, aged 20. She was officially classified as having a young status in one form and as being an adult in the next, a probable indication of doubts about where to place a 20 year old woman who may have attained her 21st birthday by the time of the second classification. In the first form, the complainant wrote on 27 March 1991: 'I was spoken to by an officer ... in a totally racist way. When locking me in my cell she said to me "Don't turn up that 'wog box' too loud." This is only the beginning of my complaint." The space for writing on this particular form was very small.

Two weeks later, the reply came on the reverse side of the same form saying, 'I have caused an investigation to be conducted with regard to your complaint.... I can find no evidence to corroborate your allegations and so conclude that your complaint is not substantiated. I do not propose to take any further action.' Notice the suggestion of absolute truth in 'I can find no evidence' which is not exactly the same as 'I did not find any evidence.' Notice also the dismissiveness of the proposal not to take any further action and the present tense of the conclusion that the complaint was not substantiated.

133

The difference between 'I can find no evidence' and 'I did not find any evidence' is that the former is finalist, absolute and dismissive in tone while the latter, phrased in the past tense, is more particularistic and more accommodating of the possibility that another investigation could yield something that was initially not found. It is true that the absolute-dismissive tone is common in bureaucratic and authoritarian discourse but the argument here is that allegations of racism are serious enough to demand greater sensitivity on the part of authoritarian bureaucrats.

It is not surprising that the complainant was not satisfied and so she appealed to the headquarters in April, detailing more abuses (sic.):

> To whom this may concern. In January 1991 I was in the educational block at Bullwood. Where I heard an Officer .... Saying to my roommate at the time (... aged 15) that 'she's going to make sure she comes to Kerstal which is her wing and make sure she goes down the block everyday. That's when I said 'You shouldn't say that to her.' She said to me "I wasn't talking to you." I said 'when you talk to one, your talking to the both of us.' When we both turned around to approach Room 3 (the officer) said loud and clear "You black Fools." Which is a racist remark. And I feel she has no right using that comment at me. I know for a fact that if it had been the other way around I would of (have?) been in serious trouble. So I decided to make a complaint to the Gov. I saw (an officer) first and she told me that was not a racist remark. I went higher up and said that I wanted to make a complaint to the area manager. Before that went through I had to see ... Gov of custody. She too told me that it was not a racist remark I said 'How could (she) sit the(re) and tell me that.' Her reply was "You are black and you are a fool." I went ahead and wrote to the Area Manager. To my disappointment his reply was "It had to be dealt with (by) the Governor at my Prison." I saw (her) again and she said what she said the first time still goes. I got my complaint sheet saying "there is no evidence of substantiate that an officer made any remark." But can I put (it to) you there is no evidence saying she did not say that because the fact is she did. From there after I've been victimised in all different ways and I'm afraid a person can only take so much .... There are so many other things to tell you but I don't have space. Today me + x roommate is on Kerstal the wing (the officer she was complaining against had threatened to take them) is majority of time and is making my sentence Hell.

The complaint is self-explanatory but it is useful to point out the deliberate limitation of the space within which a complaint has to be made on the first form. The limitation of space appears to be the reason why this woman withheld some details of her complaint the first time around. The reply to the second complaint is equally characteristic of the dismissiveness already highlighted:

> This complaint is similar in every respect to the one you sent to me 13 February. You may remember that I wrote to you stating that the matter would be dealt with by your Governor. I understand that as a result of an investigation conducted by ... you were informed that there was no evidence to substantiate your claim that the officer had made a racist comment. There is nothing in your appeal which would persuade me to change my view which is that the conversation did not initially include you and was always lighthearted. I am satisfied that no racially demeaning remark was made.

That seemed to close the case but the complainant wanted to appeal further to the Home Office and the reply was:

> I have discussed this matter at length with the Head of Custody. There are definitely no channels for your complaint to be forwarded to the Home Office. Some complaints of a particular nature can be but yours does not fit into this category. You are quite free to write to your M.P. if you are so inclined.

Perhaps this particular prisoner was a 'serial complainant' but the way the 'investigations' were conducted, without inviting her to testify or to call witnesses, indicates that prison authorities do not take such complaints seriously. It is not being suggested here that there should be a full hearing every time there is a complaint of any sort in prison. In July 1983, the 'Prison Department Circular Instruction 56/1993' was issued by the Home Office as an official statement on race relations, with emphasis on derogatory language and discriminatory work or training allocation (Genders et al, 1989: 30). Subsequently, the Race Relations Manual for prison officers re-emphasised that racist behaviour or abuse is a serious disciplinary offence. While announcing the launch of the Manual on 17 April 1991, Angela Rumbold, the Home Office Minister for Prisons, said:

> We all know that discrimination does still occur in our prisons, against both prisoners and staff. Some is overt, perhaps racial abuse of prisoners or harassment of ethnic minority officers. While some is unintentional, like stereotyping which leads to false assumptions about a person's behaviour ... I ... firmly believe that prisoners ... regardless of colour, race or religion, should be treated with equality, humanity and respect (NACRO, 1992: 8).

Note that Mrs Rumbold emphasised race and colour without mentioning gender as if racial discrimination is not often articulated with gender discrimination. Moreover, note also that she recognised that religion is articulated with race whereas the Home Office has consistently refused to recognise Rastafarianism as a religion, thereby exposing those black women that profess to be Rastas to institutionalised discrimination. In spite of the concern shown by the minister about racial discrimination or harassment in prisons, the offence is not listed under Rule 45 that is phrased one-sidedly as if only prisoners are capable of committing disciplinary offences in prisons. According to NACRO (1992: 20) the proportion of offences punished per head of the average prison population in 1990 was 1.8 for men and 2.7 for women. Similarly, punishments per 100 prisoners stood at 293 for men and 409 for women. There are no figures for disciplinary actions taken against officials.

This author believes that offences by prisoners should be treated as seriously as offences against prisoners. This is probably what the above complainant was referring to when she wrote that 'I know for a fact that if it had been the other way around I would (have) been in serious trouble.' According to the voluntary organisations, the chain of communication for complaints by prisoners starts from wing officers, who are often those against whom the complaints are made; thus not all serious complaints reach the governor or the Home Office. Far from taking prisoners' complaints seriously, Home Office research reveals that

> Like governor's applications, the petition system can serve other, less easily defined, purposes. For example, it can act as a 'safety valve': when inmates have had their requests refused, they can sometimes react by demanding to petition and then withdrawing it (or not even bothering to write it out) once they have 'cooled down' or thought the matter through. Similarly, staff sometimes suggest petitioning as a way of bringing a matter to a close or dealing with a particularly persistent complainant (Ditchfield and Austin, 1986).

However, racism is not only from whites to blacks in prison. A black woman, Martha, tells the story of how she went to prison for her white boyfriend who was a cheque forger. She thought she was in love with him and he paid her regular visits and gave her a radio that made her sentence more bearable. According to her, this relationship exposed her to a lot of 'hassle' from the other black women who used to call her a 'white man lover' and 'pagan'. Yet she believed that, in prison,

Being black wasn't a problem. Some of the girls were bitchy, some of them were National Front, some of them were Skinheads, but you knew who to mix with and who not to mix with. The black girls tended to stick together, but me, I mix with everyone, I don't care. Colour's got nothing to do with it as far as I'm concerned (Padel and Stevenson, 1988: 14-15).

A common complaint of most black women in prison, according to the agencies that worked with them, was that there were problems which were common to all female prisoners but that black women in prison faced racist problems which were not shared by white women. A South East London probation officer confirmed that, although the black women who served long sentences for drug offences were

... almost all dignified, respectful and unworldly .... (they) tend to get all the shit jobs in the prison, like working in the kitchens from 6 a.m. to 5 p.m., but they don't complain because it keeps them occupied. They prefer it because they don't have time to think about their families. In the end they have nothing (Roberts, 1989).

This shows that some black women may even volunteer for 'shit jobs' in prison but it is likely that many of them resent them. However, work in the kitchen is not necessarily a shit job given that Genders *et al* (1989: 121) found this type of work to be one of the most popular among prisoners due to the fact that the long hours 'provided a welcome break from the monotony of life on the wing' and also because of the added opportunity of smuggling out food items like sugar. Genders *et al* did not analyse the gendered nature of job allocations in prison, but a black woman who was an ex-prisoner complained that, 'Most of the work they give you (in prison) are to make you into a good housewife - cleaning, scrubbing, knitting and sewing. I hear that men get carpentry jobs, machine jobs, and all those interesting pursuits and studies' (*Channel 4*, 'Picking Oakum', 19 September 1991).

Similar racist relations were experienced by Angela Davis during her encounters with the US criminal justice system. When there was a bomb alert in one of the prisons where she was detained, the matron cuffed Angela's hands behind her back, the right arm of another black woman was chained to the left of a Chicano woman, and the only white woman present was not chained at all before they were evacuated to an underground room (Davis, 1974: 298). This was probably done to victimise the women racially and break their solidarity on the basis of gender but the latter did not succeed. For example, both white women and black women supported one black prisoner who was told that she could not watch television because she was allowed outside the prison on a 'work furlough program'. She reportedly told the matron that her badge did not give her the power to 'punish' her in that way. No, it was not intended as punishment at all, it was victimisation and the matron made this plain by informing her that she had 'overstepped her color'. In the battle of words that ensued, all the black women supported the sister and some white women also supported her (Davis, 1974: 310).

The 'fractured' solidarity of most (but not all) female prisoners in spite of racial discrimination was probably based on their consciousness that they were all oppressed on the basis of gender. Solidarity of women is being qualified here by pointing out that it is not universal, given the rivalries and quarrels that could be amplified by the austerity of prison resources. Solidarity among female prisoners is seen here to be similar to the 'fractured unity' among segments of the working class that Hall et al (1978) identified. For example, in the recreational room for women in one of the prisons where Angela was detained, the only furnishings provided were backless stools, washing machines, clothes driers, and ironing equipment. This was probably because the officials thought that women could not relax if they were separated from domestic chores. Thus the clothes and linens of men in the same prison were externally laundered while the women were expected to do their own laundering. If no woman volunteered to do the washing, some work would be imposed on them and black women would be the ones ordered to do the washing, articulating racism with sexism. However, when, out of boredom, many white women volunteered to do the washing, black women 'were consistently rejected' (Davis, 1974: 309).

Angela Davis was high profile but her politics was working class. The reference to her case was possible because it is well-known and it is well-known because she was high-profile. There could be many more Angelas out there that are not heard of who could suffer even greater victimisation as poor black women. The reference to her case is used here to demystify rather than to de-specify such incidents as the shooting and maiming of Cheryl Groce by a police inspector in Brixton or the events that sparked off the Handsworth and Broadwater Farm Estates uprisings of the 1980s.

The extent to which the insensitivity in handling complaints against racism could be generalised for all complaints procedures is reflected in the reference to the Home Office research that found that the procedure is actually regarded as a safety-valve through which prisoners have their say and officials have their way. However, the fact remains that to treat complaints against racism in the same way as every other complaint is contrary to the Race Relations Manual that singles out racism as a serious problem in prisons. This might support the assertion of Mama (1989) that, 'While prison governors express the official view that all prisoners should be treated equally, prison staff often harbour particular resentment: they are notorious for being amongst the most racist sections of the British population ....'

five out of 14 white inmates (36%) compared with 11 of the 16 minority inmates (69%) had formal action taken against them.'

Criticising the generalisation of security regimes designed for male prisoners to female prisoners, the Prison Reform Trust (1996) reports that

> ... as a result of the security crackdown following the 1995 Woodcock and Learmont Reports (both following very serious escapes from men's prisons), rigorous restraints have been imposed on women prisoners just as they have on men. This is unwarranted. Individual women who had successfully pursued activities on temporary release with no breach or negative incidents of any kind, have suddenly been deemed unsuitable for temporary release, as new criteria were applied across the board. This is unjust as well as illogical.

There was no voluntary agency that catered exclusively for black men in prison. To compare the problems facing black men and black women within prisons, discussions were held with some black men who had done time in prisons. They shared some of the problems that concerned black women but they emphasised the racism within the prisoner community itself rather than among staff. Tarzi and Hedges (1990: 23) found that foreign male prisoners had no complaints against prison staff, unlike the female prisoners. As they put it '... male prisoners found the prison staff's attitude very positive and felt that, bearing in mind the facilities available, the prison staff tried very hard and deserved praise.' This is not universally true because some of the opinions they quoted from male prisoners were very critical of the prison staff. However, it is quite likely that the prison staff conduct business in different ways in male prisons compared with female prisons due to the fact that both groups are linked by masculinity (see Sim, 1994: 105). One of the female prisoners was indeed quoted as asking, 'Why can't it be like men's prisons where I understand the officers have very positive attitude?' (Tarzi and Hedges, 1990: 23).

This is confirmed by Padel and Stevenson (1988: 10) who state that

> Women prisoners are disciplined more than twice as often as men. In 1986, 3.6 offences were punished per head of the female prison population as against 1.6 per head of the male prison population. A much higher proportion of prison rule offences committed by women fall into the 'mutiny or violence' category than by men, which is surprising given that all the major prison riots have occurred in men's prisons.

Prison staff in male prisons may claim that they operated no differently compared to their counterparts in female prisons. It could be the human inclination to believe that the grass is always greener on the neighbour's lawn. It is possible that male prisoners also believe that female prisons are feathered nests compared to their own experiences. However, it is more likely that men could take a lot of prison control practices for granted because they were designed to suit them in the first place. Behaviours that might be acceptable or tolerable from macho men could be interpreted to be undisciplined or violent if they come from 'tender' women. If officers in female prisons operated exactly like the ones in male prisons, the result would be more repression for female prisoners rather than better services. For example, a practice like strip-searching is likely to be more humiliating for a female prisoner especially if male officers are present. This was highlighted in a drama documentary by the 'Clean Break' theatre company (Channel 4, 'Picking Oakum', 19 September 1991). Hillyard (1993) analysed the humiliating impacts of strip-searching on Irish women.

Black men may emphasise the conflicts within the prisoner community because many of them frequently get into fights with fellow inmates who try to harass them racially. This exposes them to greater risks of punishment and frequent transfers from prison to prison or 'ghosting'. This was the experience of a black man who told this author that, even though he was punished for the fights, the prison officers were grateful to him for taking on the bullies and cutting them down to size. It can be inferred that black male prisoners may share certain manifestations of racist discrimination within prisons with black women while the latter bear the gender discrimination in addition. Certain gender discrimination against black women might be shared by white women and also by black men (though not in an identical way compared to the gendered discrimination against women) who were too poor, too weak, or too non-conformist to be what Naffine (1990) called the 'reasonable man of law.'

Foreign Black Women in Prison

The notion of 'black drug couriers' suggests that theories of penology, criminology and victimology should move beyond their preoccupation with the individual offender (not just because of the plural tense of 'couriers') because some of what is conceptualised as punishment goes beyond individual offenders to affect whole groups and categories who could be victimised through institutional practices that are deliberately designed to exclude, marginalise, control, alienate or even victimise the undesirable Other. Changes in the social construction of the knowledge and power about 'black drug couriers' in Britain have followed a predictable pattern. The topic itself suggests a one dimensional equation of the sort: the black immigrant equals courier, unless otherwise proven. This monolithic suggestibility in policy, theory and research is hardly surprising given that criminology and the 'war on drugs' are primarily concerned with criminality, and any focus on any group by criminologists or 'drug warriors' would necessarily be looking for degrees of criminality among such a group of people. This crime-centredness of criminology is almost unavoidable with reference to illicit drugs and black immigrants because spatial mobility is expected to imply anomie, social disorganisation, or at least, culture shock with all the predictable incidence of deviance that could be associated with exposure to a different culture. This section will critically review this apparent truism with a view to defending black women and black men against possible 'drugs war crimes' of unjustifiable stereotypes and Victimisation-As-Mere-Punishment.

The critical view is that the police focus on the black community more closely and therefore arrest black people more frequently partially for racist reasons that could be direct or indirect. This view is more persuasive because official crime figures are not provided in order to help criminologists decide which group is more crime-prone. The reason why such statistics are provided (as questions in parliament demonstrate and as section 95 of the 1991 Criminal Justice Act made clear) is for political and financial accountability. This view reverses the 'inferential fallacy' of Hood by suggesting that it is a fallacy to assume that black people commit more crimes simply because they are over-represented in the prisons. For example, the fact that 23 per cent of women in prison in 1995 were black calls for an enquiry into the ways that black women are discriminated against rather than asking whether black women are more crime-prone. There is evidence from the Institute of Race Relations (1987) that the police pick on innocent black women especially when they come looking for suspect black men.

Fitzgerald and Marshall (1996) concluded that poverty explains why so many black people are linked to crime, but they also conceded that discrimination could make this link stronger for black people than for other categories of poor people. Following Box (1983), the view favoured in this book is that it is power rather than poverty that is more strongly linked to criminality and this applies to crimes of the powerful as well as to crimes of the relatively powerless who victimise their fellow poor that happen to be weaker than themselves. The reason why the poor are over-represented in the criminal justice statistics, therefore, is because their poverty reduces their ability to effectively defend themselves even when they are wrongly accused whereas the powerful get away with murder for a similar reason.

The contention in this book that the immigrant is more marginalised than criminal is relatively uncontentious given that immigration law is mainly part of civil law rather than part of the criminal law in the United Kingdom (Agozino, 1996d). Apart from this, it can be inferred from the above Table (5.3) and from the Table below (5.4) that crime in the United Kingdom is mostly 'home grown' given that the total prison population in

England and Wales on 30 June 1995 was 51,084 whereas foreigners accounted for only 4,089.

When white foreigners are separated from black ones (Table 5.3) the claim that black immigrants are more crime prone becomes even more questionable. With specific reference to drugs offences, the total population under sentence in 1990 was 3,200, whereas foreigners accounted for only 1,248 of this category (Home Office Statistical Bulletin, Issue 24/95, *op. cit.*). Such a high proportion of foreigners among sentenced drugs-related prisoners is unquestionably artificial given that it fails to show that up to 50% of drug offenders are routinely cautioned mostly for the possession of small quantities of cannabis and that drug trafficking declined in proportion to all drugs-related offences from 20% in 1986 to 13% in 1992. These figures indicate that William Chambliss (1995) was right when he identified the 'war on drugs' in America as a disguise for the 'war on coloured people'.

The 50% cautioning rate suggests that cautions would be more readily given to British citizens for the possession of drugs whereas black foreigners are very unlikely to be cautioned even for the smallest amounts of drugs (see Tarzi and Hedges, 1990 for a suggestion that foreigners convicted of drugs trafficking recieve more severe sentences). Green et al (1994) disagree with this suggestion following their comparison of 88 Nigerians with 40 Britons who were convicted of importing class A drugs of less than £300,000 estimated street value in their sample of 573 persons sentenced between 1990 and 1992. The Nigerians received an average sentence of 67.9 months compared to 76.4 months for the Britons. However, the Britons imported drugs of higher street value (£84,900 on average compared to £72,108 by the Nigerians) Moreover, the sample does not seem representative given that there were more Britons in prison for category A drugs than Nigerians, while Nigerians in the sample were more than double the size of sampled Britons.

This evidence is inconclusive given that Green et al could not tell the racial background of the Britons in their sample, whereas Tarzi and Hedges interviewed the individual prisoners. Moreover, the higher average prison sentence for the Britons is hardly comparable to that of the Nigerians given that the latter stood little chances of caution, parole and day releases (as Tarzi and Hedges reported), while Green et al acknowledge that the judges tend to be more flexible when sentencing people for drugs with higher street values and more inflexible in their interpretation of the sentencing guidelines when drugs of lesser street values were involved. They did not indicate why this seems to be the case but it is probably related to the critical view of Steve Box (1983) and many others that the crimes of the powerful receive less severe societal reaction compared to the crimes of the relatively powerless.

The suggestion of discrimination against foreign black suspects can be illustrated by two very similar cases of Jamican women who alleged that they had been set up as 'sacrificial lambs' (Clutterbuck, 1995: 162). One of them was 'a female British-born courier' who took her first chance to visit grandparents in Jamaica by accepting an air ticket and £500 spending money in exchange for importing '250 gm of 90 per cent pure cocaine'. The drug was initially valued at £24,000 but in court the street value was raised to £57,000 and she received a sentence of four years imprisonment. The second woman was also Jamaican but apparently not British-born and she 'was caught with 200 gm of cocaine in a condom concealed in her vagina' (Ibid).

The second (non-British) Jamaican was given a sentence of six and a half years for a smaller quantity, perhaps because she did not receive any social inquiry report like all foreign defendants (the exception being the experiment by the Middlesex Area Probation Service on the preparation of such reports in 1990, as reported by Green, Mills and Read, 1994: 486). If she was given a harsher sentence because of the purer quality or higher street value of her cocaine (as Green et al, 1994, suggest) or because she had previous records or because she did not plead guilty (a la Hood, 1992), her case still starkly contrasts with the report in July 1993 that the British Prime Minister, John Major, wrote to the King of Thailand to request a Royal Pardon for Patricia Cahill and Karyn Smith who were jailed in Bangkok for 25 years and 18 years, 9 months, respectively, following their conviction for attempting to smuggle heroin out of the country. They originally claimed that their trip was organised by a black man (another bloody alien) that they met in a Birmingham nightclub but the British customs officers followed that up and found nothing. On their release after only three years of their sentences, the British press swooped in to compete for their stories as if the heroin smugglers were now heroines. This prompted the Chairman of the Press Complaints Authority, Lord McGregor, to warn the press not to pay for the stories because that would be in breach of the principle that criminals should not benefit from crime. According to him. '... the Prime Minister had not disputed the women's conviction for drug smuggling in Thailand and rested his appeal to the King of Thailand purely on humanitarian grounds' (*The Guardian*, 23 July 1993). Writing in the same newspaper a day earlier, Vivek Chaudhary reported that

> For those working with foreign female couriers, the support of the Government and other institutions for Patricia Cahill and Karyn Smith in Bangkok smacks of hypocrisy. The plight of hundreds of women from the third world languishing in British prisons, they claim, is as serious, and the desperate circumstances that lead them to become Mules are never taken into account when judges pass sentence (*The Guardian*, 22 July 1993).

The total prison population in Table 5.3 above includes detainees and immigration prisoners as well as fine defaulters who are not necessarily criminals as such. However, when the Tables 5.3 above and 5.4 below are compared, it becomes clear that any propaganda that black immigrants commit most of the crimes in the UK has no basis in reality. The over-representation of black people in the table below is an indication of the discriminatory racialisation of crime which many commentators have analysed.

In 1994, the Head of the Metropolitan Police, Paul Condon, told the world that he had invited leaders of the black community to warn them that he was about to launch operation 'Eagle Eye' against young black men because his 'intelligence' told him that 80% of muggers were young black men. No one has ever invited leaders of the white community to warn them that a special operation (call it 'Eagle's Ass') would be launched against young white men who joy-ride, drink-drive, or racist-attack in London where statistics would show that almost 99% of those involved in these serious crimes are white.

The Chinese were the first minority group in Britain to be collectively associated with drugs trafficking. This was followed in the 1980s by 'Iranians' which includes all those suspected of Islamic fundamentalism whether or not they are from Iran. The next category was the 'Pakistanis' which referred almost collectively to anyone from the Indian sub-continent. Nigeria (meaning West Africa) has only recently been recognised as a 'staging post' while Jamaica (short for West Indies) is said to be the base of violent 'Yardies' or armed drug gangs. At the same time, it is not always acknowledged that the drugs trade in Britain is still dominated by white British villains who prefer the relative safety of the drugs trade to the more hazardous bank robberies that they used to specialise in. The white professional criminals are suspected of undermining the influence of any rival ethnic criminal business by passing information to the police. This suggests that the inequalities found in the legitimate opportunity structure are reproduced in the illegitimate opportunity structure, as critics of Robert Merton's theory of individual adaptation to anomie have since pointed out (Ruggiero and South, 1995).

Furthermore, actual possession of drugs and eventual conviction may reflect Victimisation-In-Punishment because foreign convicts were not allowed Social Inquiry Reports or parole, and the provision of prison services are discriminatory against those most marginalised along the trajectory of race-gender-class relations (Green, 1991, Mama, 1989). The over-representation of black people in the prisons could also be as a result of discriminatory focus on black travellers, the marginalisation of black hustlers into the more visible lower end of the drug market and the likelihood that black people are less likely to be cautioned when found in possession of drugs compared to white people in Britain.

Foreign black women were in a peculiar predicament especially because of the drugs-related offences for which they were most frequently arrested. Racial prejudice against the 'bad' black woman may make her more vulnerable and more suspect to anti-drugs squads and immigration officials than white women. However, this does not explain why a disproportionate number of black women are lured into being used by drug barons. This may be due to their poverty in comparison with white women and with black men or due to their inadequate understanding of the penal implications of the offence.

The exploitation of black women as drug couriers and their consequent criminalisation deserve a detailed study, but it should be pointed out here that the severity of the problems facing them is more related to the seriousness attached to the offence by the criminal justice system than to their sex or race. As Penny Green (1991: 43) concluded:

> In the ideological war over who is to blame for drug abuse and other social ills the courier provides a cheap and expendable scapegoat .... Like the baron, the judiciary also exploits the courier. The drug courier has become an expressive target in the authorities' offensive against illegal drugs.

It is likely that the race and gender of black women have come to be so closely associated with this kind of crime that they are watched more closely and therefore arrested more frequently.

David Mellor, the then Secretary of State in the Home Office, in a Written Parliamentary Answer to Allan Clarke MP (on 9 November 1989), gave the following figures for women in prison for drug offences (Table 5.4). He indicated that out of a total of 323 such cases, 150 involved UK citizens. The second largest were Nigerians with 76 women in prison. The rest included 35 'Others' and those of unknown nationalities, 16 Jamaicans, 15 Ghanaians, 14 Colombians, 6 Indians, 6 from the USA, and 5 from Guyana. Yet the emphasis of the Home Office continues to be stiff penalties to discourage foreigners as if the drugs problem is entirely or even mainly foreign. Mrs Rumbold made this clear in a Written Parliamentary Answer to Mr David Porter, MP (19 March, 1991). Mrs Rumbold said: 'We are planning to publicise abroad the long prison sentences which drug smugglers can expect on conviction in this country in the hope that this may dissuade foreign nationals from bringing drugs into the United Kingdom' (*Hansard*, 187, 1990-91: 72).

Roberts (1989) and Green (1991) report that most of the couriers from Africa are poor and needy, though a few of them are well-educated. They tend to be in need of quick cash to meet some legitimate interests like raising children, paying for medical treatment, or meeting other family requirements. Unfortunately, social enquiry reports, examination of circumstances, and examination of degree of culpability are ignored by the courts and what matters are the quantity and purity of the drugs. Roberts (1989) reports a probation officer as saying, 'They are given very long sentences on a first offence.'

Analysing this phenomenon, Wilmot (1989) argues that the use of black women as drug couriers is based on the 'tortured dialectic of sexual politics' by which the exploited can also become an exploiter through the manipulation of powerful men's softness for femininity. The drug barons call the courier a 'mule' or beast of burden and she is preferred because she has more cavities for concealing drugs than her male counterpart. She is also preferred because she is supposed to be less tense than her male counterpart and she can carry a new-born baby or dress seductively to distract officials most of whom are men. However, the exploitation of powerful men's 'softness' for femininity is a questionable claim to attribute to exploited drug couriers and their alleged possession of more cavities for concealing drugs sounds very essentialist. Moreover, the alleged preference for female couriers by drugs barons is not supported by Table 5:4 which shows that the majority of the convicts happen to be men. However, it may be the case that more men than women were attempting to import their own drugs rather than merely being used as 'mules'.

The Written Parliamentary Answer to Mr Birmingham by Mrs Rumbold on 14 May 1991 shows that the majority of foreign prisoners were black people. This should have suggested to the prison services that they make allowance for the cultural and social needs of black people in prisons. However, this does not appear to be the case. The following table will show that a significant number of the foreign prisoners were convicted of drugs-related offences, which often carry very long terms of imprisonment.

Discussions of what the *Independent* (11 November 1990), called 'Rough justice (being) meted out to foreign offenders in Britain' often focus on the problems of foreign women, especially on those of Nigerian women and of women with children. This research focus is justified by the large number of Nigerian women who were in prison, mainly for drugs-related offences, as Table 5.4 shows. However, even more attention should be paid to Jamaican women because, although their national population was about two million compared with that of Nigeria (88 million), they were the second largest group of women in prison after Nigerians. The wide difference in the population sizes of the two countries indicates that the number of their men and women in prison did not have to do with national population size as such. The more important factor was the number of their citizens who were visiting or residing in Britain given that such residents stood greater chances of being arrested in Britain than their compatriots at home.

The 1991 census of Great Britain was the first to include questions on racial origin and this proved controversial because the question asked if respondents were White (implying British) White Other or Black Caribbean, Black African or Black Other (as if being black is inconsistent with being British). The census recorded that the 49,890,277 population of England and Wales was made up of 94.1% White, 1.0% Black Caribbean, 0.4% Black African and 0.4% Black Other. The highest concentration of black people was in Inner London with 74.4% White, 7.1% Black Caribbean, 4.4% Black African and 2.0% Black Other (Office of Population Census and Surveys, National Monitor, CEN 91 CM 56, December, 1992, Table J, p.21). The London figures most nearly approximate the proportion of all black people in prison, but all black prisoners are not Londoners and the overall figures indicate that white people are under-represented in the populations of prison service establishments, indicating that the prison service establishments are not equal opportunities recruiters.The large number of Nigerians and Jamaicans who were in prison for drugs-related offences suggests that most of them may have been arrested at the port of entry into Britain. The sizes of the population of Jamaica and Nigeria within their respective regions make them relatively attractive to drugs barons who need couriers. The economic crises and high levels of official corruption in these countries (Green, 1991) equally make it easy for the barons and their agents to continue recruiting 'mules' with relative ease. However, the nationals of these countries do not happen to be the only ones who traffic in drugs; they happen to be the ones who were, rightly or wrongly, the targets of close surveillance by security agents. For example, in 1992, there was a special measure to screen all visitors from Nigeria at the ports of entry. Immigration officials claimed that this was to check the large number of Nigerians allegedly travelling with forged papers. However, the then Nigerian High Commissioner, George Dove-Edwin, said that this was unfair because Nigerians were not the only ones who forged travel documents and yet they were the only ones who received special screening (The Independent, 11 April 1992). A similar practice outraged sections of the British public when a plane-load of holiday-makers from Jamaica was detained just before Christmas in 1993.

The conviction for possession does not necessarily prove guilt. Guilt is required to be proven in criminal cases only beyond all reasonable doubt but 'reasonableness' is gendered, classed and racialised rather than a given (see Naffine, 1990). This is especially so because many of the women go down still protesting their innocence (Eaton, 1993). The concept of Victimisation-As-Mere-Punishment is prepared to give such women the benefit of the doubt while the philosophy, theory and practice of Punishment-Of-Offenders is intolerant of their protestation until the tortuous processes of judicial and appellate reviews confirm their faulty convictions. The benefit of the doubt given by the concept of Victimisation-As-Mere-Punishment is reflected by the fact that its usage persuades this writer to cautiously talk about convicts while the discourse of Punishment-Of-Offenders tends to jump easily to the conclusion that all convicts are necessarily offenders (Hood, 1992). Furthermore, actual possession and conviction may reflect Victimisation-In-Punishment if the convict was not allowed Social Inquiry Reports and parole and if the provision of prison services is discriminatory against those most marginalised along the trajectory of race-gender-class relations.

Ruggiero and South (1995: 110) note that '... the vilification, persecution and victimisation of various ethnic groups for real or imagined associations with drugs has been a strong constant of drug control history, since at least the late 19th century'.

The problem of foreign black women who are in prison for drugs trafficking includes that of isolation even from other black women prisoners who do not take drugs. Adaku was one such black woman who hates drugs and hates drugs couriers especially because many of them do not take the drugs with which they were going to ruin other people's lives. She thinks that their problem is that of greed and not poverty. According to her, 'If I see a person is charged and sentenced because of drugs, I don't really like them because I think that's why there is more crime in this country' (Padel and Stevenson, 1988: 66). If a black woman could express such strong nationalist sentiments against foreign black women convicted of drugs (as the emphasis on 'this country' suggests), it can be imagined how racist prisoners and racist prison officials would regard them in prison. As Green (1991: 21) put it, 'The constructed drugs "crisis" is seen as a principally imported crisis - imported by West Africans, Asians or South Americans, fuelled by Third World supplies rather than domestic demand' and supply.

However, there was no evidence of such hostility by fellow prisoners against the drugs couriers in prison. The sentiments of Adaku might be isolated because the voluntary organisations have not noticed such problems. They claimed that prisoners who were better off tended to avoid poorer ones and that only child abusers were unpopular as an offence group among female prisoners.

All the voluntary organisations that provided information for confirmed that the reason why many black women, especially foreign ones, prefer to work in the kitchen in prison was because they got longer hours and therefore earned more money with which to meet personal needs; they did not have relatives in England who could send them presents. Yet when they finish their sentences and are about to be deported, the prison authorities tell them that the little money that they saved in order to buy presents for loved ones and pay their way from the capital cities of their country to their remote villages had been used to pay for their flight tickets. They also pointed out that it was not entirely by choice because it was almost impossible to find a

Table 5.4: Sentenced prisoners on 30 June 1990 who were known to be foreign nationals, by sex, nationality and whether sentenced for drugs

Nationality	All Offences			Drugs Offences		
	Men	Women	Total	Men	Women	Total
India	245	14	259	79	7	86
Pakistan	252	2	254	125	-	125
C'Wealth Asia	64	1	65	14	-	14
Nigeria	428	99	527	339	55	396
Ghana	42	18	60	25	13	38
C'Wealth Africa	91	9	100	33	4	37
Jamaica	432	40	472	116	18	134
C'Wealth Caribb	121	15	136	29	9	38
Cyprus	54	2	56	18	2	20
Old C'Wealth	38	3	41	9	1	10
Ireland	412	10	422	24	1	25
Other EC	196	14	210	87	10	97
USA	37	16	53	13	10	23
South America	110	29	139	90	20	110
Other Countries	347	31	378	85	12	97
Total Known	2,869	303	3,172	1,086	162	1,248

SOURCE: House of Commons, 1991, Hansard, 191, 13-23 May. Note that C'Wealth Asia, C'Wealth Afri and C'Wealth Caribb = those commonwealth countries in Asia, Africa and the Caribbean not individually listed; Old C'Wealth = Australia, Canada and New Zealand; Other EC = those European Community countries not listed; Other Countries = those countries not listed; and Total Known = all prisoners known to be foreign.

'deportee' working on a garden party due to the fear that they would abscond. For the same reason, they were not allowed day releases towards the end of their sentences as was the case with British nationals.

Furthermore, foreigners did not get field probation officers and they were not sent to open prisons for fear that they would abscond. This was supported by a white woman on day release who told this author that foreign offenders did not get into job clubs that could enable them to go outside and work to earn money that would be paid to them at the end of their sentences. She said that, although there were foreigners in all prison education classes, most of the foreign black women opted for kitchen work while British women opted for education more frequently.

However, Chigwada (1989) found that many black women, especially foreign ones, remained on the waiting lists for education classes until their sentences were over. When they complained, they were usually reminded about where they came from and how much worse services they could have been receiving back in their countries of origin. This was corroborated by a black female education officer who told Chigwada that when she wanted to know why there were never any black women in her classes, even though she was aware that many of them had applied to join, she was reportedly told that there were not enough officers to escort the black women to classes. According to Chigwada, 'This could mean either that black women were perceived as aggressive and needed more officers or that sheer racism was involved, since education was considered easy, involving no work.'

The discrimination in the allocation of jobs also affected black men, as a black man who had been to prison three times told this author:

> You never see a black guy in the officer's mess or (working) as the governor's tea boy who gets tips and favours. It is changing now because some black guys get into outside garden parties whereas they never got that in the past. They were mostly on cleaning parties (Fieldwork notes. This is supported by Genders et al, 1989, who recognised that racial discrimination in the allocation of prison jobs was a serious enough problem that the Home Office issued directives to prevent it in the 1980s).

Language is a difficult barrier against the support of foreign prisoners by probation officers, especially if the prisoners were not fluent in English (see Genders et al, 1989 and Cheney, 1993). This is further complicated by the lack of suitable referral options, information, and of resources. The result was that 'A number of foreign prisoners, particularly recent admissions, were unaware of the existence of a probation team in the prison' (Tarzi and Hedges, 1990: 43). Those who were aware of the existence of the team were confused as to what kinds of help they could get. Moreover, the probation officers were not given any training on the special needs of foreign prisoners. This problem is made more acute by the fact that, while black people were over-represented in the prisons, only one per cent of probation officers, out of a total of 6,651 were black (*H.O.S.B.*, 24/88, 'Ethnic Origins of Probation Service Staff 1987' August, 1988. p.2).

The voluntary agencies emphasised the distress that the fostering of black children to white families could cause to mothers. This was highlighted by *Voice* (10 September 1991) which stated that an increasing number of black women were leaving their children to be privately fostered under the mistaken assumption that they would get better opportunities in white families. The newspaper did not indicate that this mainly affects children of mothers who needed time to work or study and were therefore forced to foster their children privately and pay the costs personally. The black women who were arrested with babies and those who had babies while still in prison had their children publicly fostered with white families, probably because there were few black families ready to act as fosters for the Councils. The advantage in Council fostering was that the fitness of the prospective family was usually investigated beforehand whereas private fosters took as many children as possible to maximise profits. There are between six and nine thousand African children in private care in England (Voice, 10 September 1991).

The 1989 Children's Act attempted to regulate private carers by limiting the number of children per family to three. However, even then, the problem of cultural differences would remain a cause for concern even for imprisoned mothers of children who are not in care. For example, there was a woman who lost her child in Nigeria and was uncontrollable with grief. The prison officials simply locked her away when, culturally, her condition required a communal sharing of grief. Akina Mama Wa Africa said that they were ready to provide such communal support but the prison officials did not even bother to inform them (fieldwork notes).

Although most of the problems identified here, including that of isolation from family and children, affect foreign black men as well, the situation of black women is compounded by the finding that the foreign black women keep themselves to themselves more than the foreign black men in prison (Green, 1991). Green did not offer an explanation for this finding but it is likely to be related to another finding of hers regarding clothing:

> Women prisoners do not wear prison uniforms. They are therefore immediately disadvantaged if they have no friends or family to provide clothes for them. The vast majority of foreign national couriers arrive in Britain with an expectation of staying only 5 or so days - they bring enough clothes only for those few days. If they arrive in summer they have no clothing adequate for the British winters ahead. Those they have with them are then all

they have when they find themselves imprisoned for 6-10 years. One Nigerian woman interviewed burst into tears and lifted her blouse to show she had no underwear at all - her plastic sandals were broken and her lightweight African cottons totally inadequate for the British climate (Green, 1991: 31).

It is understandable that such a level of deprivation could contribute to the sense of isolation which foreign black women faced, unlike foreign black men who were provided with uniforms like all male prisoners and unlike foreign white women who could mix more easily because of their appearance and the relative ease with which their friends and families could send them supplies. The voluntary organisations that work with women in prison were campaigning on the basis that adequate clothing should be provided, especially for foreign black women, as a matter of right and not as a charitable offer from religious organisations whose faith the women might not share. The voluntary organisations were very critical of the present system of privilege - by which the prison governor uses his/her discretion to award clothing grants to successful applicants - especially because it could take a very long time before the clothing needed is purchased and supplied to the lucky applicant. This does not mean that the voluntary organisations want the individuality of personal clothing in women's prisons to be replaced with the impersonal uniforms in male prisons. What the organisations demand is that adequate clothing should be provided, if necessary with the equivalent cost of the uniforms that women are not given, but with arrangement for the clothing to be chosen and thereby personalised by the women themselves.

Conclusion

The tentative conclusion that can be cautiously drawn here is that the problems of black women in prison are more complex than the problems of black men and those of white women. This was evident especially in the difficulties of the foreign nationals who were cut off from language, young babies, diet, skin care materials, clothing, religion, and family. Some of these difficulties were shared by black male prisoners but they were likely to be better educated, to have less need for hair care creams, to be better clothed (although uniforms are far from being adequate clothing, they are better than none) and more independent of babies than the foreign black women in prison.

This conclusion is tentative in the sense that more detailed studies focusing on some of the issues raised by an exploratory study like this one would be able to confirm or modify some of the observations above. The findings presented here do not prove that the criminal justice system in England was racist, sexist, or oppressive to the poor. That was not what this book was designed to accomplish. The purpose of the book was to explore the nature of the problems that faced black women in the criminal justice system.

The problems identified include that of Victimisation-As-Mere-Punishment which was usually initiated by the police and which most likely affected the numbers and proportions of black women in courts and in prisons. The problem of commercialisation of criminal justice also runs through the system and culminates in the deprivation of black women, especially the foreign ones who were expected to buy their own provisions from monopoly shops in prisons. There were also problems of the hierarchicisation of defendants, isolation from children and inadequate support from family, attitudes, cultural differences, language difficulties, personal hygiene, and inadequate legal representation. Most of these problems were probably shared by most defendants and most prisoners, but they combined in peculiar ways (unequal race-class-gender relations) to make the situation of black women qualitatively different.

Throughout this presentation, efforts were made to avoid digressing from the criminal justice system too much. However, digressions are both necessary and desirable in a book of this length. The next chapter will indulge in such a necessary digression by returning to the theory and methods of this book to see to what extent they were reflected or refuted by the evidence provided above. There will also be a broader look at the problems identified above so that no one could get the false impression that they were isolated from other political-economic problems facing poor black women in particular and the poor in general.

6. Summary, Implications and Limitations

Introduction

set out to see to what extent the problems that face black women differ from those that face white women and black men in the criminal justice system. The book attempted to demonstrate the uniqueness of the problems that face black women along with the problems that they share with those who experience the race, class, and or gender relations that affect black women. The uniqueness of how the problem of Victimisation-As-Mere-Punishment, for example, affects black women suggests that attempts to look at black people through studies that focus on black men alone or to talk about women with what is known about only white women are myopic, misleading and inadequate for understanding even black men and white women.

For example, this writer found that many black women were victimised in the criminal justice system by actions that were originally aimed at suspected black men. This finding has not been previously highlighted by researchers probably because they have not focused attention on the articulation of race, class and gender as I have done. It is likely that black men and white women could also be victimised by actions that are aimed at people to whom they are proximate. However, it seems less likely that black men could be victimised as frequently when the black women in their lives are being proceeded against. This is because there are many more black male suspects than female ones and also because the women are seen to be more dependent on the men than otherwise even when the reverse is true such as when the woman provides accommodation to the suspected man.

Similarly, it is likely that white women would be victimised in actions originally aimed at white men (see Hillyard, 1993 for the peculiar case of the Irish). However, the Victimisation-As-Mere-Punishment that affects white women could not be exactly the same as those of black women (through actions that were originally intended for black men) because white women who are associated with black men are historically perceived to be more privileged and independent compared to the more dependent and subordinate relationship assumed to exist between black women and hegemonic masculinity (see Fanon, 1967). The similarities among all forms of victimisation suggest that the decolonisation of victimisation from the empire of punishment will have implications not only for poor black women but also for poor black men and poor white women though the uniqueness of the situation of black women (or any group) demands independent studies as part of the decolonisation process.

Decolonisation is being used here to refer to the relative autonomy of victimisation as an institutional practice that is linked to classical colonialism, neo-colonialism and internal colonialism and, consequently, to emphasise the need to resist recolonisation, as well as to demarginalise and empower the poor who inhabit the neo-colonies and the internal colonies of today. This is why I mphasise the importance of Victimisation-As-Mere-Punishment in my conclusion even though this was not the original focus of the book. What follows now is a general summary of the book, a discussion of the theoretical, methodological and practical implications of the findings, and suggestions for further research in the light of its limitations.

General Summary

Chapter one of this book outlined the methodological and theoretical background to the book . Methodologically, this author attempted to receive rather than to collect data because of ethical and technical reasons (Agozino, 1995a). Ethically, data collection tends to assume the powerlessness of the source while data reception recognises the autonomy of the subjects. Furthermore, technically, has been argued that data collection is almost impossible because of the autonomous agency of the source and so, assumes that the only thing social scientists should and can aspire to is the role of data reception. This means that the methods employed in this book are not new but, by looking at the data processes from a new perspective, this author was able to understand them better and to avoid possible distortions that the assumption of data collection could introduce into the comprehension of data. That is why this book consistently talks about receiving information from various informers rather than talking pretentiously about collecting data.

The practical difference between data reception and data collection has more to do with the politics and practicalities of access to data rather than with belief or disbelief of the researcher concerning the information received or the interpretation of tables. However, data reception may have a remote significance for belief or disbelief in a researcher's data by the reading public. If researchers, like the police, use so-called 'dirty tricks' to 'gather evidence', they could be challenged on two grounds. Firstly, evidence is not out there waiting to be collected with combine harvesters or any 'instrument' like that (as Durkheim's notion of social facts suggests), given that evidence or data is socially constructed by both the researcher and the researched (see McConville, Sanders and Leng (1991) on police investigations). Secondly, if any researcher actually collec ather than receive what is willingly given or offered and recorded, then just as the administration of justice frowns at the admissibility of such 'evidence', the researcher should examine the validity of the data so-collected.

Theoretically, the historical materialist perspective of the articulation of social relations was adopted for this book. That was because of the closeness of this perspective to the theoretical and practical struggles against Victimisation-As-Mere-Punishment to which people with different class, race and gender relations are variously vulnerable. I maintain the traditional Marxist emphasis on class relations while showing how they articulate with gender and race relations to make poor black women uniquely vulnerable to problems in the criminal justice system in particular and society in general.

This perspective is innocent of the outdated charges of economic determinism because articulation presupposes the relative autonomy of race and gender from class relations while underlining their inextricable interconnectedness in theory and practice. The perspective of articulation proved very useful because it provided a framework for the discussion of both how race, gender and class relations operate together in different ways for different categories of people and how the social practices of welfare, punishment and victimisation work together to affect different categories of people in variable ways. In short, this book suggests ways of understanding the articulation, disarticulation and rearticulation of both social relations and social practice, in both social theory and social policy.

The history of how enslavement, colonialism, and neo-colonialism affected the victimisation of black women in particular and black people or women in general was used to demonstrate the forms that Victimisation-As-Mere-Punishment took in different historically specific contexts. The focus on black women allowed this book to show that victimisation which is based on gender also affects poor black men and that similar practices based on race also affect white women but in different ways compared to how they affect black women. The latter encountered victimisation mainly because they happened to be mothers, sisters, wives, or lovers of suspected or convicted black men. The reverse was not the case for black men but it was noted that black men who supported the struggles of black women against victimisation were themselves exposed to victimisation and that black men also experienced the victimisation of black women especially when such acts of victimisation were aimed at the men in the first place.

White women were also victimised when they were closely related to suspected or criminalised black men. It could be that white women who were closely related to suspected white men would also be victimised, like the Irish women who were often assumed to be accomplices in the alleged offences of fathers, sons, lovers, or husbands (Hillyard, 1993). However, I did not investigate this directly and so the only thing to note here is that the Irish case is a special one given the virtual state of war existing in Northern Ireland. What happens to Irish women cannot be accepted as an example of what happens to white women because the Irish were at the receiving end of a racialised and militarised policing that is closer to the colonial experiences of black people.

The limited claim being made in this book is that any victimisation that is based on gender could also affect black men just as those that are based on race could affect white women especially when they share the class relations of the affected black women. Whether based on gender or on race, such victimisation is inevitably articulated, disarticulated and rearticulated with class relations that largely limit the resources available for struggles against victimisation and also maximise the vulnerability of different categories of people to such victimisation. Irrespective of the racial and gender differences between black women, black men and white women, the majority of the victimised happen to be poor. The extent to which this result can be extended to the poor of all races and gender should be left to future research.

Chapter three took off where chapter two ended. Following directly from the history of victimisation under enslavement, colonialism, neo-colonialism, and internal colonialism, chapters three. four and five opened with an attempt to understand similar (though by no means identical) practices and reactions that were still found in the policing, courts and prisons of the internal colonies of England. This made the contemporary cases appear less freaky, and references to similar cases in the US and South Africa helped to make sense of what is found in England. The discussion pointed to the fact that, just as black women and their allies struggled heroically against the manifestations of victimisation in the earlier epochs, the struggle is continuing and becoming more organised and less spontaneous against the sources and manifestations of various forms of victimisation.

Chapter three also showed that victimisation was more obvious at the level of police intervention and it was suggested that, once initiated at that level, it tended to accumulate and compound the problems that faced black women at other levels of the criminal justice process. Accordingly, the discussions of problems facing black women in the courts and in prisons touched more on what we have called Victimisation-In-Punishment than on Victimisation-As-Mere-Punishment. The former is more subtle (in the courts but likely to be deadly in prisons where the victimised were more likely to be found dead than in courts) than the latter and is suggested by the disparities and irregularities that were noted in the construction of the image of black women by officials and the responses of black women to such imagery.

However, Junger (1990) has argued that arrest statistics are less biased against ethnic minorities than court records, implying that there is more discrimination at subsequent stages of the criminal justice process. I am more interested in the form that discrimination takes than in the amount of discrimination at any given stage of the criminal justice system. Junger implicitly agrees with Bowling (1990) that there is discrimination at all levels but tried to defend her use of self-reported criminality to validate police arrest statistics. Bowling questions the validity of the self-report method for measuring "race" and delinquency.

The three major assumptions common in research (that studies of black men can tells us about black women, that studies of white women can tell us all we need to know about black women, and that studies of poor black women can tell us all about every black woman) were not upheld, showing that those researchers who implicitly make such assumptions should explicitly examine whether they are reasonable. I found that right from enslavement through the colonial period to the present, black women have not faced exactly the same problems as black men and white women. This finding is consistent with the historical materialist theory of articulation which suggests that punishment, welfare and victimisation are applied to real people with variable interests and dispositions, not exclusively to protect vested interests or through the application of force alone, but also through a manipulation of conventional morality or ideology. What is important is not whether the contention over conventional morality (especially in the colonial context) supports or condemns the victimisation of black women, but that black women are affected differently mainly because they share the uniquely subtle (and sometimes, blatant), selective and partial manipulation of race, class and gender relations in society.

The rest of this chapter will try to map out the conclusions and practical implications of the results summarised above and also try to point out the limitations of . There are two major conclusions and implications to be discussed below; one relates to the issue of the articulation of social relations and social practice and the decolonisation of victimisation, the other refers to the issue of equality, marginalisation and empowerment. It can be readily seen that different issues are grouped together under these broad conclusions and so, efforts will be made to distinguish among the related issues involved.

Articulation and Decolonisation of Victimisation

Let us return to our theoretical framework and assess its effectiveness. Our thesis statement is that victimisation is not punishment. This sounds simplistic enough but it is necessary to state the difference given the historical tendency for punishment to colonise relatively autonomous processes and reconstruct them as elements of penalty. This conceptual colonisation is most evident in the sociology of law and in criminology where efforts to understand the criminal justice system often focus on what Garland (1990) called, 'The Punishment-Of-Offenders...' This process is called different things that include correction, cure, censure, discipline, just deserts, label, response, repression, rehabilitation, treatment, etc.

Of course, these multiple concepts are not readily interchangeable because they are not synonymous. However, in spite of the ideological, methodological, and practical concerns that divide the various conceptions into rival or conflicting camps, they all seem to be united to the extent that they are all predicts of the subject variously named the offender, criminal, deviant, or delinquent. This book demonstrates that the preoccupation with penalty is both partial and misleading in the study of the criminal justice system. Punishment does not presuppose offence and offence does not guarantee punishment. It is not all those who offend that are punished and it is not all those who are 'punished' that did offend.

Furthermore, those who are punished do not receive only punishment and nothing else. The criminal justice system also has welfare policies that may be effective or ineffective, misguided or inadequate. A similar point was made by Bottoms (1983) according to whom the non-disciplinary part of penal policy is often neglected following the obsession with power and repression in the analysis of the criminal justice system. He suggested that penal policies should be understood as 'bifurcating' into disciplinary and non-disciplinary measures for minor and serious offences, respectively. However, penal policy cannot fork into itself, or into disciplinary and non-disciplinary penalty. It seems that what is forking is criminal justice policy as a whole rather than the specifically disciplinary penal policy of the system. Garland (1985: 236) recognised that penalty works through a 'penal-welfare strategy' by which 'the range of knowledge available to the authorities is extended to encompass not only the offender, but also his family and his home.' However, Garland failed to note that it is more like an articulation of penal-welfare-victimisation strategies and not simply a penal-welfare one. The point, then, is that it appears that what is going on is more than a bifurcation. It is, at least, a 'trifurcation' of criminal justice policy into punishment, welfare, and victimisation.

Incidentally, Kennedy (1976) used 'bifurcation' earlier to talk about the divergence of law into criminal and civil branches but the question being raised in connection with the thesis of Bottoms also applies. Why not represent the commercial, international, family, human rights, mercantile, land and other branches of law as well instead of assuming a simplistic divergence? Milovanovic (1992), similarly, pointed out that bifurcation is also used in chaos theory to describe 'far from equilibrium states' of divergences (instead of a single one) that make up a mechanical system especially in quantum physics. This author asked him during the American Society of Criminology meeting in Chicago, 1996, why the possible options at each point of divergence has to be limited to two as the very word divergence or bifurcation suggests. Is it not possible to have a trifurcation or even a multifurcation at any one point? Milovanovic admitted that the question revealed the inadequacy of applying models developed in the physical sciences to the social science and he admitted that the options are more indeterminate in a social system like the law. Metaphorically speaking, the idea of trifurcation can be found even in physical science where the electric plug, for instance, is designed with three prongs and not only with the more elementary two. A similar analogy that is closer to law is the three-pronged fork carried by the devil and by Britannia alike, representing, perhaps, the welfarist 'good intentions' of both hell and imperialism, their disciplinary or punitive regimes, and their unmistakable mischievousness or victimisation of the innocent. It is this third prong of Victimisation-As-Mere-Punishment (with the suggestive acronym of VAMP) that is ignored by criminologists who focus exclusively on the theory and practice of the Punishment-Of-Offenders (POO).

This is not a new discovery. The victimisation of the innocent has always been present in popular consciousness and the notion is implicit in most radical criminology. The problem here is that when victimisation is recognised as one of the impacts of the criminal justice system, it tends to be over-generalised to the extent that the other aspects of criminal justice would be neglected. However, the concept of Victimisation-As-Mere-Punishment does not assume that all those who are punished are innocent. Rather, it presupposes that victimisation is not always something one individual or group does to another individual or group, but also something that the state does to categories of people in civil society.

If the state can and does commit crimes against society as in the extreme cases of Apartheid and Nazism but also in cases of State terrorism, oppressive dictatorship and authoritarianism, how can the concerned civil society respond to the criminality of the state? Certainly, it is not enough to demand that the head of state should exercise his or her prerogative of mercy by pardoning those who are detained without trial or who are framed and unjustly convicted. It is not sufficient to say that state 'pardon' for the innocent is not enough, such a pardon should be seen as an insult added to the injury of victimisation that demands nothing less than an apology. The payment of compensations would not be regarded as adequate recompense especially because the value is arbitrarily fixed by the offending state and also because the damage done to human rights and democracy through what the Nigerian activist lawyer, Gani Fawehinmi (1993), called 'executive lawlessness' cannot be measured in monetary terms. What is needed above all else is the democratic empowerment of the oppressed to prevent further exercise of Victimisation-As-Mere-Punishment, victimisation-as-care or that of Victimisation-In-Punishment by which the guilty poor receive disproportionate punishment.

By the victimisation of black women (or of any category of people) is meant the 'punishment' inflicted on innocent people sometimes because they were wrongly suspected, stopped, arrested, prosecuted or convicted and sometimes maliciously because of their proximity to suspects and convicts. In the latter case, it may be a deliberate attempt to get at the suspect or the offender through a loved one or it may be a consequence of the operational principle of collective responsibility that apparently continues to inform criminal justice practices.

This is a departure from conventional and 'realist' studies of victimisation in criminology (see Matthew and Young, 1992, for example). Those are concerned with how little the police know about 'real crimes' and how frightened people are about 'violent crimes.' The left realists particularly wish to understand victimisation from the point of view of the 'victim' as a way of taking on board some feminist contributions to methodology. However, the survey method used by conventional and realist victimologists is very unpopular with feminists who argue that it does not capture the depth and complexity of personal experiences well enough.

Moreover, the local crime survey has not been applied by left realists with equal emphasis to all forms of victimisation - particularly victimisation by the state, by corporations and by the powerful. Victimology therefore carries on as if these forms of victimisation are not problematic enough to be taken seriously. This 'culture of silence' on crimes of the state, as Cohen (1993) puts it, does not mean that there is complete silence on the matter among victimologists, many of who are beginning to address such issues more critically. However, the almost exclusive focus on crimes of the underclass and the working class by self-professed left realists may seem to have nothing to do with the victimisation of people by the criminal justice system, but by repeatedly showing that the majority of crimes are unknown to the police, they indirectly apply the heat to the police for higher clearance rates that could result in the use of dirty tricks on poor 'victims' of criminal justice.

The belief that there are dark figures in official statistics of crime, true as it may be, tends to conceal the fact that there are 'dazzling' (or fictitious) figures as well in those same statistics. The problem with official statistics is not just that they are incomplete but also that they are superfluous. It is not all the crimes known to the police that turn out to be crimes in the end: some innocent people are convicted and later cleared and there are non-criminal populations in prisons beside the large number of inmates who are just awaiting trial and those who continue to protest their innocence. It is true that crimes would still be crimes even if they remain unsolved and even if the innocent suspect is released or acquitted and so what is emphasising is not that some crimes are fictitious but that it is not all those who are

163

suspected, convicted or imprisoned that are criminals. Those who talk only about the Punishment-Of-Offenders (POO) give the false impression that only criminals get 'punished'.

Official statistics have therefore been used in this book for the purpose for which they were provided in the first place. According to McClintock (1974), these figures are provided, often following questions in parliament, for the purpose of political accountability (inadequate as statistics may be for this purpose) rather than because of the positivistic quest for the causes of criminality nor for the secrets of its predictability. Smith (1994) argued similarly that the criminal justice system should always be analysed as if it is subject to the 1976 Race Relations Act even though it is not. Such statistical records are often discussed under the 'monitoring' of ethnicity or sex in the criminal justice system (see NACRO, 1989, for instance). Such reports are then used in electoral campaigns to present one or the other of the political parties as the party that is soft on crime or the law-and-order party. Left realists believe that the ability of Thatcherism to cling to power drew partially from the claim that the Labour Party was soft on crime and soft on criminals. It is partly for this reason that the left realists attempt to take crime seriously and to go beyond the impossibilism that nothing works and make recommendations for the next Labour government (Young, 1986). Tony Blair adopted left-realism in this sense by claiming that only Labour takes crime and the causes of crime seriously.

However, while the left realists campaign against the ideology of impossiblism in social policy, they try to sustain their own impossiblist belief - namely, that it is impossible to study and understand crime control without studying and understanding what causes crime. This author has attempted to study the politics of crime control without also searching for what causes crime and, though difficult, it has not proved to be impossible. The concern of the left realists with recommendations for the next labour government also reflects another impossiblism, that is, the belief that the victimised cannot do much about their victimisation. As Garland (1985: 126) argued, this is a widespread practice in criminal justice research where researchers interested in reforms direct their recommendations to the state because, 'Offenders only exist as such in and through the institution of the state, with the consequence that private proposals to alter or extend or mitigate the treatment of offenders must be addressed to the state.'

This is misleading in two ways. First, it is not only offenders who are caught up in the criminal justice system and so research into the system is not only about offenders but also about the victimised. Secondly, there is no reason why every recommendation 'must be addressed to the state' since the realm of the state is recognisably a contested realm where the practical struggles of people can and do produce significant changes. will therefore make its recommendations to the people who are active in the struggles against these problems not just because such people can do something about the problematic institutions and situations but also because the State has a large pool of recommendations from previous researchers to act upon.

The theoretical approach of victimology is not unprecedented. Crime is conventionally defined in criminology as the action or omission of an individual against the state. The courts dramatise the conflict as Crown vs. X. But the crimes of the state against the society are merely misrepresented as human rights violations that are addressed more like civil wrongs than like criminal acts. Such violations are often not listed in official crime statistics and therefore tend not to be seen as crimes. The concept of Victimisation-As-Mere-Punishment suggests that the state commits crimes against society just as individuals commit crimes against the state. However, while the individual may plead guilty to crimes against the state,

> The state will never look for the causes of social imperfection in the state and social institutions themselves .... In so far as the state admits the existence of social evils it attributes them to natural laws against which no human power can prevail, or to private life which is independent of the state or to the inadequacies of the administration which is subordinate to it (Marx, 1961: 221-22).

The state can afford to play this game of self-righteousness not only because the state traditionally commands consent and allegiance by appearing to care for all as an authoritarian populist (see Hall, 1979, 1988; Poulantzas, 1982) but also because the modern state insists on exercising a monopoly of coercion or institutional violence against dissenters, subversives, non-conformists, and the relatively powerless.

This is accomplished, not through force alone and not without force at all, but also through what Gramsci (1971: 57) analysed as the mechanism of class hegemony - the 'intellectual and moral leadership' of a class or the 'entire complex of practical and theoretical activities with which the ruling class not only justifies and maintains its dominance, but manages to win the consent of those over whom it rules' (Gramsci, 1971: 244). The approach of this book required a trans-legal conceptualisation of crime to include the crimes of the state, of the criminal to include the criminal state, and of 'victims' to include the 'victims' of criminal justice much along the lines advocated by Schwendinger and Schwendinger (1970) and more powerfully by Cohen (1993).

Paul Tappan (1977: 266-67) implicitly rejected the approach of the Schwedingers and Cohen in his critique of the elasticity of the concept of white collar crime. According to him, criminology is a 'science' and therefore it needs 'reasonably accurate descriptive information, it cannot tolerate a nomenclature of such loose and variable usage' as white collar crime. Crime must remain what the criminal law says it is. Tappan believes that, 'The rebel may enjoy a veritable orgy of delight in damning as criminal most anyone he pleases; .... The result may be fine indoctrination or catharsis achieved through blustering broadsides against the "existing system". It is not criminology. It is not social science.' So it is not only what is crime that is determined by the limits of the existing law; social science must also not go beyond the criminal code.

If it is accepted that oppressive social systems like slavery, Nazism and Apartheid, though well-grounded in law, organise crimes against the oppressed, then criminologists would be blindfolding themselves if they study only police records and criminal codes without also exploring how the people perceive crimes of the state and how they judge and punish these crimes through popular action. The contribution of Julia and Herman Schwendinger and that of Stan Cohen in this direction is that they argued convincingly that violations of human rights, though not listed as such under the criminal code, satisfy the legal, moral and scientific criteria for criminality and should therefore be treated as such. Similarly, the concept of Victimisation-As-Mere-Punishment suggests that even without going beyond the criminal code, criminologists should be able to go beyond the conventional picture of the offender and the 'victim' to recognise the offences of the state and the 'victims' of punishment. The rebel label which Tappan applied to theories of white collar criminality does not detract from the social scientific quality of the variable ways in which people understand the reality of oppression as crime (Agozino, 1995d).

This approach is not new; it is implicit in classical Marxism and in most critical legal studies. Naffine (1990: 150), for example, specifically talks about the gender and class based 'victims of the machineries of law' and Rodney (1975) listed 'the extension of political repression and victimisation' as one of the seven key elements that combine in various ways to reproduce petty bourgeois rule in the English-speaking Caribbean countries - an observation that could have been generalised from his earlier study of How Europe Underdeveloped Africa (Rodney, 1972). By applying this formulation to the study of black women, we have effectively extended the views of Turk (1976) beyond his narrow conflict perspective on the 'haves' and the 'have nots' and emphasised that the approach which denies the saintly innocence of the state assumes that the creation, operation, and alteration of legal institutions that affect black women reflect the mobilisation of resources by the state, black women and their allies. This does not mean that the state is invincible nor does it mean that the state is diametrically opposed to black women without any common interest.

Moreover, this approach does not mean that a majority of the black women convicted by the criminal justice system are innocent (as Pitch, 1995, accused certain unnamed 'critical criminologists' of suggesting that the criminal is a victim of both societal conditions and that of the criminal justice system itself), nor that the state commits as many crimes against black women as the latter commit against the former. We are not even saying that criminal justice officials need to violate the rules and conventions of fairness in order to victimise black women. What is implied here is that the criminal justice system is loaded in favour of the state and so playing by its discretionary rules alone would ensure that the state will continue to victimise black women with impunity.

This lends itself to easy misinterpretation by anarchists who regard absolute individualism as the essence of freedom and believe that every form of authority or force is potentially oppressive. It is not the case that every instance of punishment is victimisation and what are conceptualised in this book as Victimisation-As-Mere-Punishment, Victimisation-In-Punishment, Victimisation-As-Welfare and the struggles against these, do not necessarily result in anarchistic political tendencies whereby everyone regards everyone else as a criminal or reconstructs every aspect of punishment to be victimisation.

This book demonstrates that the social relations of class, race, and gender are articulated, disarticulated, and rearticulated in the targeting of people for victimisation by the criminal justice system as Hall (1988: 10) implied. This means that a black woman who is very rich could have her gender and race relations relatively disarticulated by her class relations in the sense that she would be less likely to be victimised by the criminal justice system since she would not be found in the symbolic locations and colonial ghettos where black people are more often targeted. Similarly, a poor woman who is not black could have her class relations relatively disarticulated by her race relations in a racist society because she would be less likely to be victimised than a black woman especially when a black man was the initial target. Moreover, a black man who is poor would have his race relations relatively disarticulated by his gender relations in the sense that he would be less likely to be the victim of attacks initially aimed at black women.

In the rearticulation of these social relations, class relations tend to occupy a central position, contrary to the assumption of Hall (1988) that race, class, gender, ideology, and culture all occupy central positions. The centrality of class relations in the process of victimisation will become clearer once we remember that in spite of gender, racial, and circumstantial differences that separate people in the criminal justice system, what unites the majority of the 'victims' and the convicts is their abject poverty or their unflinching commitment to the poor (in the cases of middle class people who are victimised for speaking out or campaigning against the oppression of the poor under dictatorial or populist authoritarian regimes). This explains why poor white men join popular protests initiated by black people, if only for the opportunity to loot some of the good things they see but cannot buy from shops. The rich white people who support the struggles of black people are most likely to be those who support the struggles of the working class. Furthermore, the black people who oppose the political struggles of black people are likely to be rich and out of touch with the conditions under which black people live. This means that class relations should be given a central position in the organisation of the defence and empowerment of the victimised in modern society.

This is in line with the choice of the Marxist frame of reference for this book. This approach has been applied to the study of black women without assuming that all black women belong to the working class but for the purpose of emphasising the exploitative and conflictual nature of sexism and racism. As Campbell (1985: 1) observes, 'Race consciousness remains an integral part of the class consciousness of African peoples as long as Euro-American culture seeks to harmonise the economic and political domination of black peoples with attempts at destroying their cultural personality.' Similarly, bell hooks (1984), Angela Davis (1981) and others have demonstrated that class consciousness is articulated with the race and gender consciousness of black women.

Campbell, hooks and Davis do not imply that all Europeans identify with the ruling class or that all black women identify with the working class. In other words, the impacts of racist domination on black people also vary with the impact of racist ideologies on the consciousness of people who share different classes, races, sexes and nationalities. Such consciousness is not just a matter of individual or group attitudes but also a manifestation of the concrete conditions of existence and institutionalised ways of doing things.

What is offered here in the analysis of race, gender and class in the problems that face people in the criminal justice system is an extension of the focus beyond race or gender (as separate relations) and the integration of the analysis of the three relations at once. By so doing, we have been able to understand that the relative victimisation of black women in the criminal justice system is based on their vulnerability due to their marginalised positions in these social relations. Although all women share a specific gender relation, rich women share a different class relation, and black women share a different racial relation. All these relations are articulated to weaken the ability of poor black women to defend themselves socially as individuals, hence they more readily form groups for self-defence or for mutual support.

This book recognises that as a result of patriarchy or the almost universal dominance of men over women, even poor men can oppress poor women under the ideology of masculinity. The same cannot be said for rich women who may be insulted by rich men but who may be relatively immune to oppression due to their power resources and who may oppress poor men and poor women. What this means is that this book emphasises concrete economic and political equality of opportunities between men and women while also considering problems of class, racial and gender oppression and how the decolonisation of victimisation could help to end all forms of oppression.

Equality, Marginalisation and Empowerment

Equality usually conjures up the opposite concept of discrimination. The former is often dismissed as an illusion that conceals subjugation of different forms and degrees. The latter is sometimes welcomed as something that could be of benefit, when it is said to be 'positive discrimination.' The approach in this book is to regard all forms of discrimination as negative, so long as they contribute to the further marginalisation of the marginalised. Those practices that are known as positive discrimination are now better known as 'affirmative action.' They are policies and 'programmes that take positive steps to redress the balance where minority groups are disfavoured' (Giddens, 1989: 262) by making a clear distinction (not discrimination) between their chances and those of the privileged.

This clarification of discrimination to mean unfair or arbitrary treatment of the disadvantaged throws a little light on the conception of equality that informs this book. Unlike those who regard equality as 'sameness' (Edwards, 1989; Mackinnon, 1987; Malik, 1996), we take the view that equality does not preclude (but in fact, presumes) heterogeneity. Of course, one thing is not equal or unequal to itself but to another thing. Equality as sameness mistakenly suspects those who agitate for equality for women, workers and black people of wanting to treat them in the same way as men, employers, and white people, respectively. Equality that is not related to the need to end oppression, marginalisation and exploitation is both abstract and metaphysical in the sense that it assumes that there is a single essence called equality that is forever elusive (hooks, 1984).

However, by relating the politics of equality to the need to end racism, sexism and class exploitation, it is clear that when one person asks for a cup of tea, another for a cup of coffee, and another for a glass of water or nothing, and each one gets what he or she needs, each has been served equally even though they were not served the same thing. It would be discriminatory for anyone to say that no one should drink coffee because his or her father died of a related addiction. It would be discriminatory to sell the limited available cups of tea to the highest bidder when clearly some of the people who need it are almost broke. It is possible to treat individuals differently but still equally on the basis of their subjective and objective needs for freedom from exploitation, deprivation, marginalisation and oppression.

Malik (1996) concludes his interesting history of The Meaning of Race with the view that it is necessary to go beyond 'race' in order to achieve equality and emancipation. He warns against moving from the 'Right to be Equal' to the 'Right to be Different' because the latter would always imply a hierarchy between core and periphery. During 'The Week' conference of Living Marxism in 1996, this author reminded him that the politics of difference has always been at the core of all successful emancipatory movements of whatever ideological persuasion. Every successful revolutionary movement in history or even in social and scientific thought has started by recognising difference and by attempting to make a difference. It is precisely on this point that Engels (1975) differentiated between utopian socialism with its phoney universal brotherhood of man from scientific socialism with its principled recognition of class divisions, gender divisions and racial divisions.

The task of the critical thinker is not to simply proclaim that we are all the same but to seek ways of mobilising the different constituencies that are working for emancipation and thereby maximise their collective efforts. Otherwise, the activists who overemphasise sameness will always be suspected of undemocratically calling on the autonomous organisations on the ground to disband and join the sole Party of Universal Humanism as a pre-condition for emancipation. Malik's answer was that the question was a tactical and not a theoretical one, whereas he was concerned with the misuse of multi-culturalism as a guise for exclusion, marginalisation and inequality (which is even more tactical). Marable (1994) reached a different conclusion while calling on us to move Beyond Black and White. To him, multi-culturalism is far from being reactionary. In the US, at least, it is about the struggle for equality without erasure based on objective and subjective needs of groups that have been traditionally excluded and ignored by the right-wing and left-wing critics of multi-culturalism especially in politicised academia.

Both the subjective and the objective requirements of the need to end oppression and exploitation are emphasised here (following hooks, 1984) to distinguish genuine needs from the selfish desire for domination and also to underscore the political nature of its pursuit. Who determines what is an objective need and whose desire is labelled selfish or universalised? These are questions which suggest that equality is not an event that occurs at any specific point in time or an object that is given out as a gift, but a contested principle of political and legal practices forever formed and transformed.

Earlier researchers have made a lot of recommendations to governments and state agencies on how to solve the problems of marginalisation in society. It can therefore be presumed that policy makers have enough recommendations to implement and so, as we have already noted, directs its recommendations to the marginalised themselves.

It can be inferred from the discussions in this book that a major reason why black women face peculiar problems in the criminal justice system is that they are the underdogs of the underdogs. On the gender hierarchy, they belong to the underdog group of women. Moreover, within this group, they are the underdogs of the underdogs on the basis of race. This race-gender hierarchy is not absolute for, as Higginbotham (1978) shows, black women were once ranked above black men but still below white women. Moreover,

James (1980) has used the Race Registration Act of South Africa to ridicule the conflicting and contradictory ranking of black people according to the lightness of their blackness.

What these hierarchies suggest is that all those who are marginalised, not only black women, must be empowered through a continuous struggle for social justice, an end to racism, sexism and class exploitation and an equal guarantee of human rights. The theoretical perspective of articulation implies that there should be no absolute specificity and it requires that the struggle in one country or class-race-gender sector should be sensitive or aligned to struggles in other sectors because the sectoral problems of race, gender, class, and nationality are closely linked.

However, the decolonisation of victimisation (meaning an end to the marginalisation, exploitation, and oppression in the criminal justice system and in society on which victimisation is based) must come to terms with the fact of internal colonialism at the institutional level of punishment and also at the levels of political space (Agozino, 1996b). The former is like the internal colonialism of Habermas (1987) who used it to describe the juridification or colonisation of economic power in particular and the life world in general by juridical power that is in turn colonised by economic power through the 'monetization' of criminal justice administration. At the level of political space, we have gone beyond the internal colonialism of Hecter (1983) which emphasises intra-national exploitation of culturally distinct categories.

To decolonise victimisation, we need to go beyond the conceptual liberation of victimisation from the constructed clutches of care and punishment. Also, we need to go beyond the Hecterian intra-national dynamics of exploitation, as Campbell (1991) has demonstrated with the 'globalisation of apartheid'. To decolonise victimisation, we also need to follow Fanon (1963) and address the international, if not global, perpetuation and extension of socio-economic exploitation and domination in spite of the gaining of formal independence. Wilmot (1986) did exactly this when he analysed 'the universality of repressed self-consciousness' and linked this to 'the schizophrenic state ... of the being of the colonized' which Fanon identified. The limitation here is that Wilmot retained the masculinist language of Fanon whereas, following Freire (1972), who now regrets the androcentric language of this earlier work, hooks (1993b: 147) insists that an international perspective on decolonisation is essential

Because the colonising forces are so powerful in this white supremacist capitalist patriarchy it seems that black people are always having to renew a commitment to a decolonizing political process that should be fundamental to our lives and is not. And so Freire's work, in its global understanding of liberation struggles, always emphasizes that this is the important initial stage of transformation - that historical moment when one begins to think critically about the self and identity in relation to one's political circumstances.

However, when internationalised and even at its institutional and intra-national levels, the struggle for decolonisation is no longer simply the 'black struggle' if it has ever been so. The struggle involves and has always involved people who are black and people who are not. The important thing to note is the need to relate the struggle for decolonisation and against recolonisation to the concrete political and economic circumstances of the people engaged in the struggle as well as to the cultural politics of the people. This means that the decolonisation process cannot afford to turn a blind eye to a cultural, political and economic problem like narcotic drugs because this is the single offence for which black women are very frequently imprisoned.

In an address to a criminology conference in London, Gilroy (1991) called for the black community to embark on serious campaigns against drug abuse and drug trafficking, but he did not suggest how this could be done without further criminalising the marginalised, impoverishing the impoverished and disempowering the relatively powerless, thereby perpetuating what he had earlier called 'The Myth of Black Criminality' (Gilroy, 1987b). Though a very outspoken critic of left realism, his call for the black community to take the drug 'crisis' seriously could be said to be a very good influence on critical criminology by left realism, but it is more likely to be evidence of the claim by Scraton (1990) that the self-professed left realists exaggerate their differences with critical criminologists whose positions cannot be realistically dismissed as idealism. However, a critical response to this problem would not focus exclusively on the poor black youth as the left realists tend to do in an ahistorical manner that ignores the dialectics of imperialism (Sim, et al, 1987).

Gilroy knew that his call was controversial and so he requested that his audience should question him on the matter but no one did. The comment this author had wanted to make on the matter is that Gilroy failed to mention that popular black artists had already gone beyond Dillinger's satirical and consumerist spelling of New York with 'a knife, a fork, a bottle and a cork', with the refrain, 'I got cocaine running around my brain' - implying that the cocaine culture of New York was so damaging that addicts no longer knew how to spell the name of their own city. The revolutionary poet, Mutabaruka (1989), avoided the ambiguity of satire and chanted directly:

> johnny used to satisfy with just smokin
> till some foreigner come and say
> man you're jokin
> a know smoking will get u high
> but that still wont make u reach the sky

i'm gonna give u a thing
that will make u sing
and everywhere you go people will swing

suh johnny stop smoke
im start sniff coke
im teck it for a joke

drug kulcha takin ova de place
yuh know dis is a damn disgrace
drug kulcha takin over de place
youth your life is gonna go to waste

With this story of how the drug culture is taking over the place, Mutabaruka provides an example of a principled pedagogy of the oppressed in which support for the campaign against drug abuse is politically selective and challenging. The selective approach prevents what Campbell (1985: 107-109) called the dilemma of 'outlawing a popular custom.' Campbell analysed the history of the initial regular importation of ganja by British plantation owners from India for sale to indentured Indian labourers in the Caribbean. This was gradually adopted among the African people who saw the parallel between it and the kola nuts that their ancestors brought from West Africa. However, because a majority of the people who adopted ganja as a popular culture were poor Rasta and working class people who were understandably rebellious, it was easy to criminalise the drug even though scientists have since proved that 'alcohol is 1000 times more lethal than marijuana' (Goode, 1973, 1993). The example of the politicisation of marijuana is given here in some detail to illustrate the point that the struggle for decolonisation could tackle problems of common interest to the people as well as to the state and still retain an independent agenda, success for which depends mainly on the organisational ability of the people.

Mutabaruka's poem continues the tradition of artists like the self-styled 'Bush Doctor', Peter Tosh, who called for marijuana to be legalised because 'judges smoke it' and because it is a safer alternative to cigarette-smoking which is a hazard to health. It is paradoxical that Rasta people who are stereotyped as drug-crazed people are actually at the front-line of the campaign against addictive drugs. So black people are already campaigning against the drug culture and the call by Gilroy should serve to promote such a campaign rather than to launch it. However, the anti-drugs campaign by black people, as Mutabaruka demonstrates, has its own agenda that is fundamentally subversive of official definitions of dangerousness.

The United States Drug Enforcement Agency (USDEA) defined marijuana as a dangerous threat and launched 'Operation Buccaneer' against ganja planters in Jamaica with the support of the Labour Party government in the 1970s (Campbell, 1985). However, the popularity of ganja all over the world coupled with the scientific evidence that it is still the safest known drug (Goode, 1973, 1993) guaranteed a huge income for the drugs barons who employed poor black women and men as vulnerable couriers who frequently got arrested and thrown into jail. A convicted black man who was on a day release to attend a conference on Drug Couriers, London, 26 March 1992 argued that the campaign against drug trafficking would be more successful if accompanied by a campaign for the legalisation of marijuana because the majority of convictions involve cannabis through which a lot of poor people can make an honest living.

Home Office figures show that between 1979 and 1989, the number of all drugs offenders rose from 16,056 to 52,131. Of these, cannabis offenders were 14,116 in 1979 and rose steadily to 23,592 (compared to a total of 28,560 for all drugs offender) in 1984. The figures for cannabis offenders dramatically shot up to 44,920 in 1989 (*H.O.S.B.*, 24/90, 'Statistics of the misuse of drugs: seizures and offenders dealt with, United Kingdom 1989', 6 September 1990). What is obvious but unstated by the Home Office is that such massive increases are not simply indicative of increased offending but evidence of the law and order policies of Thatcherism that strongly emphasised the 'war on drugs' as a key part of its electoral politics of crime control. The huge increases in the arrests for cannabis could give the misleading impression that this is a very serious crime whereas cannabis is not among category A drugs that the authorities perceive as the greatest threat, hence many of the arrests for possessing cannabis are dealt with by a caution rather than a charge. On the contrary, the arrest figures for cannabis suggest that the drug is part of a popular culture that the authorities wish to repress even though there is no reported case of cannabis users being hospitalised or treated for addiction since cannabis is non addictive (Goode, 1993). Further evidence of politicisation is the 1994 Crime and Public Order Act which increased the fine for the possession of cannabis from £500 to £2,500 (*New Statesman & Society*, 24 June 1994).

The relative safety of the drug and relative ease of growing the plant in any climate would provide alternative employment for millions of people who could be forced into drug trafficking for economic reasons. According to Green (1991: 43),

> Drug couriers do not conform to the ungrounded imagery which vilifies them in the public mind. The research profile suggests a reality of Third World poverty and despair, of men and women generally naive about drugs and the First World's war against them, of men and women whose offence was not motivated by greed but by familial concerns and economic deprivation.

Drug offenders may be naive about hard drugs but they appear knowledgeable about the even more severe war being waged by the Third World against drugs just as they seem to know that marijuana is relatively safe and very popular. Far from being generally naive, many of the convicts happen to be what Green called 'educated destitutes'.

According to Campbell (1985: 168) 'the ganja traders paid EC$1,000 per pound of the weed while the State paid only 6 cents per pound for bananas.' Although the traders organise violence to protect their monopoly trade and run cartels that involve highly placed agents of the state, they would not want to see marijuana legalised. This is because legalisation would remove their comfortable monopoly since ganja could be easily planted and grown with two harvests per year unlike most other crops. The end products could be easily patented, colourfully packaged and competitively marketed by big business with enormous value-added tax by the state.

This means that the selling price to the consumer would still be too high for some people and the products could carry health warnings like cigarettes which are more harmful than marijuana (Goode, 1993). However, it is likely that legalisation would considerably reduce the price of marijuana and this would make ganja more competitive against more dangerous drugs that are equally more expensive. This suggests that some poor youth who could be driven to crime to finance their fix could turn their backs on the expensive and more dangerous drugs and grow their own marijuana or buy some at more or less the same price as cigarettes and thereby help throw the gun-running drug barons out of business.

At the same time, the price of what the reggae band, Culture, calls 'the international herb' will likely be cheap enough to make the cultivation of food crops equally attractive to farmers who could justifiably abandon bananas to grow cash crops for drug barons. The call by Gilroy for the black community to take the drug problem seriously has already been taken up by popular black artists in a way radically different from the intimidating approach of Black Muslims in the USA where drug peddlers could be displaced from one estate to another. Also unsuitable is the individualist example of Tai Solarin, the non-alcoholic Nigerian social critic who confronted the colonial authorities with a bottle of 'illiticised' local gin and demanded to be arrested in open challenge to a law that he saw as a design for the protection of the monopoly of British distillers. Such heroic individualism is inappropriate in the principled campaign against the drug culture because collective action would be more effective.

The cultural activists who campaign for the legalisation of marijuana as part of the campaign against hard drugs could be said to be acting as what Becker (1963) called 'moral entrepreneurs' whose strong interest in the matter makes them take it upon themselves to persuade the public that the legalisation of marijuana is for the general good of those who take it and those who do not. However, the tag of moral entrepreneurship seems inappropriate here because many of the supporters for legalisation have nothing to gain from it.

For example, the black US Surgeon General, Jocelyn Elders told a conference on 8 December 1994 that the government should seriously study the experience of countries that decriminalised drugs and thereby reduced drug addiction and violent crimes. This prophetic statement cost her the job as President Clinton, who allegedly smoked but did not inhale, dismissed the messenger with the message even though all available evidence indicates that the war on drugs was yet, 'another lost war' (Chambliss, 1995: 101).

That the war is lost was partially conceded by the black man known as President Clinton's 'drug czar', Lee Brown, former New York and Houston Police Chief (Cockburn, 1993). Brown's rhetoric is said to give the impression that the government had declared the war on drugs over and moved on to rehabilitation whereas the reality remained that simple possession was still increasingly being punished with imprisonment. Lee Brown was continuing the two agendas from the new right and the new left. Congressman Charles Rangel for Harlem called legalisation 'the moral equivalent of genocide of black people'. This agrees with Mr Clinton's favoured option of increased enforcement and Mr Brown underlined this option when he echoed the Nixon-Carter-Reagan-Bush-Clinton promises of increased military aid for tackling drugs trafficking at source, that is, waging the war abroad.

It is up to sufficiently large segments of influential and respected opinion in the black community in particular and the intellectual community at large to support the publicity provided by the popular artists to neutralise the objections of those whose authoritarian interests are threatened by the legalisation of marijuana. When the Liberal Party Congress of 1994 voted in support of the legalisation of marijuana, the party leader, Paddy Ashdown, took the unprecedented step of distancing himself from that decision. Similarly, when Claire Short, a member of the Labour Party executive, made a similar call in 1995, she was forced to withdraw the statement by leaders of the opposition. Even when Paul Boateng made the mild call for 'a national strategy against drug trafficking' during debates on the 1994 Drug Trafficking Bill, he was interrupted with shouts of 'churlish' soon denied by Sir Ivan Lawrence. In response to Boateng, the Solicitor General accused him of not paying attention to 'the national drug strategy which the government have pursued for a long time.' Boateng emphasised that the existing strategy was not adequate and that it was not targeted at drug trafficking specifically but at drugs as a whole (*Hansard*, Vol. 248, 1993-94, Oct. 17 - Nov. 3). So, according to Labour, the Tories are not being tough enough on crime, a concern that Labour (1964) saw as a 'concern for us all'.

Janet Paraskeva, a magistrate and director of the official National Youth Agency, recently told a Home Office sponsored London Drug Policy Forum that it is a waste of time and resources to ask the police to pick up young people who had little quantities of marijuana. According to her, 500,000 people had been prosecuted for cannabis use in the past 25 years and yet there is no marijuana user among the 28,000 registered drug addicts. She concluded her address by pleading as follows; 'Let's at least discuss separating cannabis from hard drug use; let's separate its source of access .... The removal of criminal status from cannabis would hardly affect the numbers of young people using. Most young people use it because they enjoy it, not because it is against the law.' She received a louder ovation from the audience of drug workers, local authority representatives and police officers than Mr Tony Newton, Leader of the House of Commons, who said that the government had no intention of decriminalising or legalising any drugs (*The Guardian*, Saturday, 25 March 1995). The existing policy is reflected in the 1995 Criminal Justice and Public Order Act which increased the fine for possession of cannabis from £500 to £2,500.

The existing national strategy is clearly a strategy of all-out 'war' on drugs. This includes the provision of military equipment and training for foreign governments to assist them in their own 'war' on drugs. However, the fact that every new administration re-launches this 'war' suggests that there is no victory in sight for the warriors. A radical alternative was proposed more than twenty years ago by urging the US to spend a fraction of its military aid to dictators on compensating peasant farmers who cultivate the raw materials for narcotics and also buying up and burning the existing supplies. The US responded by providing more military equipment and instructors to the Burmese dictators simply because those who made the proposal were guerrillas fighting what the aide to president Jimmy Carter called the 'legitimate government' of Burma (*Channel 4*, 'The Opium Convoys, Saturday, 6 July 1996).

However, a series of reports implicating CIA agents in organised supply of crack cocaine to inner-city black and poor communities in the US as part of the clandestine operation to raise money for arms with which to support Nicaraguan Contra rebels under presidents Ronald Reagan and George Bush were being investigated by the CIA at the time of writing this book. In the People's Weekly World, 21 September 1996, Tim Wheeler reported that there was widespread protest against fresh evidence in the San Jose Mercury News linking the CIA with the smuggling of tons of cocaine into Los Angeles in the 1980s. The $50 million annual profit from that smuggling was allegedly used 'to bankroll the CIA's mercenary army which murdered 45,000 or more Nicaraguans during the eight-year Contra war.' A week later, the same reporter wrote in the same medium that Celerino Castillo III, a former agent of the Drug Enforcement Administration, revealed that he saw the CIA operatives load planes with drugs bound for the US while he was stationed at the Ilopango Air Force Base, El Salvador, in 1986. When he reported the traffic to his superiors, he was told that his career would end if he stepped on 'a White House operation.' When some activists went to the DEA headquarters to demand that the files mentioned by Castillo be investigated, they were arrested and charged with 'impeding traffic'. Apparently, the Senate Committee on Foreign Relations report 'Drugs, Law Enforcement and Foreign Policy', 12/88, indicated that Oliver North, who was in charge of the Ilopango Air Force Base operation, had noted in his personal diary that he was told about the drug smuggling, including the type of aircraft used and the route. He testified that he passed the information to the DEA but DEA officials said that they had no such evidence. If these allegations prove to be true, they will only confirm the belief of many people that the hypocritical war on drugs has a hidden agenda that is aimed against the poor in favour of the rich and powerful drugs barons.

The political economy of the war on drugs is summarised by Cockburn (1993) as follows:

> The career of the DEA tells the whole story. Back when the 'war on drugs' began, in the late 1960s, there were two federal agencies enforcing the drug laws on a total budget of less than $10 million. Today there are 54, including the DEA, National Security Army, Internal Revenue Service, Defence Intelligence Agency, Bureau of Alcohol, Tobacco and Firearms, State department, Customs, Coast Guard, Army, Navy, Air Force, Marines; and the overall budget is $13 billion of which more than $100 million goes to the DEA alone.

If the agencies could spend so much to tackle any trade, it is inconceivable that such a trade would continue to thrive without any collusion by the officials themselves. In this connection, it is important that the hegemonic ideology must be made more responsive to the needs of the poor in its structure, purpose and operation. This cannot be achieved without the marginalised groups being given equal access to participation in and, more importantly, control of the apparatuses of hegemony. The struggle against social injustice continues but all marginalised groups must make conscious efforts to acquire the necessary knowledge and contest for the right to control the machinery of justice.

This is not unrealistic, although the idea of hegemony has come to represent a forceful prevention of the empowerment of the groups of people under domination. As Terry Eagleton (1995: 27) pointed out:

> The word 'hegemony' nowadays means something like dominance or supremacy. But in the annals of Marxism it has a more exact meaning which stretches back far beyond the work of its most celebrated theorist, Antonio Gramsci. The concept of hegemony first springs to light in a series of debates within the

Second International over the question of leadership within the revolutionary movement itself - of how the proletariat is to rally other oppressed groups and classes to its standard, or how it is to set the pace for the forces of bourgeois democracy. Since such alliances are obviously not to be achieved by coercion, the idea of hegemony begins life as the very opposite of the repressive power which it sometimes suggests today. It is rather about the way in which the working class can win political authority over other radical movements, unifying them into a revolutionary bloc. The originality of Gramsci, then, is to have boldly transferred this concept to the question of the ruling class, and the means by which it secures its power.

It follows from this that the struggle for emancipation is not anti-hegemonic but counter-hegemonic. It is reasonable to expect more marginalised individuals and groups to struggle and gain access into the legal professions, the academia, the media, the legislature and even criminal justice services. This will enable them to exert pressure from outside and from within for better training on, and monitoring of, gender, race, class, and nationality issues in the criminal justice system and in society as a whole.

News reports suggest that more marginalised people are leaving the criminal justice service than are joining it due to frustration and discrimination. However, it is not enough to complain that the system is discriminatory; the marginalised people must see the struggle for participation in the operation and control of the system as a necessary part of the struggle to overcome the material basis of marginalisation that is reflected in, and constituted by, the law and other hegemonic institutions.

Hawkins and Thomas (1991) traced the history of 'white policing of black populations' in America and concluded that black political power has significantly impacted on previously white-dominated police departments. Such impacts were criticised as being too limited and being bought at too high a cost by Cashmore (1991: 101) but even Cashmore acknowledged that 'black representation at senior levels has had some practical consequences' such as '...general decline in allegations of police brutality; further increase in ethnic minority recruitment; lower crime all round ...; and either a continuance of "softer" community-oriented policy or a change towards it.'

Black men and women who join the criminal justice services may have to cope with the double jeopardy of being regarded as sell-outs by sections of the black community and being racially abused and discriminated against by colleagues but the alternatives of an all-white or non-black criminal justice system in particular and state power structure in general are too frightening to contemplate. However, it is not enough to campaign for more black people to join the criminal justice personnel without also demanding that

179

more opportunities for black journalists, scholars, parliamentarians, lawyers and judges should be guaranteed. To limit the chances that such officers and professionals would sell out on the black community, they should be unionised and kept in touch with black community organisations without exposing the latter to repressive surveillance from the former.

Conclusion: Lessons for Future Research

This author hopes to learn from the limitations of in order to improve on future attempts to understand the articulation of race, class and gender in practical or theoretical problems and the struggles to overcome such problems. The major limitation of this book is the deliberate exclusion of white men and men and women of other ethnic minorities from the discussion. This was not an oversight but a convenient strategy to narrow the discussion down within the acceptable limits. While the experiences of those excluded can be inferred from parts of this book, there is the need for a more definitive study that will carry the comparisons to their necessary bounds.

Another limitation is that the fieldwork did not concentrate exclusively on black women who have individually experienced the criminal justice system and, therefore, it was not possible to directly measure the attitudes of black women. Although certain references to existing publications and some information from individuals and organisations indicate the influence of attitudes, an empirical study is required to make this clearer.

This book could be said to have a misleading title. It is called 'Black Women and the Criminal Justice System' and yet it is epigraphed with the greetings of a black brother to his brothers and sisters. Perhaps a better title would be black people and the criminal justice system. Such a title will seem to reflect the fact that the book is considerably about black men as well. However, the original title was retained because it reflects the goals and methods of better. It is true that this book is not exclusively on black women, whatever the title may suggest. However, neither is it exclusively on black people as the alternative title would suggest. The brothers and sisters that Rodney (1981) was hailing in his last public address were of all racial groups.

The focus on black women more effectively captures the articulation of race, class and gender. The class element is not visible in the title unlike the race and gender elements but the analysis emphasised the importance of class. The emphasis on the struggles by black women also appears misleading because many of the organisations mentioned here were not struggling in the revolutionary sense that Rodney implied. They were more exactly support agencies that were highly vulnerable to co-optation by the state (Kelly and Radford, 1987) but the fact that they were there for the affected women to contact is a very welcome development (Scraton and

Chadwick, 1987; Pitch, 1995). The emphasis on struggles of resistance is consistent with Rodney's acknowledgement that the struggle is not the prerogative of any one group. As he put it, 'We feel more confident because of the demonstrated ability and capacity of the people as a whole.'

Another possible critique is that claims to be couched on the historical materialist theoretical perspective of articulation and yet it is not a mode-of-production analysis. The book could even be said to be idealist and not materialist because a lot of the analysis concerns the interpretation of imagery, symbolism and appearances. However, the interpretations offered can be said to remain within the chosen perspective because appearances are interpreted here in the 'strong sense' in which Marx always used the term (see Hall, et al, 1978: 198). In this sense, what is apparent is not necessarily illusory, false, or fantastic. Rather, it refers to the representation of a complex social formation demonstrating that 'there is no necessary identity or correspondence between the effects a relation produces at its different levels' (ibid). This is why tried to point out what the different results appear to be saying rather than overstating the case by making absolute claims.

It is not for this author to judge whether his claim to commitment in this book is objective enough or whether his attempt to be objective is committed enough. He made his value-position obvious from the beginning and he has tried not to conceal opposing value-positions in an approach that he has called committed objectivity or objective commitment (Agozino, 1993, 1995a). He is aware that evidence of disparities in the problems facing black women, black men and white women may not be adequate proof of discrimination. This is why he has been cautious to claim that these findings merely suggest the forms that discrimination could take. This is consistent with some of the conclusions of Hudson (1989), Gordon and Shallice (1990) and Hood (1992).

Finally, this book was not out to prove anything in particular nor to discover any fundamental truth about black women and the criminal justice system, but simply attempted to reach a better understanding of the problems constituted for the former by the latter. This author does not claim to have understood the problems completely since understanding is an infinite process that grows or diminishes in line with concrete conditions in the struggle for social transformation and deeper knowledge.

Bibliography

ABDULAI, N. ed., (1994) *Genocide in Rwanda: Background and Current Situation*, London, Africa Research and Information Bureau.

ADEBAYO, A., (1985) *White Men in Black Skin*, Ibadan, Spectrum.

AFIGBO, A. E. (1972) The Warrant Chiefs, London, Longman.

AGOZINO, B. (1991) 'Victimisation As Punishment' in *African Concord*, 6, 7, June.

AGOZINO, B. (1993) *'Committed Objectivity in Social Research'*, *TeleTimes* International, May.

AGOZINO, B. (1995a) 'Methodological Issues in Feminist Research', in *Quantity & Quality: International Journal of Methodology*. Vol. 29, No.3, pp287-298.

AGOZINO, B. (1995b) 'Matigari's Gender, Labour and Law in Africa' in *Africa World Review*, May-September, London, 1995, pp13-16.

AGOZINO, B. (1995c) 'The Social Construction of Deviance, Psychiatry, Gender & Race in a Feminist Performance' in *The Journal of Contemporary Health*, Number 3, Winter, pp61-67.

AGOZINO, B. (1995d) 'Radical Criminology in African Literature' in *International Sociology: Journal of the International Sociological Association*, Vol. 10, No.3, pp315-329, September.

AGOZINO, B. (1996a) 'Football and the Civilising Process: Penal Discourse and the Ethic of Collective Responsibility in Sports Law' in the Law and Popular Culture special issue of *the International Journal of the Sociology of Law*. Vol.24, No.2, June. pp163-188.

AGOZINO, B. (1996b) 'The Third Debt to the Third World: The Politics of Law and Order in Camp de Thiaroye' in *Third Text*, 36, Autumn, pp3-13.

AGOZINO, B. (1996c) 'The Victimisation of Black Women, Slavery, Colonialism and the Globalisation of the Judicial Process', a paper presented to the meeting of the American Society of Criminology, Chicago, November.

AGOZINO, B. (1996d) 'Transformations in the Social Construction of Crime among Immigrants in the United Kingdom', solicited excerpts in *Trends in Organized Crime*, Winter, Vol. 2, No. 2, pp80-81.

AGOZINO, B. (1996/97) 'The African Charter and Executive Lawlessness' in *Africa World Review*, September 1996 - March 1997.

AGOZINO, B. (1997) 'Is Chivalry Colour-Blind? Race and Gender Discrimination in the Criminal Justice System' *in International Journal of Discrimination and the Law*, Vol.2, No.3, 199-216.

AHIRE, P.T. (1991) *Imperial Policing: the Emergence and Role of the Police in Colonial Nigeria 1860-1960*, Milton Keynes, Open University.

AIDOO, A.A. (1992) *An Angry Letter in January*, Coventry, Dangaroo.

ALLEN, H. (1987a) 'Rendering them Harmless: The Professional Portrayal of Women Charged with Serious Violent Crimes.' In Carlen P. and Worrall, A. eds, *Gender, Crime and Justice*. Milton Keynes, Open University.

ALLEN, H. (1987b) *Justice Unbalanced*, Milton Keynes, Open University.

ALLENDE, I. (1991) *The Stories of Eva Luna*, London, Quality Paperbacks Direct.

AMNESTY INTERNATIONAL (1992) *Women on the Frontline*, London, A.I.

ATTOE, S. D. (1988) 'Aspects of Colonial Experience in Biase Land' in S.O. Jaja, et al, eds, *Women in Development*, Calabar, Media Women.

BALDWIN, J. and McCONVILLE, S. (1982) 'The Influence of Race on Sentencing in England' in *Criminal Law Review*, 652-658.

BECKER, H.S. (1963) *Outsiders: Studies in the Sociology of Deviance*, New York, The Free Press.

BELL, Jr., D.A. (1973) *Race, Racism and American Law*, Boston, Little, Brown and Company.

BENALLEGUE, N. (1983) 'Algerian Women in the Struggle for Independence and Reconstruction' in *International Social Science Journal*, Vol. 35.

BILBY, K. and STEADY, F. C. (1981) 'Black Women and Survival: A Maroon Case' in F. C. Steady, ed, *Infra*.

BOTTOMS, A.E. (1967) 'Delinquency amongst Immigrants' in *Race*, VIII, 4.

BOTTOMS, A.E. (1983) 'Neglected Features of Contemporary Penal Systems' in D. Garland and P. Young, eds, *The Power to Punish: Contemporary Penality and Social Analysis*, London, Heinemann.

BOWLING, B. (1990) 'Conceptual and methodological problems in measuring "race" differences in delinquency: a reply to Marianne Junger', *British Journal of Criminology*, 30, 4.

BOX, S. (1983) *Power, Crime, and Mystification*, London, Tavistock.

BRAKE, M. and HALE, C. (1992) *Public Order and Private Lives: The Politics of Law and Order*, London, Routledge.

BROGDEN, M. and SHEARING, C. (1993) *Policing for a New South Africa*, London, Routledge.

BRYAN, B., DADZIE, S. and SCAFE, S. (1985) *The Heart of The Race*, London, Virago.

BUJURA, J. M. (1982) 'Women "Entrepreneurs" of Early Nairobi' in C. Sumner, ed, Crime, *Justice and Underdevelopment*, London, Heinemann.

CABRAL, A. (1972) *Return to Source*, New York, Monthly Review Press.

CAIN, M. (1990) 'Towards Transgressions: New Directions in Feminist Criminology' in *International Journal of the Sociology of Law* 18.

CALLAWAY, H. (1987) *Gender, Culture and Empire*. London, Macmillan.

CAMPBELL, H. (1985) *Rasta and Resistance: From Marcus Garvey to Walter Rodney*, London, Hansib.

CAMPBELL, H. (1991) 'Africans and the "New World Order": Democracy or the Globalisation of Apartheid?' An Address to the Holdane Society of Socialist Lawyers Conference, London.

CARLEN, P. (1976) *Magistrates' Justice*, London, Martin Robertson.

CARLEN, P. (1983) *Women's Imprisonment*, London, Routledge & Kegan Paul.

CARLEN, P. (1988) *Women, Crime and Poverty*. Milton Keynes, Open University.

CARLEN, P. (1992) 'Women's Criminal Careers' in D. Downes, ed., *Unravelling Criminal Justice*, London, Macmillan.

CASHMORE, E. (1991) 'Black Cops Inc.' in E. Cashmore and E. McLaughlin, eds, Supra.

CASHMORE, E. and McLAUGHLIN, E. (1991) 'Out of Order?' in E. Cashmore and E. McLaughlin, eds, *Out of Order? Policing Black People*, London, Routledge & Kegan Paul.

CHAMBLISS, W.J. (1995) 'Another Lost War: The Costs and Consequences of Drug Prohibition' in *Social Justice*, Vol. 22, No. 2, pp 101-124.

CHENEY, D. (1993) *Into the Dark Tunnel: Foreign Prisoners in the British Prison System*, London, PRT.

CHIGWADA, R. (1989) 'Black Women's Experiences of Prison Education.' *Gender and Education*, 1, 2.

CHIGWADA, R. (1991) 'Policing of Black Women' in E. Cashmore and E. McClaughlin, eds, Supra.

CIIR (1988) *Cries of Freedom: Women in Detention in South Africa*, London, CIIR. (originally published as *A Woman's Place is in the Struggle, not Behind Bars* by DPS/Descom, Johannesburg, 1988).

CLIFFORD, W. (1974) *An Introduction to African Criminology*, Nairobi, Oxford.

CLUTTERBUCK, R. (1995) *Drugs, Crime and Corruption: Thinking the Unthinkable*, London, Macmillan.

COCKBURN, A. (1993) 'America Kisses its grass goodbye' in *New Stateman & Society*, 12 November.

COHEN, S. (1972) *Folk Devils and Moral Panics*, London, MacGibbon & Kee.

COHEN, S. (1985) *Visions of Social Control*, Cambridge, Polity Press.

COHEN, S. (1993) 'Human Rights and Crimes of the State: The Culture of Denial' in *Aust. & NZ Journal of Criminology*, 26.

COOK, D., and HUDSON, B., eds, (1993) *Racism and Criminology*, London, Sage.

COOPER, C., et al, eds, (1990) *Race Relations Survey 1989/90*, Johannesburg, S.A. Institute of Race Relations.

CRE, Commission For Racial Equality (1989) *Racial Justice in Magistrate Courts*, London, CRE.

CRENSHAW, K. (1991) 'Demarginalizing the Intersection of Race and Sex: A Black Feminist Critique of Antidiscrimination Doctrine, Feminist Theory, and Antiracist Politics' in K.T. Bartlett and R. Kennedy, eds, *Feminist Legal Theory: Readings in Law and Gender*, Boulder, Westview Press.

CROW, I. and COVE, J. (1984) 'Ethnic Minorities and the Courts', *Criminal Law Review*.

DALY, K. (1987) 'Structure and Practice of Familial-Based Justice in a Criminal Court.' *Law and Society Review*, 21,2.

DALY, K. (1993) 'Class-Race-Gender: Sloganeering in Search of Meaning' in *Social Justice*, 20, 1-2.

DAVIS, A. (1974) *An Autobiography*. New York, Random House.

DAVIS, A. (1981) *Women, Race and Class*. London, The Women's Press.

DILL, B.T. (1987) 'The Dialectics of Black Womanhood' in S. Harding, ed., *Feminism and Methodology*. Milton Keynes, Open University.

DITCHFIELD, J., and AUSTIN, C., (1986) *Grievance Procedures in Prisons: a study of prisoner's applications and petitions*, London, HMSO.

DORN, N., SOUTH, N., and MURGI, K. (1992) *Traffickers: Drug Markets and Law Enforcement*, London, Routledge.

DUNN, J and FAHY, T.A. (1987) 'Police admissions to a psychiatric hospital: demographic and clinical differences between ethnic groups' in *British Journal of Psychiatry*. 156.

DURKHEIM, E. (1973) 'Two Laws of Penal Evolution', *Economy and Society*, 2, 3.

DURKHEIM, E. (1982) *The Rules of Sociological Method and Selected Texts on Sociology and its Method*, S. Lukes, ed., W.D. Halls, trans., London, Macmillan.

EAGLETON, T. (1995) *Heathcliff and the Great Hunger: Studies in Irish Culture*, London, Verso.

EATON, M. (1987) 'The Question of Bail on Behalf of Men and Women', in Carlen and Worrall, eds, *Supra*.

EATON, M. (1993) *Women After Prison*, Buckingham, Open University.

ECHENBERG, M. (1991), *Colonial Conscripts: The Tirailleurs Senegalais in French West Africa*, 1857-1960. London, Heinemann.

EDWARDS, A.R. (1989) 'Sex/Gender, Sexism and Criminal Justice: Some Theoretical Considerations', *IJSL*, 17.

ENGELS, F. (1975) *Socialism: Utopian and Scientific*, Peking, Foreign Languages Press.

ERICSON, R.V., BARANEK, P.M. and CHAN, B.L. (1989), *Negotiating Control*. Milton Keynes, Open University.

FANON, F. (1963) *The Wretched of the Earth*, Middlesex, Penguin.

FANON, F. (1965) *A Dying Colonialism*, trans. H. Chevalier, Monthly Press, New York.

FANON, F. (1967) *Black Skin, White Masks*, New York, Monthly Review Press.

FARRINGTON, D. and MORRIS, A. (1983) 'Sex, Sentencing and Reconviction.' *British Journal of Criminology*. 23, 3.

FAULKNER, A. (1989) 'Women and Section 136 of the Mental Health Act 1983' in C. Dunhill, ed., The Boys in Blue. London, Virago.

FAWEHINMI, G. (1993) 'Human Rights are Non-Negotiable', *Nigeria Now*, Vol. 2, No. 6, June.

FITZGERALD, M. (1993) *The Royal Commission on Criminal Justice: Ethnic Minorities and the Criminal Justice System*, London, HMSO.

FITZGERALD, M. and MARSHALL, P. (1996) 'Ethnic Minorities in British Prisons: Some Research Implications' in R. Matthews and P. Francis, eds, *Prison 2000: An International Perspective on Current State and Future of Imprisonment*, London, Macmillan.

FITZPATRICK, P. (1995) *Nationalism, Racism and the Rule of Law*, Aldershot, Dartmouth.

FOUCAULT, M. (1977) *Discipline and Punish: the Birth of the Prison*, London, Allen Lane.

FREIRE, P. (1972) *Pedagogy of the Oppressed*, Harmondsworth, Penguin.

FRENCH, L. (1981) 'The Incarcerated Black Female ...' in F. C. Steady, ed., Infra.

GARLAND, D. (1985) *Punishment and Welfare: a History of Penal Strategies*, Aldershot, Gower.

GARLAND, D. (1990) *Punishment and Modern Society: a Study in Social Theory*, Oxford, Clarendon.

GELSTHORPE, L. (1986) 'Towards a Skeptical Look at Sexism.' *International Journal of the Sociology of Law*, 14.

GENDERS, E., PLAYER, E., with JOHNSTON, V. (1989) *Race Relations in Prisons*, Oxford, Clarendon.

GIDDENS, A. (1989) *Sociology*, Cambridge, Polity.

GIDDENS, A. (1996) 'There is a Radical Centre-Ground' *in New Statesman*, 29 November.

GILL, P. (1994) *Policing Politics: Security Intelligence and the Liberal Democratic State*, London, Frank Cass.

GILLIGAN, C. (1982) *In a Different Voice*. London, Harvard.

GILROY, P and SIM, J. (1987) 'Law, Order and the State of the Left' in P. Scraton, ed., *Law and Order and the Authoritarian State*, Milton Keynes, Open University.

GILROY, P. (1987a) *There Ain't No Black in the Union Jack*, London, Hutchinson.

GILROY, P. (1987b) 'The Myth of Black Criminality' in P. Scraton, ed., *Law, Order and the Authoritarian State*, Milton Keynes, OUP.

GILROY, P. (1990) 'The End of Anti-Racism' in *New Community*. 17, 1.

GILROY, P. (1991) 'The Politics of Race and the Criminal Justice System', address to 'Criminology Into the 1990s Conference' on Women and Ethnic Minorities and the Criminal Justice System, London, 29th May.

GILROY, P. (1993) *The Black Atlantic*, London, Verso.

GOFFMAN, E. (1979) *Gender Advertisements*, London, Macmillan.

GOODE, E. (1973) 'Major Drugs of Abuse Among Youths and Young Adults' in E. Harmis, ed., *Drugs and Youth: the Challenge of Today*, New York, Pergamon.

GOODE, E. (1993) *Drugs in American Society*, New York, McGraw-Hill.

GORDON, P. (1992) 'The Racialization of Statistics' in R. Skellington and P. Morris, eds, *'Race' in Britain Today*, London, Sage.

GORDON, P. AND SHALLICE, A. (1990) *Black People, White Justice?* London, Runnymede Trust.

GRAMSCI, A. (1971), *Selections From the Prison Notebooks*, London, Lawrence and Wishart.

GREELEY, R.A. (1992) 'Image, Text and the Female Body: Rene Magritte and the Surrealist Publications' in *The Oxford Art Journal* 15:2.

GREEN, P. ed., (1996) *Drug Couriers*, London, Howard League.

GREEN, P. (1991) *Drug Couriers*, London, The Howard League for Penal Reform.

GREEN, P., MILLS, C., and READ, T. (1994) 'The Characteristics and Sentencing of Illegal Drug Importers' in *British Journal of Criminology*, Vol. 34, No. 4, pp 479-486.

GREGORY, J. (1987) *Sex, Race and the Law*. London, Sage.

HABERMAS, J. (1987) *The Theory of Communicative Action*, Volume 2. Lifeworld and System: A Critique of Functionalist Reason. Cambridge, Polity.

HACKING, I. (1991) 'How Should We do the History of Statistics?' in G. Burchel, C. Gordon and P. Miller, eds, *The Foucault Effect. London*, Harvester.

HALL, R.E. (1985) *Ask Any Woman*. Bristol, Falling Walls.

HALL, S. (1979) *Drifting into a Law and Order Society*, London, Coben Trust.

HALL, S. (1980a) 'Race, Articulation and Societies Structured in Dominance' in UNESCO, ed., *Sociological Theories: Race and Colonialism*. Paris, Unesco.

HALL, S. (1980b) 'Encoding/Decoding' in S. Hall, et al, eds, *Culture, Media and Language*, London Hutchinson.

HALL, S. (1987) 'Urban Unrest in Britain' in J. Benyon and J. Solomos, eds, *The Roots of Urban Unrest*, Oxford, Pergamon.

HALL, S. (1988) *The Hard Road to Renewal*. London, Verso.

HALL, S. (1996) *Critical Dialogues in Cultural Studies*, London, Routledge.

HALL, S., CRITCHER, C., JEFFERSON, T., CLARKE, J. and ROBERTS, B. (1978) *Policing The Crisis*. London, Macmillan.

HARRIS, R. (1992), *Crime Criminal Justice and the Probation Service*, London, Tavistock/Routledge.

HASTEDT, G. (1991) *Controlling Intelligence*, London, Frank Cass.

HAWKINS, H. and THOMAS, R. (1991) 'White policing of black populations: a history of race and social control in America' in E. Cashmore and E. McLaughlin, eds, *Supra*.

HEADLEY, B. D. (1983) '"Black on Black" Crime ...' *Crime and Social Justice*, Number 20.

HECTER, M. (1975) *Internal Colonialism: The Celtic Fringe in British National Development 1536-1966*, Beverly Hills, University of California Press.

HECTER, M. (1983) 'Internal Colonialism Revisited' in D. Drakakis-Smith and S.W. Williams, eds, *Internal Colonialism: Essays Around a Theme*, Edinburgh, Department of Geography.

HEIDENSOHN, F. (1985) *Women and Crime*, Basingstoke, Macmillan.

HEIDENSOHN, F. (1986) 'Models of Justice: Portia or Persephone?' *International Journal of the Sociology of Law*. 14.

HIGGINBOTTAM, A.L., Jr., (1978) *In The Matter of Color: Race and the American Legal Process*, New York, Oxford University Press.

HILLYARD, P. (1993) *Suspect Community: People's Experience of the Prevention of Terrorism Acts in Britain*, London, Pluto.

HINE, D. C. and WITTENSTEIN, K. (1981) 'Female Slave Resistance: The Economics of Sex' in F. C. Steady, ed., *Infra*.

HOOD, R. with GORDOVIL, G. (1992) *Race and Sentencing: A Study in the Crown Court*, Oxford, Clarendon.

hOOKS, b. (1981) *Aint I a Woman*. London, Pluto.

hOOKS, b. (1984) *Feminist Theory: From Margin to Center*, Boston, South End Press.

hOOKS, b. (1993a) *Yearning: race, gender, and cultural politics*, London, Turnaround.

hOOKS, b. (1993b) 'bell hooks Speaking About Paulo Freire - The Man, His Work' in P. McLaren and P. Lepnard, eds, *Paulo Freire: A Critical Encounter*, London, Routledge.

hOOKS, b. (1994) *Outlaw Culture: Resisting Representations*, London, Routledge.

HUDSON, B. (1987) *Justice Through Punishment*, London, Macmillan.

HUDSON, B. (1989) 'Discrimination and Disparity: The Influence of Race on Sentencing.' *New Community*, 16, 1.

IRR, Institute of Race Relations (1987) *Policing Against Black People*. London, IRR.

ISIKALU, N. (1988) 'The Revolt and Civil Liberties of Women.' in S. Jaja et al, eds., *supra*.

JACOBS, S. (1983) 'Women and Land Resettlement in Zimbabwe' in *Review of African Political Economy*, 27/28.

JAMES, C.L.R. (1980) *The Black Jacobins: Toussaint L'Ouverture and the San Domingo Revolution*, London, Allison and Busby.

JAMES, S.M. and BUSIA, A.P.A., eds, (1993) *Theorizing Black Feminisms: the visionary pragmatism of black women*, London, Routledge.

JEFFERSON, T. (1990) *The Case Against Paramilitary Policing*, Milton Keynes, Open University Press.

JEFFERSON, T. (1991) 'Discrimination, disadvantage and police work', in E. Cashmore and E. McLaughlin, eds, *Out of Order? Policing Black People*, London, Routledge.

JEFFERSON, T. (1992) 'The racism of criminalisation: policing and the reproduction of the criminal other', in L. Gelsthorpe, ed., *Cropwood Roundtable on Ethnic Minority Groups and the Criminal Justice System* Cambridge, Institute of Criminology.

JEFFERSON, T. and WALKER, M. A. (1992) 'Ethnic Minorities in the Criminal Justice System' in *Criminal Law Review*, February.

JEWSIEWICKI, B. (1991) 'Painting in Zaire: From the Invention of the West to the Representation of the Social Self' in S. Vogler and I. Ebong, eds, *Africa Explores: 20th Century African Art*, New York, The Centre for African Art.

JOHNSON, C. (1982) 'Grass Roots Organizing: Women in Anticolonial Activity in Southwestern Nigeria', *African Studies Review*, 25/2-3.

JOSHUA, H., WALLACE, T. and BOOTH, H. (1983) *To Ride the Storm: the 1980 Bristol 'Riot' and the State*, London, Heinemann.

JUNGER, M. (1990) 'Studying ethnic minorities in relation to crime and police discrimination: answer to Bowling', *British Journal of Criminology*, 30, 4.

JUPP, V. (1989) *Methods of Criminological Research*, London, Unwin Hyman.

KEITH, M. (1993) *Race, Riots and Policing: Lore and Disorder in a Multi-racist Society*, London, UCL.

KELLY, L. and RADFORD, J. (1987) 'The Problem of Men: Feminist Perspectives on Sexual Violence' in P. Scraton, ed., *Law, Order and the Authoritarian State*, Milton Keynes, Open University.

KENNEDY, H. (1992) *Eve Was Framed*, London, Vintage.

KENNEDY, M.C. (1976) 'Beyond Incrimination: Some Neglected Facets of the Theory of Punishment' in W.J. Chambliss and M. Mankoff, eds, *Whose Law What Order?*, London, John Wiley & Sons.

KINSEY, R., LEA, J., and YOUNG, J., (1989) *Losing the Fight Against Crime*, Oxford, Basil Blackwell.

KITSUSE, J.I. and CICOUREL, A.V. (1963) 'A note on the use of official statistics' in *Social Problems*, vol. 2, pp 328-38.

KUPER, L. (1965) *An African Bourgeoisie*, London, Yale U.P.

LABOUR PARTY (1964) *Crime: A Challenge to Us All*, London, Labour.

LACEY, N. (1988) *State Punishment: Political Principles and Community Values*, London, Routledge.

LANDAU, S. F. and NATHAN, G. (1983) 'Selecting Delinquents for Cautioning in the London Metropolitan Area.' *B.J.C.* 23, 2.

LARDNER, J.A. (1987) 'Introduction to Tomorrow's Tomorrow: The Black Woman.' in Harding, ed., *Supra*.

LEA, J. (1992) 'The analysis of crime' in J. Young and R. Matthews, eds, *Infra*.

LEA, J. and YOUNG, J. (1984) *What is to be Done about Law and Order?* Middlesex, Penguin.

LENG, R., McCONVILLE, M., and SANDERS, A. (1992) 'Researching the Discretions to Charge and to Prosecute' in D. Downes, ed., *Unravelling Criminal Justice*, London, Macmillan.

LETUKA, P., MAMASHELA, M.P., MOCHOCHOKO, P., MOHALE, M., and MBATHA, L. (1991) *Women and Law in Southern Africa Research Project*, Harare, WLSA.

LUGARD, F.J.D. (1965) *Dual Mandate in British Tropical Africa*, London, Cass.

LUMUMBA, P. (1962) *Congo My Country*, Tr. G. Heath, London, Pall Mall.

MAcCORMICK, N. (1981) 'Adam Smith on Law' in *Valparaiso University Law Review*, 15, 2.

MACEWEN, M. (1991) *Housing, Race and Law: The British Experience*, London, Routledge.

MACK, B.B. (1992) 'Women and Slavery in Nineteenth-Century Hausaland' in *Slavery & Abolition*, 13, 1.

MACKINNON, C.A. (1987) 'Feminism, Marxism, Method, and the State: Towards Feminist Jurisprudence' in S. Harding, ed., *supra*.

MACKINNON, C.A. (1989) *Towards a Feminist Theory of the State*, London, Harvard University Press.

MADEN, A., SWINTON, M., and GUNN, J. (1992) 'The Ethnic Origin of Women Serving A Prison Sentence' in *British Journal of Criminology*, vol. 32, No. 2.

MAIR, G. (1986) 'Ethnic Minorities and the Magistrates' Courts', *British Journal of Criminology*, 23.

MAIR, G. and BROCKINGTON, N. (1988) 'Female Offenders and the Probation Service', *The Howard Journal*, 27, 2.

MALIK, K. (1996) *The Meaning of Race: Race, History and Culture in Western Society*, London, Macmillan.

MAMA, A. (1989a) 'Imprisoned in Exile' in *African Woman*, Journal of Akina Mama Wa Africa, Spring.

MAMA, A. (1989b) *The Hidden Struggle*, London, London Housing and Race Research Unit.

MAMDANI, M. (1983) *Imperialism and Fascism in Uganda*, London, Heinemann.

MANDELA, W. (1984) *Part of My Soul* in A. Benjamin, ed., M. Benson, Middlesex, Penguin.

MARABLE, M. (1994) *Beyond Black and White*, London, Verso.

MARS, M. (1985) 'Prison and Education', Paper at conference on Black Women In Prisons, London, Black Female Prisoners Scheme.

MARX, K. (1961) *Selected Writings on Sociology and Social Philosophy*, T. Bottomore and M. Rubel, eds, London, Penguin.

MARX, K. (1981) *Capital, Vol. Three*, Middlesex, Penguin/NLR.

MATHIESEN, T. (1983) 'The Future of Control Systems - the Case of Norway' in D. Garland and P. Young, eds, *The Power to Punish*, London, Heinemann.

MATTHEWS, R. and YOUNG, J. (1992) *Issues in Realist Criminology*, London, Sage.

MBA, N. E. (1982) *Nigerian Women Mobilized*, Berkeley, California University Press.

MBILINYI, M. (1988) 'Runaway Wives in Colonial Tanganyika ...' *International Journal of the Sociology of Law*, 16.

191

McCLINTOCK, F.H. (1963) *Crimes of Violence*, London, Macmillan.

McCLINTOCK, F.H. (1974) 'Facts and Myths about the State of Crime' in R. Hood, ed., Crime, *Criminology and Public Policy*, London, Heinemann.

McCONVILLE, M. and BALDWIN, J. (1982) 'The Influence of Race on Sentencing in England', *Criminal Law Review*, October.

McCONVILLE, M. and SHEPHERD, D. (1992) *Watching Police, Watching Communities*, London, Routledge.

McCONVILLE, M., SANDERS, A., and LENG, R. (1991) *The Case for the Prosecution*, London, Routledge.

MEEK, C.K. (1955) 'Igbo Law' in J. D. Jennings, et al, ed., *Readings in Anthropology*, New York, McGraw-Hill.

MEMMI, A. (1990) *The Colonizer and the Colonized*, H. Greenfeld, trans., London, Earthscan.

MERCER, K. and JULIEN, I. (1988) 'Race, Sexual Politics and Black Masculinity: A Dossier' in R. Chapman and J. Rutherford, eds, *Male Order*, London, Lawrence & Wishart.

MIDGLEY, C. (1992) *Women Against Slavery: the British Campaigns*, 1780-1870, London, Routledge.

MILOVANOVIC, D. (1992) *Postmodern Law and Disorder: Psychoanalytic Semiotics*, Chaos and Juridic Exegeses, Liverpool, Deborah Charles.

MORRIS, A. (1987) *Women, Crime and Criminal Justice*, Oxford, Basil Blackwell.

MORRIS, A. (1988) 'Sex and Sentencing.' *Criminal Law Review*, 163-71.

MORRISON, T. (1992) *Jazz: a Novel*, London, Chatto & Windus.

MUTABARUKA (1989) *Any Which Way ... Freedom*, Newton, Shanachie Records.

NAANEN, B.B.B. (1991) 'Itinerant Gold Mines': Prostitution in the Cross River Basin of Nigeria, 1930-1950' *in African Studies Review*, 34, 2.

NACRO (1992) *Criminal Justice Digest*, London, NACRO.

NACRO (1988) 'Some Facts and Findings About Black People in the Criminal Justice System,' *Briefing*, June.

NACRO (1989) *Race and Criminal Justice*, London, NACRO.

NACRO (1991) 'The Resettlement Needs of Women and the Lessons of NACRO'S Women Prisoners' Resource Centre', Mimeograph.

NAFFINE, N. (1990) *Law and the Sexes: Explorations in Feminist Jurisprudence*, Sydney, Allen & Unwin.

NDEM, E.B.E. (1988) 'Women in Constitutional Development' in Jaja, et al eds., *Supra*.

NKRUMAH, K. (1968) *Neo-Colonialism: The Last Stage of Imperialism*, London, Heinemann.

NORRIS, C., FIELDING, N., KEMP, C., and FIELDING, J. (1992) 'Black and blue: an analysis of the influence of race on being stopped by the police' in *British Journal of Sociology*, vol. 43, No. 2.

O'DOWD, L. (1990) 'New Introduction' to Memmi, supra.

O'DWYER, J., WILSON, J. and CARLEN, P. (1987) 'Women's imprisonment in England, Wales and Scotland: recurring issues' in P. Carlen and A. Worrall, eds, *Gender, Crime and Justice*, Milton Keynes, Open University.

OAU (1981) *African Charter on Human and Peoples' Rights*, Nairobi, OAU.

OLORUNTIMEHIN, O. (1981) 'A Preliminary Study of Female Criminality in Nigeria.' in F. Adler, ed., *The Incidence of Female Criminality in the Contemporary World*, New York, New York U. P.

PADEL, U. and STEVENSON, P. (1988) *Insiders: Women's Experience of Prisons*, London, Virago.

PAREKH, B. (1987) 'Preface' to J.W. Shaw, P.G. Nordie and R.M. Shapiro, eds, *Strategies for Improving Race Relations*, Manchester, Manchester University Press.

PASHUKANIS, E.B. (1989) *Law and Marxism: a General Theory*, London, Pluto Press.

PCA, Police Complaints Authority (1991) *Annual Report 1990*, London, HMSO.

PITCH, T. (1995) *Limited Responsibilities: Social Movements & Criminal Justice*, J. Lea, trans., London, Routledge.

POULANTZAS, N. (1982) 'Law' in P. Beirne and R. Quinney, eds, *Marxism and Law*, New York, John Wiley & Sons.

PRISON REFORM TRUST (1996) *Women in Prison: Recent Trends and Developments*, London, PRT.

PRYCE, K. (1979) *Endless Pressure: A Study of West Indian Life-Style in Bristol*, Harmondsworth, Penguin.

REINER, R. (1992) 'Race, crime and justice: models of interpretation', in L. Gelsthorpe, ed., *Cropwood Roundtable on Ethnic Minority Groups and the Criminal Justice System* Cambridge, Institute of Criminology.

REX, J. (1987) 'Life in the ghetto' in J. Benyon and J. Solomos, eds., *The Roots of Urban Unrest*, Oxford, Pergamon.

RFSC, ROACH FAMILY SUPPORT COMMITTEE (1989) *Policing in Hackney 1945-1984*, London, Karia/RFSC.

RICE, M. (1990) 'Challenging Orthodoxies in Feminist Theory: A Black Feminist Intervention.' in L. Gelsthorpe and A. Morris, eds, *Feminist Perspectives in Criminology*. Milton Keynes, Open University.

RICHARDS, A.J. (1950) 'Some Types of Family Structure Amongst the Central Bantu.' In A.R. Radcliffe-Brown, et al, eds, *African Systems of Kinship and Marriage*, Oxford, Oxford U.P.

ROBERTS, J. A, QC (1991) 'Black People and the Legal Profession', address at the 'Criminology into the 1990s conference' on Women and Ethnic Minorities and the Criminal Justice System, London, 29th May.

ROBERTS, Y. (1989) 'To the Slaughter' in *New Statesman & Society*, 13 Oct.

RODNEY, W. (1969) *The Groundings With My Brothers*. London, Bogle-L'Overture.

RODNEY, W. (1970) *A History of the Upper Guinea Coast, 1545-1800*, Oxford, Clarendon.

RODNEY, W. (1972) *How Europe Underdeveloped Africa*. London, Bogle-L'Ouverture.

RODNEY, W. (1975) 'Contemporary Trends in the English-Speaking Caribbean' in *Black Scholar*, Vol. 7, No. 1.

RODNEY, W. (1981) *Sign of the Times*, London, W.P.A. Support Group (UK).

RUDÈ, G. (1978) *Protest and Punishment: The Story of the Social and Political Protesters Transported to Australia 1788-1868*, Oxford, Clarendon.

RUGGIERO, V. (1992) 'Realist Criminology: a Critique' in J. Young and R. Matthews, ed., *Infra*

RUGGIERO, V., and SOUTH, N. (1995) *Eurodrugs: drug use, markets and trafficking in Europe*, London, UCL.

RUSCHE, G. and KIRCHHEIMER, O. (1968, c1939), *Punishment and Social Structure*, New York, Russell & Russell.

SAID, E. (1993) *Culture and Imperialism*, London, Chatto and Windus.

SCHWENDINGER, H. and J. (1970) 'Defenders of Order or Guardians of Human Rights?' in *Issues in Criminology*, 5.

SCRATON, P. (1990) 'Scientific Knowledge or Masculine Discourse? Challenging Patriarchy in Criminology' in L.Gelsthorpe and A. Morris, eds, *Feminist Perspectives in Criminology*, Milton Keynes, Open University.

SCRATON, P. and CHADWICK, K. (1987) 'Speaking ill of the dead': Institutionalized Responses to Deaths in Custody' in P. Scraton, ed., *Law, Order and the Authoritarian State*, Milton Keynes, Open University.

SELLIN, J.T. (1976) *Slavery and the Penal System*, New York, Elsevier.

SHAW, M. (1984) 'Marxism and the Problem of Law and Order in Britain' in P. Norton, ed., *Law, Order and British Politics,* Aldershot, Gower.

SHIVJI, I. G. (1982) 'Semi-Proletarian Labour and the Use of Penal Sanctions in the Labour Law of Colonial Tanganyika, (1920-38)' in C. Sumner, ed., *Supra*.

SIM, J. (1994) 'Tougher than the Rest? Men in Prison' in T. Newburn and E.A. Stanko, eds, Men, *Masculinities and Crime: Just Boys Doing Business?*, London, Routledge.

SIM, J., SCRATON, P. and GORDON, P. (1987) 'Introduction: Crime, the State and Critical Analysis' in P. Scraton, ed., *Law, Order and the Authoritarian State*, Milton Keynes, Open University.

SMART, C. (1990) 'Feminist approaches to criminology or postmodern woman meets atavistic man' in L. Gelsthorpe and A. Morris, eds, *Feminist Perspectives in Criminology*, Milton Keynes, Open University Press.

SMITH, D.J. (1994) 'Race, Crime and Criminal Justice' in M. Maguire, R. Morgan and R. Reiner, eds, *The Oxford Handbook of Criminology*, Oxford, Oxford University Press.

SMITH, D.J. and GRAY, J. (1983) *Police and People in London, iv. The Police in Action*, London, Policy Studies Institute.

SOLOMOS, J. and RACKETT, T. (1991) 'Policing and urban unrest: problem constitution and policy response' in E. Cashmore and E. McLaughlin, eds, *Supra.*

STEADY, F.C. ed. (1981) *The Black Woman Cross-Culturally*, Cambridge, Massachusettes, Shenkman.

STERN, V. (1987) *Bricks of Shame: Britains' Prisons*, Middlesex, Penguin.

SUDARKASA, N. (1981) 'Female Employment and Family Organisation in West Africa' in F. C. Steady, ed., *Supra.*

SWAANINGEN, R.V. (1989) 'Feminism and Abolitionism as Critiques of Criminology.' *IJSL* 17.

TAPPAN, P.W. (1977) 'Who is The Criminal?' in G. Geis and R.F. Meier, eds, *White-Collar Crime*, New York, The Free Press.

TARZI, A. and HEDGES, J. (1990) *A Prison Within a Prison: A Study of Foreign Prisoners*, London, Inner London Probation Service.

TAYLOR, I. (1982) 'Against crime and for socialism', *Crime and Social Justice*, No. 18, Winter.

TAYLOR, I. (1994) 'Fear of Crime, Urban Fortunes and Suburban Movements', Paper presented to the World Congress of Sociology, University of Bielefeld, Bielefeld, Germany, July.

TAYLOR, I., WALTON, P. and YOUNG, J. (1973) *The New Criminology*, London, Routledge & Kegan Paul.

THOMAS, D.A. (1970) *Principles of Sentencing*, London, Heinemann.

THOMPSON, E.P. (1979) *The Poverty of Theory & Other Essays*, London, Merlin.

TOMBS, J. (1982) *Law and Slavery in North America: The Development of a Legal Category*, Ph.D. Thesis, University of Edinburgh.

TURK, A.T. (1976) 'Law, Conflict and Order: From Theorizing Toward Theories' in *Canadian Review of Sociology and Anthropology*, 13, 3, August.

URDANG, S. (1983) 'The Last Transition? Women and Development in Mozambique' in *Review of African Political Economy*, 27/28.

VAN BINSBERGEN, W.M.J. (1979) *Religious Change in Zambia: Exploratory Studies*, Haarlem, In de Knipscheer.

VAN DIJK, T.A. (1993) *Elite Discourse and Racism*, London, Sage.

VAN ONSELEN, C. (1982) *New Babylon*. London, Longman.

VOAKES, R. and FOWLER, Q. (1989) *Sentencing, Race and Social Enquiry Reports*, Bradford, West Yorkshire Probation Service.

WADDINGTON, P.A.J. (1984) 'Black Crime, the 'Racist' police and fashionable compassion' in D. Anderson, ed., *The Kindness that Kills*, London, SPCK.

WALKER, M.A. (1988) 'The Court Disposal of Young Males, by Race in London in 1983.' *British Journal of Criminology*, 28, 4.

WALKLATE, S. (1992) 'Appreciating the Victim: conventional, realist or critical victimology?' in J. Young and R. Matthews, eds, *infra*.

WARE, C. (1970) *Woman Power: The Movement for Women's Liberation*, New York, Tower Publications.

WEATHERITT, M. (1986) *Innovations in Policing*, London, Croom Helm/The Police Foundation.

WEBER, M. (1954) *Law in Economy and Society*, M. Rheinstein, ed., M. Rheinstein and E. Shils, trans., Cambridge, Harvard University Press.

WEST, C. (1993) *Beyond Eurocentrism and Multiculturalism, vol.2: Prophetic Thought in Postmodern Times*, Monroe, Common Courage.

WILLIAMS, S.W. (1983) 'The Theory of Internal Colonialism: An Examination' in D. Drakakis-Smith and S.W. Williams, eds, *Internal Colonialism: Essays Around a Theme*, Monograph No.3, Developing Areas Research Group, Institute of British Geographers, Edinburgh, Department of Geography.

WILMOT, P. (1986) *The Right to Rebel: The Phenomenology of student revolutionary consciousness*, Oguta, Zim Pan-African Publishers.

WILMOT, P.F. (1989) 'Stooping to Couriers' *African Concord* 7 August.

WILSON, J.Q. and HERRNSTEIN, J.H. (1985) *Crime and Human Nature: The Definitive Study of the Causes of Crime*, New York, Touchstone.

WILSON, P. (1985) 'Black Female Prisoners and Political Awareness.' Conference paper, Black Women In Prison. London.

WIPPER, A. (1989) 'Kikuyu women and the Harry Thuku disturbances: some uniformities of female militancy' in *Africa*, Vol. 59, No. 3.

WOLPE, H. (1972) 'Capitalism and Cheap Labour in South Africa' in *Economy and Society*, 1, 4.

YOUNG, C. and TURNER, T. (1985), *The Rise and Decline of the Zairian State*, London, University of Wisconsin.

YOUNG, J. (1986) 'The Failure of Criminology: the need for a radical realism' in R. Matthews and J. Young, eds, *Confronting Crime*, London, Sage.

YOUNG, J., and **MATTHEWS, R.**, eds (1992) *Rethinking Criminology: The Realist Debate*, London, Sage.

YOUNG, P. (1976) 'A Sociological analysis of the early history of probation', *British Journal of Law and Society*, Vol.3.

YOUNG, P. (1987) *Punishment, Money and Legal Order: An Analysis of the Emergence of Monetary Sanctions With Special Reference to Scotland*, Ph.D. thesis, Edinburgh University,

YOUNG, P. (1992) 'The Importance of Utopias in Criminological Thinking' in *British Journal of Criminology*, Vol. 32, No.4, Autumn.